W9-BUX-203

REMOVED
from Collection

A Gift for

Presented by

1/10/12

I Wish
I Knew
That
Geography

I Wish I Knew That

Geography

Cool Stuff You Need to Know

James Doyle

Reader's Digest

The Reader's Digest Association, Inc.
New York, NY / Montreal

A READER'S DIGEST BOOK

Copyright © 2012 Michael O'Mara Books Limited

All rights reserved. Unauthorized reproduction, in any manner, is prohibited.

Reader's Digest is a registered trademark of The Reader's Digest Association, Inc.

First published as *Where on Earth?* in Great Britain in 2010 by Michael O'Mara Books Limited, 9 Lion Yard, Tremadoc Road, London SW4 7NQ

FOR MICHAEL O'MARA BOOKS
Editors: Sue McMillan, Elizabeth Scoggins, and Sally Pilkington
Maps: David Woodroffe
Illustrator: Andrew Pinder
Designer: Zoe Quayle

FOR READER'S DIGEST TRADE PUBLISHING
Consulting Editor: Andrea Chesman
U.S. Project Editor: Kimberly Casey
Manager, English Book Editorial, Reader's Digest Canada: Pamela Johnson
Project Production Coordinator: Rich Kershner
Senior Art Director: George McKeon
Executive Editor, Trade Publishing: Dolores York
Associate Publisher, Trade Publishing: Rosanne McManus
President and Publisher, Trade Publishing: Harold Clarke

Library of Congress Cataloging in Publication Data
Doyle, James, 1972-
I wish I knew that geography : cool stuff you need to know / James Doyle.
   p. cm.
"A Reader's Digest Book."
Includes bibliographical references and index.
ISBN 978-1-60652-347-6
1. Geography--Juvenile literature. I. Title.
G133.D63 2012
910--dc23

2011027524

Reader's Digest is committed to both the quality of our products and the service we provide to our customers. We value your comments, so please feel free to contact us: The Reader's Digest Association, Inc., Adult Trade Publishing, 44 S. Broadway, White Plains, NY 10601

For more Reader's Digest products and information, visit our website:
       www.rd.com (in the United States)
       www.readersdigest.ca (in Canada)

Printed in the United States of America

1 3 5 7 9 10 8 6 4 2

For Oonagh, Conall,
Erin, and Cara

CONTENTS

INTRODUCTION:
WHY IN THE WORLD . . . ?

Have you ever wondered why we don't have kangaroos in North America? Or why earthquakes happen more frequently in some parts of the world than others? Or why some hot places are deserts and some are rain forests? And why do people talk about rain forests all the time, anyway? These are questions that geographers think about all the time. Geography is the science that explains where in the world things are and how they got there. Geography looks at the whole world and brings together geology, meteorology, history, and biology to help describe the world.

The earth is constantly changing. Did you know that mountains actually grow? New islands form, too. And floods and tsunamis (giant ocean waves) change the surface of the planet. Why does this happen?

Whew! Lots of questions. Let's take a look at the always-changing earth from the inside out, and then look at the oceans and the seven continents, the mountains, the rivers—how to find it all on a map. Words in bold will help you pay attention to key terms as you go. Soon you will be able to answer anyone who asks, "What is the difference between an ocean and a sea?" or "Where on earth is the longest river?"—and lots more.

Impress your friends, your parents, and your teachers with all the cool new stuff you know! The world is at your fingertips.

WELCOME TO PLANET EARTH

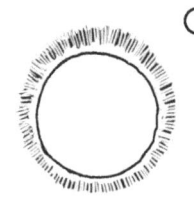

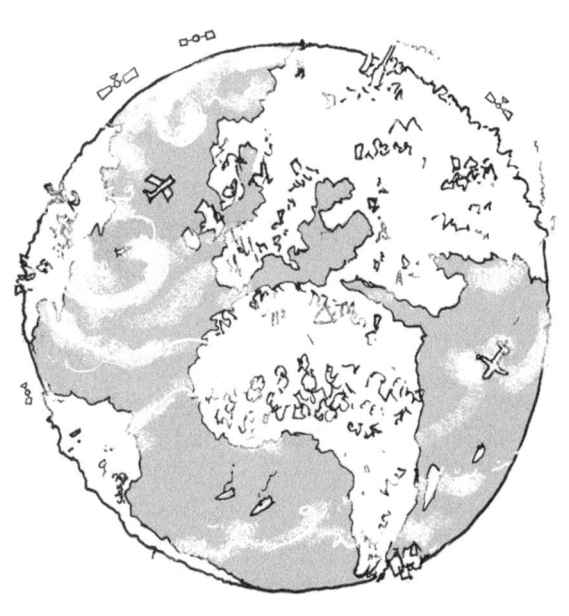

HOME SWEET HOME

Earth, the planet we call home, is one of a group of eight planets that move around the sun. These planets in order of closeness to the sun are: **Mercury, Venus, Earth, Mars, Jupiter, Saturn, Uranus,** and **Neptune.** Together, they make up the **solar system**.

Until recently, **Pluto** was considered the ninth planet in the solar system. Pluto still exists, but since it is smaller than the earth's moon, scientists decided it should be called a "dwarf planet." (Pluto isn't the only dwarf planet. There are also Ceres and Eris, not to mention plenty of asteroids, comets, and meteoroids orbiting the sun.)

Earth is a special planet because on it there is life—you, me, and all the people, animals, plants, and microorganisms. Scientists think Earth may be the *only* planet with living creatures in the whole **universe** (all of outer space, including all the stars, planets, moons, comets, asteroids, you name it).

It's a Small World after All

The earth feels like a huge place, but in fact it is only the fifth largest planet in the solar system. Jupiter is the biggest—its diameter is 11 times greater than that of Earth's.

WHAT IS THE WORLD MADE OF?

The earth is a **terrestrial planet**, which means it is mostly made from rock rather than gas. It has three main layers. These layers are kind of like the layers of a piece of fruit, with a thin crust (or skin), thick center, and core.

The Crust. The outer layer of the earth—where people, animals, and plants live—is the **crust.** It is the thinnest layer, measuring from about 5 miles (8 km) thick under the oceans to about 25 miles (40 km) thick in places under land. Two types of volcanic rocks, granite and basalt, make up most of the earth's crust.

The Mantle. Under the crust lies the **mantle,** which is about 1,800 miles (2,900 km) thick. The mantle is made up of thick, gooey, partially melted rock called **magma.** Magma isn't solid because the temperature of the mantle is about 3,600°F (2,000°C)—and that's hot enough to melt rock.

The Core. The earth's core is so deep below the surface that scientists aren't entirely sure what it is made of—although they believe the core contains mostly two metals: iron and nickel.

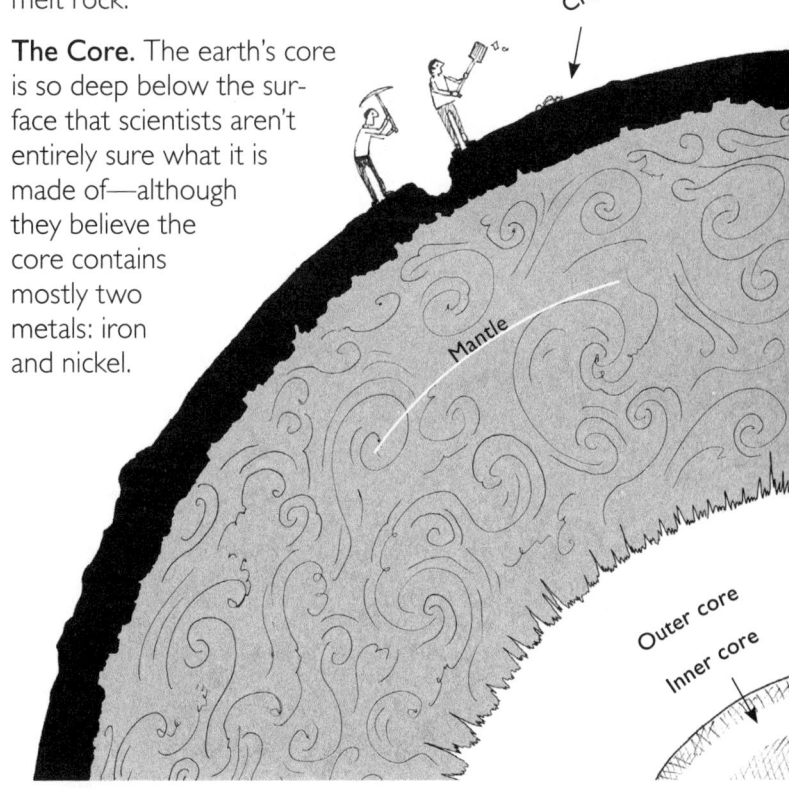

Crust

Mantle

Outer core

Inner core

They think it is extremely hot, with temperatures greater than 12,600°F (7,000°C). The **outer core** is about 1,400 miles (2,250 km) thick and is liquid. The **inner core** is about 1,600 miles (2,600 km) in diameter (all the way across). It is probably scorching hot there, too, but scientists think the inner core is solid because the weight of all the other layers press down on it.

Journey to the Center of the Earth

The distance from the earth's surface to the center is about 4,000 miles (6,400 km). But you could never actually make a journey to the center of the earth—you'd either be fried to a crisp in the scorching heat or crushed to death by the pressure of the layers of rock in the crust and mantle.

CONTINENTS AND OCEANS

A continent is a large landmass. It is thought that at one time (about 250 million years ago), all the land on the earth was part of one big landmass that split apart into seven continents: **North America, South America, Europe, Africa, Asia, Australia/Oceania,** and **Antarctica.** Europe and Asia form a single landmass divided by the Ural Mountains and the Caspian and Black seas. Europe and Asia are the only continents that are so tightly joined. Some geographers say the two should be called "Eurasia" or "Europe/Asia." The combination continent many people agree on is Australia/Oceania, which includes many of the Pacific Islands as well as Australia itself.

Continents account for just one-third of the earth's surface. Oceans cover the rest of the planet's crust, which is why the earth looks blue from outer space. There are five oceans:

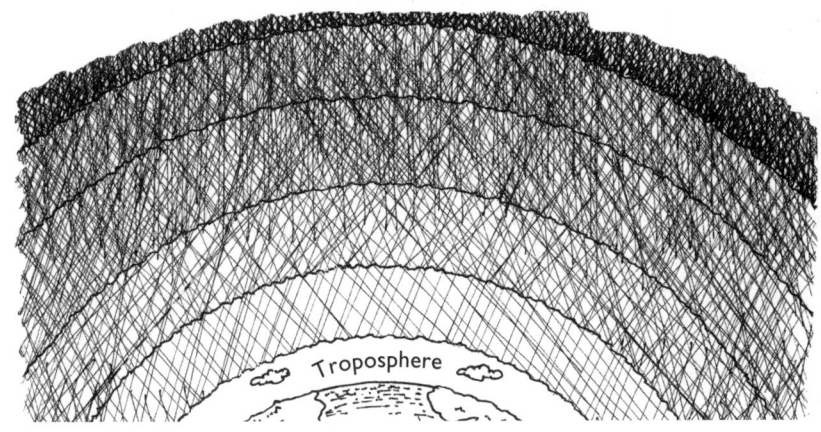

Troposphere

the **Pacific, Atlantic, Indian, Southern,** and **Arctic.** Some people call the Southern Ocean the "Antarctic Ocean."

AWESOME ATMOSPHERE

The **atmosphere** wraps the planet in a thin layer of gases, which protect the earth from the sun's burning hot temperatures. The atmosphere of the earth is made up mostly of the gases oxygen, nitrogen, and argon. There are also trace (small) amounts of other gases and little particles, like dust, water, and pollen. The part of the atmosphere where we live and breathe is called the **troposphere.** This is also where the earth's weather happens.

THE HOT AND THE COLD OF IT

Planet Earth is a spinning ball of rock. It takes 24 hours—one day—for the earth to complete one spin, or rotation. As it

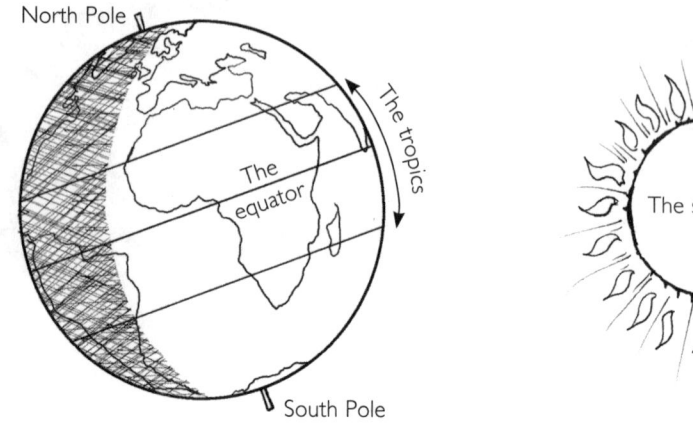

spins, the earth is also moving in an **orbit** (a circular path) around the sun. Radiation from the sun heats the planet, but it hits the planet unevenly. An area around the middle of the planet, called the **tropics,** which includes the **equator,** receives more heat than the parts at the top and bottom, which are known as the **Arctic Circle** and the **Antarctic zone.**

That uneven heating explains why we find warm, wet, tropical rainforests and hot, dry deserts near the equator and why polar bears and penguins call the frozen lands at the North and South poles home. Temperatures would be even more extreme in these areas if there weren't some helpful conditions in the atmosphere.

Earth's Air-Conditioning System

Heat from the sun moves from warmer parts of the earth to cooler areas by the constant movement of ocean currents, winds, and big storms, such as hurricanes. Without this movement, the tropics would be too hot and the poles too cold for most forms of life to survive, and maybe even too hot and cold for people! So currents too strong to swim against and wind that blows dirt in your eyes are good things—sort of.

THE REASON FOR SEASONS

Even though we think of the North Pole as up, the earth actually tilts to one side as it travels around the sun. As the earth moves, different parts of the planet get more sunshine at different times of the year.

When it is winter in the North, the **Northern Hemisphere** (the northern half of the planet) is tilted away from the sun. Because the Northern Hemisphere is farther from the sun at this time, not as much heat and light reaches it, and the weather feels cooler. Meanwhile, it is summer in the **Southern Hemisphere** because that half of the planet gets more hours of sunlight each day, and the weather feels warmer. As the earth continues on its orbit, the Northern Hemisphere starts to get more sunlight each day, the weather heats up, and summer arrives. That is when winter begins in the Southern Hemisphere.

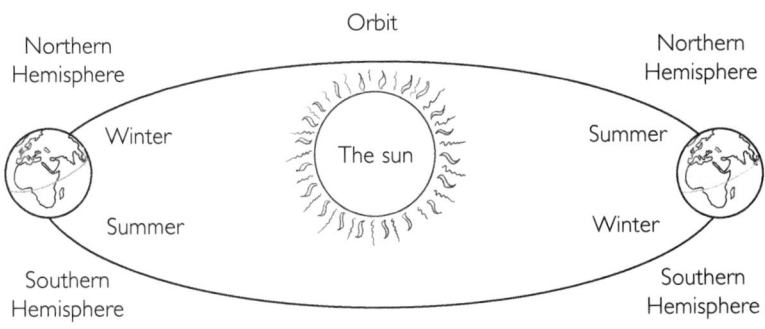

Earth Fact Sheet

Age	4.5 to 4.6 billion years
Distance from the Sun	93,000,000 miles (150,000,000 km)
Distance from the Moon	239,000 miles (384,000 km)
Distance around the equator (the middle)	25,000 miles (40,075 km)
Surface area	196,938,500 square miles (510,065,700 km^2)
Surface area of land	57,500,000 square miles (148,940,000 km^2)
Surface area of ocean	139,400,000 square miles (361,132, 000 km^2)
Mass	13,131,920,000,000,000,000,000,000 pounds or 6,000 billion, billion tons

POLAR OPPOSITES

The exact **North Pole,** located in the Arctic Circle, is the one point on the planet where you cannot go any farther north. If you stood at the North Pole and walked in any direction, you would be heading south. Of course, you'd actually be walking on a floating sheet of ice. At the North Pole, and the area around it, there is no land at all—just hundreds of miles of ice.

The exact **South Pole,** located in the Antarctic, is the most southern point on the planet, so if you stood at the South Pole and walked in any direction, you would be heading north. Unlike the North Pole, the South Pole is located on land, but it's buried under ice that is more than 1¼ miles (2 km) thick. What else sets the poles apart? Their seasons are entirely opposite due to the tilt of the earth's axis (see page 17). So on a balmy summer's day in the Arctic, when it might be as "warm" as 32°F (0°C), it's a teeth-chattering winter's day in Antarctica, where the temperatures can reach as low as −56°F (−49°C).

It's Been a Long Day . . .

Did you know that at the North and South poles, a summer "day" can last up to six months and a winter's "night" can be just as long? As the earth spins, the top of the planet, the North Pole, points at the sun for six months and then points away from it for the next six months. This means that when the Arctic is bathed in summer sunshine, the Antarctic is plunged into a long, dark winter, and vice versa.

Even though the poles get so many hours of sunshine, their summers are still very cold and temperatures rarely climb above freezing. This is because the sun is always low in the sky; its rays are weakened because they have to travel farther to reach the poles than they do to reach the equator. The poles are also covered in white ice, which reflects heat back into the atmosphere.

Solid Ice?

Until recently, many explorers and scientists thought the Arctic, like Antarctica, was a landmass covered by ice. In 1958 a submarine journeyed beneath the ice cap and came out the other side, proving that there is no land at all and that the Arctic is nothing but ice.

Polar Bear versus Penguin

Polar bears live in the Arctic, and penguins live in the Antarctic and parts of the Southern Hemisphere. Both need cold weather to survive, but which animal can withstand the toughest climate?

The Polar Bear. This animal is the largest meat eater living on land. It is well-suited to temperatures below zero and can travel over snow and ice easily. The polar bear is a great swimmer, too. A thick layer of fat beneath the skin acts like thermal underwear to keep the polar bear warm and helps it float in icy water. It can smell food—seals and other marine animals—over great distances and is armed with powerful jaws and large claws. The polar bear must survive winter temperatures of −22°F (−30°C) in the Arctic, but that's nothing . . .

The Penguin. The emperor penguin is the largest species of penguin. Like the polar bear, it is a super swimmer and has a thick layer of fat under its skin to keep it warm. But that's not what makes it the winner of this polar contest. The emperor penguin breeds during the bone-chilling Antarctic winter. While the female penguin goes in search of food, the male protects their egg through the harshest winter on Earth. He faces temperatures of −76°F (−60°C), fierce winds, and four months without sunlight, food, or water. He huddles with other males on the polar ice, waiting for the mother penguin to return, the egg to hatch, and the mother penguin to take over and feed the chick. That may make the penguin the winner in a contest of polar bear versus penguin. What do you think?

Planet Earth's Designer Sunglasses

Believe it or not, the ice, snow, and freezing temperatures at the planet's poles help keep the rest of the world at a comfortable temperature range. The icy poles are bright white in color and this maximizes their **albedo.** The word albedo (pronounced al-bee-doh) is used to describe how reflective the surfaces on Earth are. Earth's oceans and dark soils aren't very good at reflecting the sun's rays, so they have a very low albedo—about 10 percent. This means they absorb more heat from the sun than they reflect. Fresh snow has a high albedo—around 85 percent or more. So large, icy areas, such as the North and South poles act like giant mirrors, reflecting most of the sunlight they receive back into space, helping the planet stay cool. If there were no ice at the earth's poles, the planet would be a much warmer place.

The Warm Pole

The Arctic is the warmer of the two poles. Its temperature ranges from 32°F (0°C) in the summer to a very cold −22°F (−30 °C) in the winter. The Antarctic is much colder. The average summer temperature there is around −22°F (−30°C), and in the winter it can reach below −76°F (−60°C). The coldest temperature ever recorded on Earth was −128°F (−89°C) at Vostok Station, Antarctica, in July 1983.

CLIMATES ARE COMPLICATED

Weather is the hour-to-hour or day-to-day state of the atmosphere. **Climate** describes the state of the atmosphere over a much longer period (usually at least 30 years).

If climate were just a result of how close to (or far away from) the equator or the North or South poles a certain place is, climate would be easy to understand. But the picture is complicated by whether the land is mountainous, whether it is near an ocean, where the wind comes from, and more.

Prevailing Winds. Places nearer the equator receive more sunlight and are much warmer than places nearer the poles. The heat causes air currents that rise and drive the general circulation of the atmosphere, moving heat away from the equator toward the poles. The wind belts that form are sometimes called the **prevailing winds.** They blow east-west more often than north-south due to the rotation of the earth.

Land Features. Topography is the word we use to describe whether there are mountains or valleys or flat open land. Mountain ranges act like walls, blocking the movement of air. In North America, the coastal mountain ranges and the Sierras block prevailing winds from the west that carry moisture from the Pacific Ocean. The warm air hits the mountain barrier and rises. As it rises, it cools. As it cools, it can't hold as much moisture, so rain falls. So on the west side of the mountain, lots of rain falls, but on the east side of the mountain . . . not so much. Sometimes deserts form on the dry sides of mountains.

Elevation. As you hike up a mountain, you feel the air temperature drop and maybe have to add more layers of clothing. That's because as air rises, temperatures fall. On some mountains, the tops are covered with ice and snow all year long. The higher the **elevation** of a place, the cooler the climate. Mount Kilimanjaro (located in the United Republic of Tanzania) lies about 200 miles (320 km)

> ### Whether the Weather?
>
> Whether the weather be hot,
> Or whether the weather be not,
> We'll weather the weather,
> Whatever the weather,
> Whether we like it or not.

A Brief Time Line of the Earth

4.6 billion years ago	Earth formed, along with the other planets
3.7 billion years ago	Earth's crust solidified
3.5 billion years ago	First life appeared in oceans
I billion years ago	Plants and fungi appeared
600 million years	Simple animals started to appear
500 million years	Fish and early amphibians appeared
475 million years	Plants moved onto land
300 million years	Reptiles evolved on land
245 million years ago	Age of Dinosaurs began
200 million years	Mammals appeared
150 million years ago	Supercontinent broke up and birds took to the air
65 million years ago	Age of Dinosaurs ended, with mass extinctions
2.5 million years ago	Early ancestors of man made an appearance
100,000 years ago	First Homo sapiens appeared
10,000 years ago	Recorded human history began

Note: The dates above are only estimates, and new information continually forces science to revise the "facts."

south of the equator, well within the tropics, but ice and snow cover the summit all year long.

Land versus Oceans. The oceans absorb heat far more slowly than land. During the summer, bodies of water are cooler than the adjoining land, which is why swimming in the ocean or in a big lake is so refreshing. But in winter the big waters are warmer, and that keeps the land they border warmer as well. Also there are warm ocean currents, such as the Gulf Stream in the Atlantic, for example, that help keep the weather in places like England and Cape Cod, Massachusetts, warmer than it would be otherwise. Coastal regions generally experience mild and humid **maritime climates,** while the interiors of large landmasses boast **continental climates,** with warmer summers and colder winters. The summers stay cooler and the winters are milder in Portland, Oregon, for example, than in Minneapolis, Minnesota, even though the two cities are located in nearly the same latitude (see page 59).

THE EARTH NEVER STOPS CHANGING

CRACKS IN THE CRUST

Most of the time change happens slowly on planet Earth, over periods of millions of years. Then there are changes—like earthquakes or the eruption of volcanoes—that happen in an instant.

The earth's crust is one of those changeable parts. Many pieces, called **plates,** fit together to form the crust, like a giant jigsaw puzzle. There are seven enormous plates, and many smaller ones. The study of how these plates move is called **plate tectonics.** The plates float on the partially melted mantle (see page 13), which moves them slowly over the earth's surface. Most of the **boundaries** (edges) are under the sea and move only a few inches a year, but they do move.

Drifting Apart

Today the land is divided into continents and islands, but about 250 million years ago, all the land was joined together

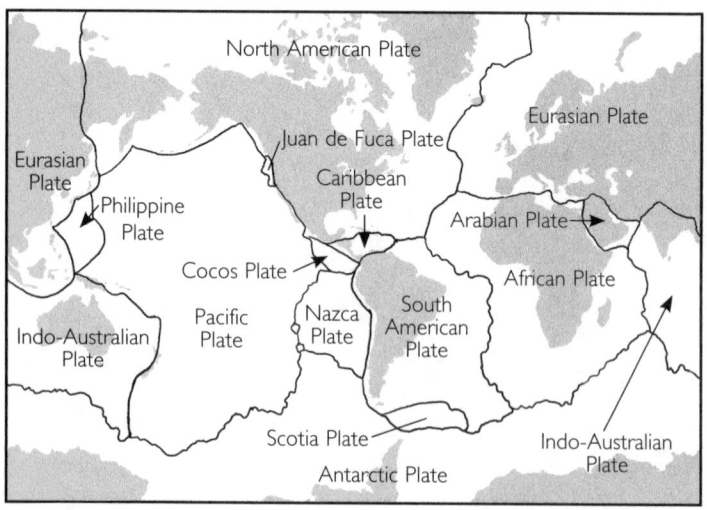

as one big continent called **Pangaea** (pronounced pan-gee-a), which means "all lands" in ancient Greek. It was surrounded by a huge ocean called **Panthalassa,** which means "all seas."

A German geographer named Alfred Wegener (1880–1930) noticed that on a map the shape of the east coast of South America looked as if it fit into the west coast of Africa. Did South America break off from Africa? Wegener asked himself. When he watched icebergs drifting out to sea in Greenland, Wegener realized that continents could be moving, too. Most people thought he was crazy at the time, but in the 1960s scientists proved his theory.

One piece of evidence was the fossilized remains of the mesosaurus, a dinosaur that lived about 300 million years ago. This dinosaur was found only in Africa and South America, two continents separated by a huge ocean—and this particular dinosaur couldn't swim or fly. But what if those continents had once been attached? Problem solved! Another puzzle: You can dig below the ice in certain spots to find coal in

Antarctica. Coal is made from decaying plants. No plants can live in Antarctica these days because it is just too cold and dry there. So either the weather at the South Pole has changed a lot (unlikely given the distance from the equator) or the continent of Antarctica moved from a warm spot on the globe. Bingo! More evidence for continental drift.

CONTINENTS ON THE MOVE

The world has changed a lot in the last 250 million years because the tectonic plates move, carrying the continents with them. These maps show how the continents are thought to have moved during this time.

250 Million Years Ago. The continents were joined in one enormous landmass, called Pangaea.

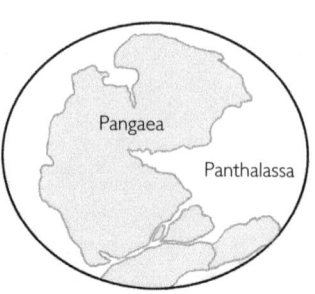

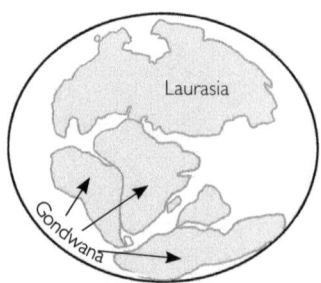

200 Million Years Ago. Pangaea started to split into two giant continents—**Laurasia** in the north and **Gondwana** in the south.

135 Million Years Ago. The two giant continents started to split once more as Gondwana divided into Africa and South America, separated by the Atlantic Ocean. India broke off from Africa to form a separate island continent and drifted north.

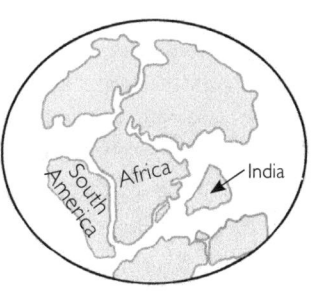

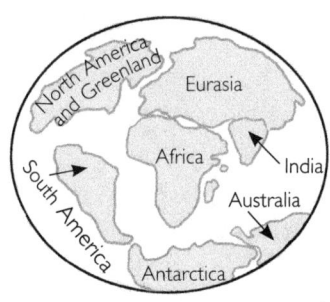

40 Million Years Ago. The continents began to look as they do today. Australia/Oceania and Antarctica started drifting apart. India collided with Eurasia. North America and Greenland shifted west, splitting away from Eurasia. Later, Greenland became an island when rising sea levels cut it off from North America.

The world has not stopped changing because the earth's tectonic plants still move. Some plates are moving toward each other on a collision course. As these plates bump into each other, one plate gets pushed under the other, the rock melts, and it becomes part of the earth's mantle. These boundaries are called **destructive boundaries** because land is destroyed.

At the same time, new land is created all the time. When plates pull away from one another, molten rock, or magma, is released into the gap, hardening to form new land. These points are known as **constructive boundaries.** Most of these points are located under the sea.

ENORMOUS EARTHQUAKES

Earthquakes take place where two tectonic plates meet, called a **fault plane.** When two plates slip past each other, the rock and magma below the planet's surface shakes and rolls. Sometimes you can hardly feel this movement, and sometimes it can destroy whole cities.

Although many plate boundaries are under the oceans, there are some on land. The San Andreas Fault, for example, stretches for more than 560 miles (900 km) along the west coast of the United States, passing through two large cities, San Francisco and Los Angeles. There are frequent earthquakes along this fault.

Whose Fault Is It?

More than 80 percent of all earthquakes happen in the **Ring of Fire,** an area in the Pacific Ocean that is famous for its volcanoes and earthquakes. It's the shakiest place on the planet! But earthquakes can happen wherever plate boundaries come together. While most plates move past each other, some plate boundaries get stuck. And although the plate edges are stuck, the rest of the plate continues to move. The energy that would usually help the plates slide past one another is stored up, so when the faults finally slip apart, the stored-up energy is released, causing the land to shake violently. The energy radiates in all directions from the fault in what are known as **seismic waves.** When the waves reach the earth's surface, they are felt as vibrations. These may be anything from a little wobble to huge tremors. Seismic waves are measured by seismographs that assign a number based on the **Richter scale,** developed by a man named Charles Richter (1900–1985). Each whole number on the scale represents a tenfold increase in the size of an earthquake, so a medium-size earthquake might measure 5.3 on the Richter scale, but one that measures 6.3 would be considered a strong earthquake because it is 10 times greater. The strongest earthquake ever measured took place in Chile in 1960; it measured 9.5 on the Richter scale.

How Shocking!

Some earthquakes begin with **foreshocks,** or little tremors, that happen in advance of the main shock. The main shock is the largest and most violent part and is followed by smaller earthquakes called **aftershocks.** If the main shock is really big, the aftershocks can go on for days, months, or even years.

PRESSURE POINTS

Earthquakes are in the news a lot. What makes them so dangerous is that no one can say exactly when or where the next one will happen.

Pacific Ring of Fire. The earthquakes that occur frequently in Japan and California are all part of the Ring of Fire, a horseshoe-shaped fault line that stretches from Indonesia and the Philippines, past China to the Aleutian Islands in the United States, then down through Alaska, the Pacific Northwest, down the San Andreas Fault to Mexico, and into South America.

Alpine-Himalayan Zone. The Alpine-Himalayan zone goes through India, Tibet, and China, down to Myanmar and across to the Middle East, and then over to the Mediterranean.

East Africa Rift. Africa is ripping apart along a 2,400-mile (3,862 km) crack that stretches from the Red Sea to Mozambique. This big split started in the north some 25 million years ago and has been creeping south, apparently on the way to splitting the African Plate into two new tectonic plates.

The Caribbean. The Caribbean Plate is small, but it borders the North American Plate, the South American Plate, the Nazca Plate, and the Cocos Plate (see page 26). Where there are boundaries between plates, you can expect a lot of earthquake action, like the devastating 2009 earthquake in Haiti.

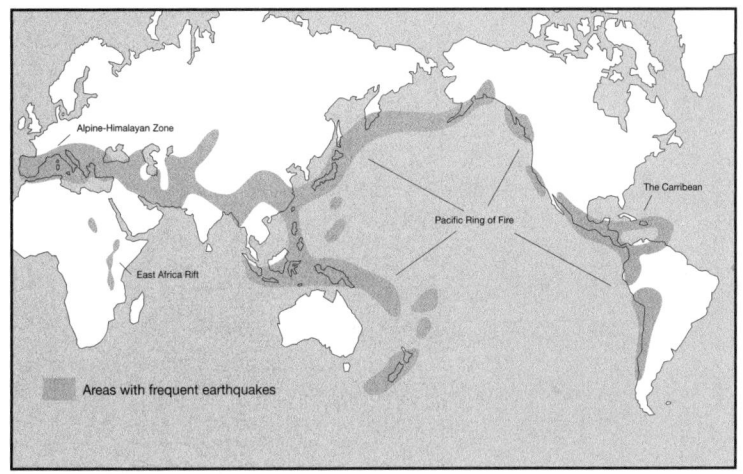

Areas with frequent earthquakes

EARTH-SHATTERING EFFECTS

Major earthquakes can be deadly, causing buildings to collapse and roads and bridges to be destroyed. The shaking can make the ground feel like jelly, damaging electric and gas lines, which cause fires. Landslides and avalanches can also be triggered by earthquakes. If the **epicenter** (center of the earthquake) is located in the ocean, an earthquake can create a huge wave, called a **tsunami**.

Towering Tsunamis

A tsunami is triggered when water in the ocean is moved violently. This sets off a ripple effect, and the waves travel across the oceans. In open water, the waves travel fast and a great distance apart, but as they reach shallower water, they slow down and pile up to form a wall of water up to 130 feet (40 m) high. In December 2004, a huge tsunami struck in Indonesia, Southeast Asia, after an earthquake in the Indian

Ocean measuring more than 9.0 on the Richter scale. The tsunami struck across a huge part of the globe, including Thailand, Sri Lanka, Indonesia, and the coast of Somalia, in Africa. More than 200,000 people were killed, and more than 1.5 million people were left homeless. A tsunami in March 2011 followed an earthquake off the east coast of Japan, which measured 9.0 on the Richter scale. The tsunami caused a partial meltdown of a nuclear power plant, killed an estimated 25,000 people, and left many homeless.

VOLCANIC ACTION

Volcanoes are destructive when they erupt and spew molten lava or hot, volcanic ash. But at the same time, they are famous for being builders of mountains and islands.

Nasty Eruptions

A volcano is the point at which magma, or liquid rock, from the earth's mantle, erupts through the ground. Pressure forces either magma or hot volcanic ash out of the ground through a **vent,** or hole, in the earth's surface.

Molten Mountains

Volcanoes can form anywhere on Earth, even on the ocean floor! They usually form along the edges of tectonic plates, where the different sections of the planet's surface push toward or pull away from each other. Magma builds up in huge underground chambers and erupts as **lava,** the name for magma once it is aboveground. Lava is destructive and dangerously hot, like 1,290°F (700°C) hot, and can even reach a temperature of 2,280°F (1,250°C). It can be thick and slow-moving like jam, runny like melted ice cream, or any consistency in between. As it cools, lava hardens and forms new rock, including **pumice** (pronounced puh-miss). Over time, different volcano shapes build up depending on the viscosity, or thickness, of the lava. The thickness varies according to the type of melted rock and how much pressure is inside the volcano.

ATTACK OF THE VOLCANO

Lava flows can destroy pretty much anything in their path, but there's even more to the dangers of volcanoes. Here are just a few of them:

Lahars. These volcanic mudflows of ash and debris mix with water to form deadly mudslides. The water can be a result of heavy rain just after an eruption, or when eruptions melt ice on a snow-capped volcano. On steep slopes a lahar can travel at speeds fast enough to knock down trees and bury houses. **Mount Ranier** in Washington State is the type of volcano likely to generate a lahar flow, but the last time that happened was about 500 years ago.

Dust Clouds. Volcanoes can spread dust clouds across the globe, blocking out the sun and lowering temperatures. If the layers of ash are very thick, the temperature can be lowered for years. In 1815 **Mount Tambora** in Indonesia erupted, sending so much dust into the atmosphere that 1816 was known as "the year without a summer" in parts of North America.

Flooding. Volcanic eruptions can also cause flooding—especially when they occur underwater. They can create giant waves called tsunamis (see page 33). In 1883 the eruption of **Krakatau,** in Indonesia, created a wave that was 130 feet (40 m) high. It is estimated that the Krakatau tsunami killed more than 36,000 people.

Volcanoes Up Close

Some volcanoes that aren't in imminent danger of exploding and killing visitors have turned into tourist attractions. Here's some you can visit:

- Mount St. Helens National Volcanic Monument, Washington State
- Volcanoes National Park, Hawaii (Kilauea and Mauna Loa volcanoes)
- Arenal Volcano, Costa Rica
- Popocatepetl National Park, Mexico
- Santa Maria/Santiaguito Volcano, Guatemala
- Vesuvius, Mount Etna, and Stromboli volcanoes, Italy
- Kilimanjaro, Oldoinya Lengai, Meru volcanoes, Tanzania
- Fuji Five Lake Region, Japan (Mount Fuji)

Hot Spots!

Hot spots are superheated areas below the earth's crust. The high temperatures cause the crust to melt, allowing magma to escape and build volcanoes—even away from plate margins. A hot spot can keep a volcano erupting for centuries, but as the earth's tectonic plates shift, the land moves away from the hot spot and its magma, so the volcano becomes **dormant,** or resting, and cannot erupt.

Some volcanic places, such as Iceland and New Zealand, have **geysers,** or hot springs. These produce hot water and jets of steam that can be used to heat homes and provide electricity. They are also popular tourist destinations. Volcanic eruptions also produce mineral-rich rock, creating some of the world's most fertile farmland.

CLIMATE CHANGE

These days many people worry about global warming. Most scientists understand that actions of humans are causing global temperatures to rise. Global warming and chilling have happened before on planet Earth, and these changes in temperature changed the land.

Periods of cold are known as **ice ages,** and they usually last millions or tens of millions of years. The latest ice age began about 2.5 million years ago. During that time, giant ice sheets called **glaciers** advanced and retreated many times in North America and Europe. During each ice age, the average temperatures around the world dropped. The areas around the equator stayed warm, but the rest of the planet was very, very cold. Many species of plants and animals couldn't adapt to the changing climate and became extinct.

Those giant glaciers did a good job of bulldozing the land to make the five Great Lakes that border the United States and Canada. They also created the Finger Lakes in New York State, Walden Pond in Massachusetts, and any number of lakes in North America and Canada. The glaciers also carved out the Colorado, Missouri, and Mississippi rivers. As glaciers move, they pick up large amounts of rock and soil and then drop their loads in new places.

Glaciers lock up a lot of water. As more and more water freezes, sea levels drop, and land bridges appear between continents and islands. Those land bridges allowed early man to migrate to new lands, which is how people came to occupy North and South America and Australia.

The worry with global warming today is how it will affect the earth in the long term. Global warming will cause storms to increase in power, which increases the potential damage from storms, especially flooding. If the polar ice caps melt, sea levels will rise, and islands and coastal land will be submerged under water. Florida's Everglades could be

Glacial ice carves away the rock.

Glacier

Cirque

Rocky debris scours away the base, forming a hollow.

A lip forms as some debris is deposited at the edge of the cirque.

completely submerged. In some areas, such as low-lying islands in the Pacific, a 3-foot (1-m) rise in sea levels would be catastrophic. Low-lying countries, such as Bangladesh off the coast of India and the Netherlands, a country in Europe, are also at risk, as are parts of southeast England. If this happened, the world map could look very different, with the shape of some countries and continents changed forever. Some islands like the Maldive Islands in the Indian Ocean could disappear off the map completely.

If *all* the polar ice were to melt (which would probably never happen), scientists think that the sea level all over the world would rise about 230 feet (70 m). This could create some big changes in how maps look. The United States could be split by a newly formed Mississippi Sea, which would connect the Great Lakes with the Gulf of Mexico!

The earth—it keeps changing.

OCEANS IN MOTION

OCEANS AND SEAS

Oceans cover more than 70 percent of the earth's surface and are home to some of the deepest valleys and tallest mountains in the world. They have a lot of influence on the weather and are jam-packed with life—yet much about them remains a mystery.

The earth's oceans are all connected and form one gigantic body of water, which is sometimes known as the global ocean. Geographers have divided the global ocean into five enormous oceans. In order of size, these are the Pacific, the Atlantic, the Indian, the Southern—or Antarctic—and the Arctic.

The five oceans include many smaller parts known as **seas.** Most seas are partly enclosed by land, but each sea is part of one of the oceans. One of the largest seas is the South China Sea in Asia. It is more than 1,158,000 square miles (3,000,000 km^2) in size and is part of the Pacific Ocean. Another word that describes a part of an ocean is *gulf.* The Gulf of Mexico and the Caribbean Sea, for example, are both parts of the Atlantic Ocean. Some inland saltwater lakes, such as the Dead Sea in Israel, are also called seas, because the water in them is so salty.

The table on the right tells you where in the world you'll find the earth's oceans and how big they are.

Never Peaceful Pacific

Ferdinand Magellan, the first explorer to sail around the world, named the Pacific in 1519. *Pacifica* means peaceful in Portuguese, Magellan's native language. But the Pacific is anything but a peaceful ocean.

What follows are some fascinating facts about this important body of water.

Our Oceans

OCEAN	AREA	WHERE IN THE WORLD?
Pacific	60,610,00 sq. mi. (155,557,000 sq km)	Pacific Ocean
Atlantic	29,638,000 sq. mi. (76,762,000 sq km)	Atlantic Ocean
Indian	16,979,000 sq. mi. (68,556,000 sq km)	Indian Ocean
Southern	7,848,000 sq. mi. (20,327,000 sq km)	South Pole / Southern Ocean
Arctic	5,427,000 sq. mi. (14,056,000 sq km)	North Pole / Arctic Ocean

- The Pacific is the largest ocean; it covers more than a third of the earth's surface. It contains more than half of the earth's water.

- The Pacific is home to the **Pacific Ring of Fire,** an area of intense earthquake and volcanic activity. More than 75 percent of the world's volcanoes lie within this ring.

- The deepest spot on the surface of the earth, the **Mariana Trench,** is located in the Pacific Ocean, just east of the island of Guam. The bottommost point of the trench, called **Challenger Deep,** is about 36,000 feet (11,000 m) below sea level. If you were able to pick up and move Mount Everest, the highest mountain on Earth, and place it on this spot, it wouldn't even break the surface of the water; there would be about 1 mile (1.6 km) of ocean concealing it.

- The greatest amount of the world's fish supply is caught in the Pacific Ocean.

- Hurricanes that start in the Pacific are called **typhoons.**

The Mountainous Atlantic

The second largest ocean, the Atlantic Ocean, separates the Americas from Europe and Africa. It is the most mountainous ocean because undersea volcanoes constantly build new mountains under the water along the **Mid-Atlantic Ridge.** This is the longest mountain range in the world, snaking along the ocean floor for 7,000 miles (11,265 km).

Here are important facts about this vast ocean.

- The Atlantic was formed when the supercontinent Pangaea broke apart (see page 27). As the western and eastern landmasses drew apart, a great rift was formed, creating the Atlantic Ocean basin.

- **Hurricanes** form in the Atlantic. From June 1 to November 30, tropical storms originate off the coast of Africa and cross the Atlantic, taking up vast amounts of moisture. The storms blow over the Caribbean, coastal areas of the Gulf of Mexico, and the southern Atlantic coast of the United States with damaging winds, devastating amounts of rain, and **storm surges** (water levels far higher than the expected tides).

- Waters from many of the world's largest rivers flow into the Atlantic, including the **Amazon, Congo,** and **Niger** rivers. The **Nile River** flows into the Mediterranean Sea, which is part of the Atlantic. The Atlantic is the **saltiest ocean** because so much river water, which carries dissolved minerals, flows into it.

- The largest island in the Atlantic Ocean is **Greenland.**

- The newest island in the Atlantic is **Surtsey,** formed off the coast of Iceland in 1963.

Tropical Indian Ocean

The Indian Ocean surrounds India and stretches from Africa to Australia.

What else do we know about this tropical body of water?

- The Indian Ocean is the warmest ocean. It lies mostly below the equator. The **Arabian Sea, Persian Gulf,** and **Red Sea** are all part of the Indian Ocean.

- Forty percent of the world's offshore oil drilling takes place in the Indian Ocean.

- The Bay of Bengal is sometimes called **Cyclone Alley** because

Sunken Continent

Submerged in the Indian Ocean is a microcontinent (small continent) called the Kerguelen Plateau. A series of large volcanic eruptions beginning 110 million years ago started its formation. Rocks found on the plateau are similar to ones found in Australia and India, suggesting they were once connected. Evidence also suggests that the plateau was above sea level for some of its history, perhaps covered by dense forest. The plateau finally sank underwater about 20 million years ago and is now 1 to 1¼ miles (1 to 2 km) below sea level.

of all the storms that begin there. (A cyclone is a type of tropical storm.)

- An earthquake under the Indian Ocean caused the disastrous **Indonesian tsunami** of 2004. It generated waves recorded at a height of 49 feet (15 m).

- Changing air pressure systems over the Indian Ocean trigger the famous **monsoon** (rainy) **seasons** of Asia.

- The Maldive Islands, 8 feet (2.4 m) above sea level at their highest point, are expected to be the first casualties of rising sea levels caused by global warming.

Penguins' Southern Ocean Paradise

Some geographers call this body of water the Antarctic Ocean. Others think that it shouldn't be an ocean at all! Instead they want the Atlantic and Pacific oceans to claim this area of the globe. However, *most* geographers agree to make space on the map for the Southern Ocean, which extends north from the coast of Antarctica to 60° south latitude. But even this aspect of the ocean provokes fighting. Some Australian geographers say it extends all the way to Australia's shore. Work it out, people!

Here is even more surprising information about this chilliest of oceans.

- The Southern Ocean has the coldest waters of all the oceans.

- It is the **least salty** of the oceans.

- Penguins like to swim in the Southern Ocean.

- The **Antarctic Circumpolar Current** (ACC) flows west to east around Antarctica and is the strongest ocean current in the world. This current prevents warm waters from

Why Is the Ocean Salty?

Oceans are salty because fresh water flows into them. Okay, that answer doesn't *seem* to make sense, but fresh water flow is the major contributor of salt. The original oceans were probably only slightly salty. Over millions of years, rivers flowed over the newly formed land, carving out canyons, dissolving mountains, and picking up lots of dissolved minerals—including salt. These dissolved minerals all eventually flow into the ocean. Meanwhile, the sun heats the ocean surface, causing water to evaporate. What's left behind are those dissolved minerals—a cycle that continues today. The Atlantic Ocean has the greatest amount of river water flowing into it, so it is the saltiest of the oceans.

reaching Antarctica and enables that continent to maintain its huge ice sheet.

Icy Arctic Ocean

Much of the Arctic Ocean lies north of the Arctic Circle. It is a sea of ice but that may be changing due to global warming.

Take a look at these fascinating facts.

- The Arctic Ocean is the smallest ocean.

- It is the shallowest ocean.

- Polar bears swim and hunt in the Arctic Ocean.

- It is bordered by North America, Europe, and Asia.

- During winter, the Arctic Ocean is almost completely covered in sea ice.

- The North Pole is located in the middle of the Arctic Ocean.

- For centuries, explorers tried to find what is called the **Northwest Passage,** a route through the Arctic Ocean from the Atlantic to the Pacific; none succeeded. Today ice-breaking ships travel ahead of trade ships sailing on the Arctic Ocean, making a path through the ice.

IN HOT WATER

Oceans aren't just fun for sailing on or swimming in, they work hard regulating the planet's temperature. Within the oceans are vast **currents** of warm and cold water (a current is a movement of water). The currents determine how warm or cold ocean water is all over the world. The sun warms water in the oceans around the equator more than at the poles. Ocean currents then continually move this warm water from the equator toward the colder regions.

Warm ocean currents heat the air above them as they travel.

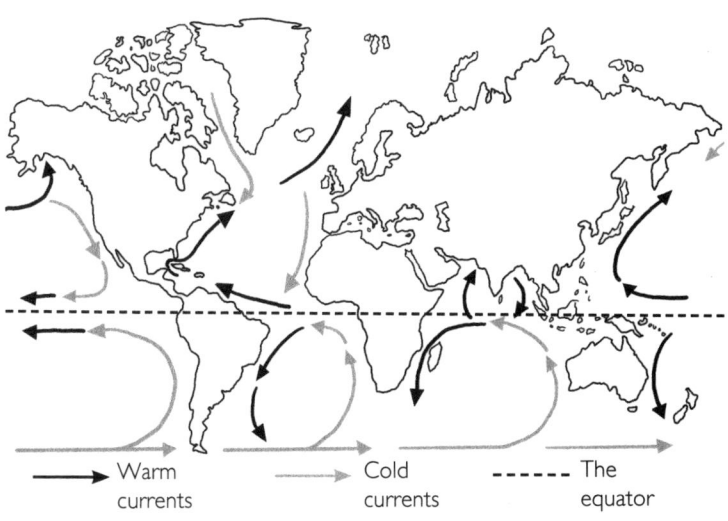

| → Warm currents | → Cold currents | ------ The equator |

Cold ocean currents cool the air above them and move cold water away from polar regions and toward the equator. This way, the ocean balances the earth's temperature. Without currents, the warmest parts of the planet would be much hotter, and the coldest parts would be even colder.

A JOURNEY ACROSS THE OCEAN FLOOR

Below the surface of the ocean there are mountains, hills, and valleys, just as there are on land. If you were to take a trip across the ocean floor, you would discover some interesting deep-sea details along the way.

Continental Shelf. A continental shelf forms at the edges of continents, where the land gently slopes away underwater. The water is usually less than 425 feet (130 m) deep along a continental shelf.

Continental Slope. The land slopes more steeply toward the ocean floor at the edge of a continental shelf.

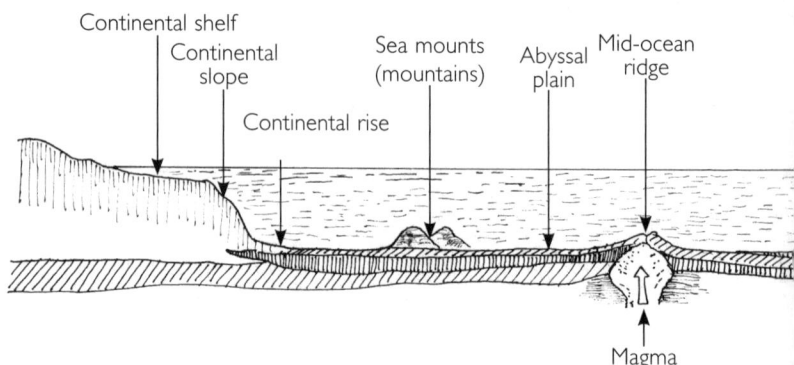

Continental shelf
Continental slope
Continental rise
Sea mounts (mountains)
Abyssal plain
Mid-ocean ridge
Magma

Continental Rise. A continental rise is a gentle hill formed by sediment like sand and rocks that build up at the foot of a continental slope, leading to the deep ocean.

Abyssal Plains. Continuously covered in thick sediment, the abyssal plains are the flattest areas on Earth and form most of the ocean's floor. They may be as much as 16,000 feet (5,000 m) from the surface of the ocean.

Sea Mounts. These tall, solitary mountains rise at least 3,300 feet (1,000 m) from the seafloor.

Mid-Ocean Ridges. Across the ocean floor, long ranges of underwater mountains form an almost continuous chain around the world. When two tectonic plates move apart underwater, magma erupts as lava to build these underwater mountains.

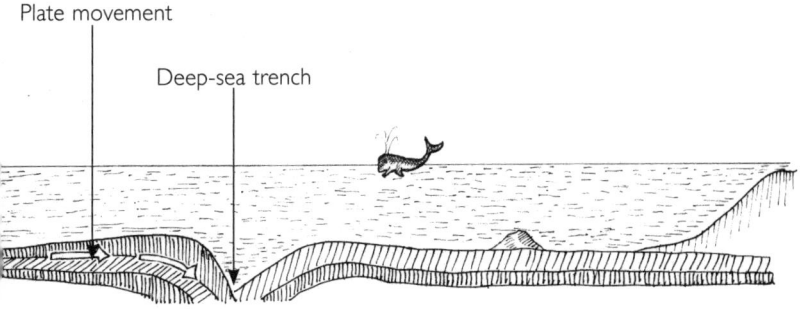

Plate movement

Deep-sea trench

Too Cold for a Swim?

The average water temperature of the combined oceans is about 39°F (2°C). But some oceans are warmer than others, and currents such as the Gulf Stream make cold waters warmer. If you are looking for a swim, the Indian Ocean is your warmest bet.

Deep-Sea Trench. The deepest points of an ocean floor can be more than 36,000 feet (11,000 m) below the surface. The deepest trench of them all is the Mariana Trench in the Pacific Ocean.

Under Pressure

Scientists are eager to discover more about the ocean floor, but exploring the deep ocean can be even more dangerous than going into space. As you dive underwater, the weight of the water above you increases the **pressure.** At great depths the pressure is so great that you would be crushed to death unless you were in a specially adapted submarine.

That's not all. In the lower zones of the ocean, it is pitch black and very cold, because the sun's rays can't travel that far. There are pockets of very high temperatures, too, caused by holes in the ocean floor called **hydrothermal vents,** which spew out hot liquids and gases.

DWELLERS OF THE DEEP

The ocean provides a variety of habitats for ocean creatures and plants, and life in the ocean is incredibly diverse. It ranges from microscopic bacteria to the largest mammal on earth—the enormous blue whale, which can grow to 110 feet (34 m) in length. Some of the ocean's animals are migratory, traveling huge distances from where they mate or have their babies to feeding grounds, while other critters stay in the same place on the ocean floor their entire lives. Some burrow beneath the sand, while others swim near the surface. Scientists believe that there may be as many as 10 million species of plants and animals in the ocean that no one has ever seen, much less named.

Most of the diverse marine life lives in the top layer of the ocean, within the reach of sunlight but where the ocean temperatures are relatively cool.

Fisheries

The oceans are an important source of food, but modern fishing methods may put this source at risk. So many fish are taken out of the ocean that not enough fish are left to spawn (release fertilized eggs to grow more fish) and grow to full size. Researchers have found that about 75 percent of the major marine fish supplies are in danger of disappearing because of overfishing. Pollution, habitat destruction, and global warming also threaten marine life. Species of fish endangered

Is the Dead Sea Really Dead?

Depends on what you mean by "dead." Certainly it is too salty to support much marine life, though it does support swimmers who can float easily in the water.

by overfishing include: tuna, salmon, haddock, halibut, and cod—some of the most popular fish to eat. In the nineteenth century, codfish weighing up to 200 pounds (90.7 kg) were not uncommon; today a 40-pound (18.1-kg) cod is considered huge. Fish farming may one day solve this problem, but farmers must be careful to avoid pollution and overharvesting fish food.

Coral Reefs

Thousands of animal and plant species inhabit the busy underwater communities of coral reefs. Coral looks like rocks or petrified plants, but it is actually made from the limestone skeleton of a tiny, spineless, carnivorous animal called a **coral polyp.** Coral polyps live in groups called **colonies.** Colonies grow quickly. One polyp can become a colony of 25,000 polyps in just three years. Each polyp uses calcium from the water to build a case of limestone around itself like a house, with a floor and walls. Polyps cannot move from their limestone homes, and their cases remain after the polyps die. Each case forms a foundation for another polyp to build a house on, and as the cases build up and out, the formation is called a **coral reef.**

The **Great Barrier Reef** off the coast of Australia is so big that it can be seen from space, making it the largest structure created by any group of animals. These tiny builders have existed on the earth for more than 200 million years. They grow in clear, fairly shallow warm water (64° to 91°F / 18° to 33°C). Coral cannot grow in polluted water or in water carrying soil from the land, such as at the mouths of rivers.

Coral reefs are mostly found in shallow tropical water and are among the world's most endangered ecosystems.

LIFE ON THE OCEAN FLOOR

Most of the fisheries and marine ecosystems are near the water surface, dependent on solar energy to support the plants and microscopic organisms that help life flourish in the ocean. But solar energy can reach only so deep into ocean waters, and photosynthesis (the sun-dependent process organisms use to grow) cannot occur below 660 feet (200 m). This lack of energy, along with the sinking of cold, subpolar water, makes most of the deep ocean floor a frigid environment with few life forms. However, geothermal hot springs do exist along the centers of mid-ocean ridges, sending dissolved minerals and heat into the water, allowing specially adapted bacteria to survive. These bacteria are the bottom of a food chain that supports a surprising diversity of marine life, including giant tubeworms, clams, and mussels. These miraculous animals don't mind the water pressure of up to 65 pounds per square foot (0.03 kg per cm^2)—but humans would be crushed to death at that pressure.

Animals that can survive with no sunlight, at extreme temperatures, and despite bone-crushing pressures help scientists to understand the planet better. And the fact that creatures have adapted to these extreme conditions makes some scientists believe that there may be life on other planets in the universe, or even in our own solar system.

WHERE IN THE WORLD ARE YOU?

THE MARVEL OF MAPS

Not so long ago, travelers needed maps to figure out how to get from one place to another. Without maps, hikers couldn't find their way out of the woods, pirates couldn't find buried treasure, and vacationers couldn't find their hotels. Today Global Positioning Satellites (**GPS**) and the Internet make traveling easier, but that doesn't mean that maps are old-fashioned.

A map is a two-dimensional picture of the world. It shows you a bird's-eye view of places. There are many different types of maps—from street maps, to **topographical maps,** to survey maps. Every type of map tells you something different about a place. Some, like topographical maps, show physical features such as mountains and rivers. Others show concepts—things that our human minds have figured out—like political boundaries, names of places, or even climate zones; these are things that satellite images can't show.

Maps are also useful when comparing places. It is easy to see that Asia is the largest continent or that the tip of South America is close to Antarctica when you look at a world map. Maps often include a **scale** that tells you how to figure out distance on that particular map. They often contain a **legend** that explains the symbols used on a map. For example, the capital city might be marked with a star and other cities marked with a dot. Or blue lines might indicate rivers and black lines might indicate roads.

Maps use points, lines, and shapes to tell you what you need to know. Points usually show where a specific place is located. Depending on the map, that place can be a city or a special landmark, such as a mountain peak (or a buried treasure). Lines represent borders, roads, and rivers (or the path to a buried treasure). What the shaded areas mean usually depends on the map. A map of rivers might have watersheds shaded in. A climate map might use different colors to indicate different climate zones. A historical map might use shaded areas to show where things used to be.

READING MAPS

The four main points of a **compass,** the device used to determine direction, are **n**orth, **e**ast, **s**outh, and **w**est. Remember them easily with this saying: **N**ever **E**at **S**hredded **W**heat. The initial letter of each word reminds you of the order of the compass directions clockwise from the top. North is always at the top of the map.

Lines of **longitude** (from the North Pole to the South Pole) and **latitude** (parallel to the equator) divide maps and globes into a kind of grid. These divisions come to us from Ptolemy (c. 100–170), the world's first geographer. Longitude and latitude give us a reasonably easy, precise, and universal way of pinpointing any specific location on Earth, especially in the ocean, where landmarks are scarce.

Why Is North Always at the Top of Maps?

In the early days of mapmaking, north was not always at the top. It used to be that Jerusalem, a holy site in many religions, often was set at the top of maps. But once globes became popular during the period of European cultural development called the Renaissance, it seemed logical to mapmakers to put north at the top of maps, for easy viewing of the "important" landmass they called home—Europe.

If you drew an imaginary line on the earth's surface exactly the same distance from the North Pole and South Pole, you would have drawn the equator. It's the line that divides the earth into a Northern Hemisphere and a Southern Hemisphere at the earth's widest point. And, it is the place where the sun passes directly overhead at noon on March 21, the spring equinox, and at noon on September 21, the fall equinox. Most of the landmasses are in the Northern Hemisphere.

The equator lies at 0° latitude. The equator was an obvious place to call ground zero because it is based on the sun's position. But where on earth to call 0° of longitude? Mapmakers puzzled, and various solutions were proposed, mainly using a country's capital as zero degrees for maps made in that country. But in 1884, when Great Britain was a superpower, the International Meridian Conference adopted the Greenwich meridian as the universal **prime meridian,** or 0° longitude. The Greenwich meridian runs through the Royal Observatory in England.

HOW GPS WORKS

GPS stands for Global Positioning System. Dreamed up by the U.S. military, the system is made up of 24 satellites that orbit the earth about 12,000 miles above us, transmitting data about their location and the current time to a GPS receiver. Using solar power as fuel and traveling at about 7,000 miles (11,265 km) per hour, they each orbit the earth about every 12 hours.

Here's how GPS works: A satellite tracks your vehicle's location or the location of your handheld GPS device and, based

on maps that have been loaded via CD into the GPS unit, the device guides you using visual and voice prompts to whatever address you've selected—be it a small town, an airport, or a specific street address.

High-Tech Hide and Seek

Most GPS devices are sold with cars, and kids can't drive. But you don't have to drive to get involved with **geocaching,** a worldwide, high-tech hide-and-seek activity. Participants use a GPS receiver or other navigational techniques to hide and find containers called "geocaches" on all seven continents (even Antarctica!).

Generally, geocaching begins with registering on a Web site. A typical geocache is a small waterproof container with a book inside. The geocacher uses coordinates from the Web site to search for the cache, enters the date found into the logbook, and signs it with an established code name. The containers also may contain items for trading, usually toys or souvenirs of little value. If you take something out, you are expected to leave something behind for the next person to find.

CONTINENTALLY SPEAKING

DIVIDING UP THE MAP

The earth's large pieces of land are called continents. **Asia** is the largest continent, followed by **Africa, North America, South America, Antarctica, Europe,** and **Australia.** Some geographers group Australia and many of the Pacific Islands, including New Zealand, into a continent they call **Australia/ Oceania.**

Continents, with the exception of Antarctica, are divided into different countries. Some borders between the countries are based on natural land features, such as rivers or lakes. For example, the Rio Grande (*rio* means river in Spanish) forms part of the border between Mexico and the southern United States.

Sometimes borders between countries change because of war. In 2005, for example, southern Sudan became a semi-autonomous region within the country of Sudan after years of civil war. A January 2011 popular vote held in the region split Sudan into two countries, and the Republic of South Sudan became the newest country on the world map in July. A peaceful separation happened in 1991 when the USSR (Union of Soviet Socialist Republics) broke apart to form 15 different countries—Armenia, Azerbaijan, Belarus, Estonia, Georgia, Kazakhstan, Kyrgyzstan, Latvia, Lithuania, Moldova, Russia, Tajikistan, Turkmenistan, Ukraine, and Uzbekistan.

Sometimes countries change their names. When resource-hungry European powers started exploring Africa in the 1800s, armies were sent into Africa to unify different tribes into colonies under European rule. When those African colonies gained their independence in the 1900s, they sometimes chose new names. For example, French Sudan became Mali and German Southwest Africa became Namibia.

ENORMOUS ASIA

The largest continent on Earth, Asia accounts for 30 percent of the world's land area and contains **Russia,** the world's largest country. With a population of 4 billion, Asia is home to 60 percent of the world's population and includes three of the four most populous countries—**China, India,** and **Indonesia.** Asia is the only continent that borders two other continents: Africa and Europe. In the winter when ice forms in the Bering Sea, it sometimes joins with a third continent: North America.

What Else Is Special about Asia?

Asia has more going for it than just its size. Here are more fun facts about this continent.

• The equator passes through Indonesia, a nation of 17,508 islands. The rest of Asia is north of the equator.

• The northern reaches of Asia lie within the Arctic Circle. This region is part of Russia and is called **Siberia.** Siberia is sparsely populated because the climate is so harsh. Eastern Siberia has winter temperatures as low as −94°F (−70°C). Siberia is rich with mineral resources, but it is most famous for its prison system, including the labor camps where Russians were sent for political crimes in the twentieth century.

• China is the most populous country in Asia. It is both an ancient civilization—with roots that can be traced back 8,000 to 10,000 years—and a modern nation that was created in 1949 as the People's Republic of China. China's huge population makes it important to the rest of the world. All those people need jobs, and Chinese manufacturing supplies many of the things people in other countries want to buy. But China buys things, too—such as the fossil fuels needed (including oil) to power those factories. As the country becomes wealthier, more people buy consumer goods made in other countries, such as refrigerators, computers, televisions, and designer clothes.

• India is the second most populous country in Asia. Its large population, like that of China, provides many goods and services important to the rest of the world, buys imported goods, and uses resources from its own country and around the world.

- The Asian country of Japan sits where the Pacific, Philippine, and Eurasian tectonic plates meet (see page 26). Earthquakes are frequent in Japan, and occasionally they do serious damage, as in 2011 when an earthquake just off the coast caused a tsunami that killed an estimated 25,000 people.

- The mountains of Japan include about 200 active volcanoes. That means that 10 percent of the world's most active volcanoes are located in this one country! **Mount Fuji** is Japan's tallest and most famous mountain, with an elevation of 12,388 feet (3,776 m); it is a dormant (sleeping but not extinct) volcano that last erupted in 1707.

- **Tokyo,** the capital city of Japan and a major economic and political center, is the world's largest city. It has an estimated population of 35.1 million people.

- **Seoul,** South Korea, is the second largest city in the world with an estimated population of 20.6 million people.

- The **Himalayas,** the highest mountain range in the world, stretch about 1,860 miles (3,000 km) across Asia, running through six countries: Bhutan, Tibet, India, Nepal, Pakistan, and Afghanistan.

- **Mount Everest** is the tallest mountain in the world with an elevation of 29,035 feet (8,850 m). It is located in Nepal.

- Three mighty rivers—the **Indus, Brahmaputra,** and **Yangtze**—originate, or start, in the Himalayas.

- **Hong Kong** is an island off the coast of China. It is one of the most densely populated places in the world and has more skyscrapers than any other city. There are more people who live or work above the fourteenth floor of the many buildings in Hong Kong than anywhere else on earth.

• The **Arabian Peninsula,** on the western edge of Asia, is the largest peninsula (a piece of land surrounded on three sides by water) in the world.

• The **Middle East** is part of Asia. It is made up of the countries of the Arabian Peninsula and those that border the Persian Gulf. The Persian Gulf is an extension of the Indian Ocean located between Iran and the Arabian Peninsula. The Middle East includes the countries of Syria, Jordan, Lebanon, Israel, Saudi Arabia, Yemen, Oman, United Arab Emirates (U.A.E.), Qatar, Bahrain, Kuwait, Iraq, and Iran.

• Many countries in the Middle East have large quantities of crude oil underground and available for drilling. The oil is used to made gasoline to fuel cars and heating oil to warm buildings.

• Cherrapunji, India, may be the wettest place on Earth. Between August 1860 and July 1861, a record of 905 inches (2,299 cm) of rain fell.

• The country of **Qatar** in the Arabian Peninsula is the wealthiest nation in the world.

• Asia is the only continent where tigers and giant pandas are found in the wild.

• Russia is so big that it stretches across 11 time zones. Its two largest cities, **Moscow,** the capital, and **St. Petersburg,** are both located on the western (European) side of the country but most of its land is located on the eastern (Asian) side.

FRACTURED AFRICA

The second largest continent, Africa accounts for about 20 percent of the Earth's landmass. Surrounded by water on all sides, Africa was once connected to Asia in its northeast

corner by the Sinai Peninsula, where the Suez Canal now joins the Red Sea and the Mediterranean Sea.

Why is it a "fractured" continent? Because when the African and Arabian tectonic plates (see page 26) separated about 35 million years ago, a huge fault line was created in Africa. That fault line is the **Great Rift Valley.** In a few million years, the eastern part of Africa—the eastern portion beyond the Great Rift Valley—will probably split off from the African plate and form a new plate. The sea will invade the gap created by the separation and form a new ocean basin. And that means Africa will become two continents—or one continent and one big island.

With all this tectonic plate action, it is not surprising that the Great Rift Valley is home to 30 active and semi-active volcanoes and countless hot springs. Volcanic eruptions are responsible for the landscape along the length of the rift—perpendicular cliffs, mountain ridges, rugged valleys, and a series of about 30 very deep lakes along its entire length, including **Lake Tanganyika,** the second deepest lake in the world.

What Else Is Special about Africa?

Africa isn't just interesting for its moving and shaking. Here are more things to know about this continent.

• Africa has a population of 922 million people, which makes it the second most populous continent.

• **Nigeria** is Africa's most-populous nation. With 146 million people, it is the eighth most populous nation in the world.

• The people of Africa are divided into several thousand different ethnic groups, which speak an estimated two thousand different languages.

• The world's longest river is the **Nile.** It runs through the African countries of Burundi, Democratic Republic of Congo, Egypt, Ethiopia, Rwanda, South Sudan, Sudan, Tanzania, and Uganda.

• The world's largest hot desert is the **Sahara** in northern Africa. It is part of the landscape of the African countries of Algeria, Chad, Egypt, Libya, Mali, Mauritania, Morocco, Niger, Sudan, Tunisia, and Western Sahara.

- **Mount Kilimanjaro** is the highest mountain in Africa, with an elevation of 19,340 feet (5,895 m). It is snowcapped all year even though it is only 230 miles (370 km) miles from the equator!

- The equator runs through Africa, making it the most tropical of all the continents.

- **Madagascar** is the largest island off the coast of Africa. About 75 percent of the species found in Madagascar live nowhere else on Earth. This includes dozens of species of lemurs and chameleons—and even giant hissing cockroaches.

- Most of the world's gold and diamonds come from Africa, which is also rich in other natural resources, such as minerals.

- Around 60,000 B.C., early man left Africa and settled in India and Australia, and then West Asia, Europe, and China.

RESOURCE-RICH NORTH AMERICA

The third largest continent, North America stretches south from the Arctic Circle, through the country of Panama, and to the northern tip of South America, just 500 miles (800 km) north of the equator. North America includes an area called Central America. The islands of the Caribbean are also part of North America. (To view Central America see the maps on pages 72 and 75.)

Water and other natural resources are abundant in most of the continent. The sheer variety of environments—arctic tundra, grasslands, temperate forest, desert, and rain forest—means an incredible variety of plants and animals, too.

What Else Is Special about North America?

Natural resources are just part of this continent's big picture. Here are additional facts about North America.

• North America is surrounded on three sides by ocean— the Arctic, Atlantic, and Pacific oceans.

• North America includes many islands, including **Greenland,** the world's largest island.

• The **Caribbean Sea** has the greatest concentration of islands in North America—about 7,000.

- The island nations of the Caribbean are sometimes called the **West Indies** because that's what the explorer Christopher Columbus (1451–1506) thought he had found when he landed there.

- The largest country in North America is **Canada.** It is the second largest country in the world. The **United States of America** is the third largest country in the world.

- The largest city in North America is **Mexico City,** the capital of the country of Mexico. It has a population of 20.4 million people. It is ranked as the third largest city in the world. New York City comes in fourth with an estimated population of 19.8 million people.

- **New York City,** a city of immigrants, is the most diverse city in the world, with 800 different languages spoken.

- The **San Andreas Fault** runs through the state of California. The fault is a boundary line between two tectonic plates: the Pacific plate and the North American plate (see page 26). All the land west of the fault on the Pacific plate is moving slowly to the northwest, and all the land east of the fault is moving southwest at a rate of about $1\frac{1}{3}$ to $1\frac{1}{2}$ inches (3.4 to 3.8 cm) each year. Earthquakes are frequent along the fault.

- **Mount McKinley,** also called Mount Denali, is located in Alaska. It is the highest peak in North America at 20,324 feet (6,194 m). **Mount Kea** in Hawaii would be taller, but much of its height is below water, which doesn't count toward its elevation.

- The most reported tornadoes happen in the United States, where there are around 1,000 per year. The majority of them take place in what is known as **Tornado Alley**—in the states of Nebraska, Kansas, Oklahoma, and Texas. Texas alone has an average of 125 tornadoes a year!

• Most of **Central America** rests on the small but geologically active **Caribbean plate** (see page 26), accounting for the region's numerous deadly earthquakes and volcanoes.

• The **Isthmus of Panama** connects North America to South America. An isthmus is a narrow strip of land with water on both sides that connects two large land areas.

• Parts of the Arctic Circle are covered by a permanent ice cap. Greenland and far northern Canada have an arctic climate, which is better for polar bears than humans so the farther north you go, the smaller the population.

• The lowest point in North America is **Death Valley,** California, at 282 feet (86 m) below sea level.

• **Lake Superior,** on the border between the United States and Canada, is North America's largest freshwater lake. It covers 31,700 square miles (82,100 km^2).

• The first human inhabitants of North America crossed over to Alaska on a land bridge from northeastern Asia roughly 20,000 years ago and then moved southward.

• North America is important to the rest of the world because it produces the greatest amount of the world's corn, meat, cotton, soybeans, tobacco, and wheat, along with a variety of other food.

LONG AND LEAN SOUTH AMERICA

At 6.9 million square miles (17.9 million km^2), South America ranks as the fourth largest continent, but much of the land—rugged mountains and inaccessible rain forest—is virtually uninhabited by humans. This long, narrow continent runs from the equator nearly to the South Pole. The northern part of

South America, near the equator, is generally hot and wet. In the southern part, near the South Pole, it can be very cold.

Three centuries of **European colonization** shows in the cultures of South America. Roman Catholicism, introduced by Spain, is the majority religion of the region. Spanish and Portuguese (in Brazil, the largest country) are the dominant languages. The biggest impact the Europeans had on the continent was the spreading of many diseases, which quickly sickened the native population. Shortly after the first European contact with the **New World,** as explorers called North and South America, about 80 percent of the native population died of smallpox, diphtheria, measles, mumps, typhus, and other **Old World** diseases.

What Else Is Special about South America?

From mountain peaks to crashing surf, South America claims some unique geographic features. Here are extra facts about this continent.

• The **Andes Mountains** run all the way down the west coast of South America. It is very cold on the peaks of these high mountains, even in the warm north of the continent.

• From its main source in the Andes, near the equator, the **Amazon River** runs east to the Atlantic Ocean. The Amazon isn't the longest river in the world, but it does send the largest volume of water into the ocean of any river in the world.

• Grassland south of the Amazon rain forest is known as **pampas.** The **Atacama Desert,** which is mostly uninhabited, is found along the southern west coast of South America, between the Andes Mountains and the Pacific Ocean.

• The vast majority of South Americans live in cities. The largest South American country in both size and population is **Brazil,** which is the fifth largest country in the world. The largest city in South America is **São Paulo,** Brazil.

• The harbor at **Rio de Janeiro** on Guanabara Bay in the Atlantic Ocean is considered one of the natural wonders of the world. The bay creates a huge natural harbor protected by two tall mountains that stand guard at the mouth of the bay: Sugar Loaf Mountain and Corcovodo Mountain. Sugar Loaf Mountain got its name because its bare ground and lopsided shape makes it look like a "loaf" of sugar, which is how sugar used to be sold. Corcovado means "hunchback" in Portuguese, and the mountain has a humped shape. On top of Corcovado is the statue of Christ the Redeemer, one of the seven wonders of the modern world.

• The **Amazon River basin** is the world's largest tropical rain forest, at 2.5 million square miles—which is just about the same size as the continental United States (that means without Hawaii and Alaska). The rain forest covers about one-third of the South American continent.

• The **Galápagos Islands,** off the coast of the country of Ecuador, are famous as the place that led scientist **Charles Darwin** (1809–1882) to develop his famous theory of evolution. Residents of the Galápagos include **finches, tortoises, penguins, albatrosses,** and the **blue-footed booby.**

• The world's southernmost city is **Puerto Toro,** Chile.

• South America is important to the rest of the world because it has abundant natural resources, grows an important share of the world's food supply, and is a growing presence on the global economic stage.

FROZEN ANTARCTICA

Antarctica is the most extreme location on the planet. This frozen land of snow and rock is the coldest, windiest, driest, loneliest, and least hospitable landmass. It's the planet's southernmost continent and does not belong to any one country—at least for now. In the past various countries have tried to claim ownership of the land, but an international treaty now governs Antarctica. Today only a few thousand scientists live and work there.

Including its permanent sheet of ice, Antarctica has an area of about 5.5 million square miles (14.3 million km^2), which makes it the fifth largest continent. It is the most isolated continent on Earth, and you'd have to sail a distance of 600 miles (1,000 km) to reach the southernmost tip of South America, its nearest neighbor.

What Else Is Special about Antarctica?

If learning about extreme Antarctica makes you want to read on, you're in luck. Here are even more facts about this wild continent.

• Surrounded by the Southern Ocean, Antarctica is an ice-locked landmass located at the South Pole.

• The average annual temperature inland is −70°F (−57°C). The lowest temperature ever recorded on Earth was in the Antarctic, an incredible −128.5°F (−89°C).

• Underneath its ice cap, the eastern part of Antarctica is rock, mostly above sea level.

• West Antarctica was formed by volcanic action. Under the weight of its ice, much of the land, which seems to be a group of islands held together by permanent ice, is actually below sea level.

• Probably the best-known volcano on Antarctica is **Mount Erebus,** which is part of the Pacific Ring of Fire. With a summit elevation of 12,448 feet (3,794 m), it looms over McMurdo Station, an American research base on Ross Island.

• Antarctica is technically a **frozen desert.** It is thought that in some spots, such as McMurdo Sound, rain or snow hasn't fallen for more than two million years!

New Year's Moving Day

If someone could insert a rod through the entire planet to show how the earth rotates, it would go through the North and South poles. In the Arctic the rod would have to be inserted into the seabed of the Arctic Ocean. In Antarctica the South Pole lies inland. Norwegian polar explorer Roald Amundsen (1872–1928) and his team of adventurers planted the first flag on the South Pole, and today the geographic South Pole is the site of the Amundsen-Scott Station, a United States scientific base. But the exact place where the South Pole is located moves every year because it is on an ice sheet that migrates about 33 feet (10 m) annually. So the pole that marks the spot is ceremoniously moved every New Year's Day.

But don't confuse the *geographic* South Pole (0° longitude) with the *magnetic* South Pole. That's about 1,700 miles (2,740 km) away!

• With the exception of a few bare peaks and "dry" valleys, almost all this land is covered by an immense **ice sheet** an average of 1 mile (1.6 km) thick. Its greatest known thickness is about 3 miles (4.8 km)—that's 15,670 feet (4,776 m).

• Because the snow on Antarctica never melts, it never goes away—ever. So it builds up, and up. The average elevation of Antarctica is about 7,500 feet (2,286 m), which makes it the highest continent on Earth.

• The high elevation of Antarctica explains why it is colder at the South Pole than the North Pole. The North Pole is at sea level, an elevation of zero, and the South Pole is at 9,300 feet (2.9 m); air is cooler at higher elevations.

• The annual snowfall in the interior of the continent is only 1 to 2 inches (2.5 to 5 cm), although more snow falls along the coast and on the windward side (the side the wind is blowing) of coastal mountains—10 to 20 inches (25 to 51 cm) per year.

All about Icebergs

When a big chunk of ice breaks off from a glacier, the process is called **calving**. Generally 10,000 to 15,000 icebergs are calved each year. Chunks of ice smaller than an iceberg are called bergy bits and growlers.

Icebergs are larger than they appear, since only 10 to 15 percent can be seen above the surface of the water. To be classified as an iceberg, the ice must be at least 16 feet (5 m) tall, 98 to 164 feet (30 to 50 m) wide, and the ice must cover an area of at least 5,382 square feet (500 m²). The largest iceberg ever measured was 208 miles (335 km) long and 60 miles (97 km) wide. Scientists estimated that if that iceberg melted and the water were captured, it would provide enough freshwater to supply London, England, for 700 years.

- The ice that covers the Antarctic holds 70 to 90 percent of the earth's freshwater reserves. Along the coast, the ice sometimes forms enormous floating sheets called **ice shelves.** The largest are the Ross Ice Shelf, the Ronne Ice Shelf, the Larsen Ice Shelf, and the Filchner Ice Shelf.

- The ice shelves are fed, in part, by huge **freshwater glaciers** moving down mountain valleys to the coasts. Glaciers also flow directly into the sea like long floating tongues; these are called glacier tongues or iceberg tongues.

- The **Lambert Glacier** on the eastern half of the continent is 25 miles (40 km) wide and more than 248 miles (400 km) long, making it the largest glacier on earth.

- Each summer tons of icebergs break off the edges of the ice shelves and float north. Sea ice—frozen seawater that forms during the winter—also breaks up during the summer, creating freely floating ice known as **pack ice.**

WELL-SETTLED EUROPE

When you look at a world map you might wonder why Europe is considered a continent. After all, it is physically attached to Asia. Some geographers call Europe a peninsula, part of "Eurasia." But the two areas are culturally distinct—even if a few countries (such as Russia) fall within both Europe *and* Asia. So we consider Europe a continent, separated from Asia by the Ural and Caucasus mountains.

Covering 3.9 million square miles (10.1 million km^2), Europe is the second smallest of the continents and has been fully settled for centuries. With a total population of 731 million, it comes second only to Asia in terms of population density. Europe's agriculture and industry also are well developed. It was once covered with temperate forests, but little of that remains. The land has been grazed and farmed for centuries. Few areas of untouched wilderness are left, except in Scandinavia and northern Russia.

What Else Is Special about Europe?

When it comes to settling down, Europe is king! Here are some fabulous facts about this continent.

- Most of Europe lies within 300 miles (483 km) of a seacoast.

- There are no deserts in Europe.

- **Vatican City,** which is located within the city of Rome, Italy, is the world's smallest country in terms of population (829). And most of the people are not even permanent residents. Covering an area of just 0.17 square miles (0.44 km^2), Vatican City is the world's smallest country by area as well. It serves as the residence of the pope, the head of the Catholic Church.

- Besides Vatican City, there are other tiny nations in Europe. **San Marino,** located within the borders of Italy, is the oldest

surviving sovereign state and constitutional republic in the world. It was founded on September 3, 301. Densely populated, **Monaco** is a city state on the Côte d' Azur, bordered on three sides by its neighbor France. Monaco is famous for its casinos, tourism, and beautiful location on the French Riviera. The small, landlocked nation of **Liechtenstein** has the highest Gross Domestic Product (GDP) per person in the world.

• The island country of **Iceland** is basically one big volcano, formed over millions of years as molten rock bubbled up from the sea floor. Other features of Iceland include glaciers, lava wastes, ice caps, and boiling lakes.

• The mountains in northern Norway are home to the largest glacier on mainland Europe, **Jostedal Glacier.**

• Norway is famous for its **fjords** (pronounced fee-yords). A fjord is a narrow, steep-sided inlet to the sea carved by glaciers.

• Lapland, in northern Norway, and parts of Sweden and Finland lie within the Arctic Circle.

• The Netherlands is a whole country with an elevation that is basically below sea level. Since the Middle Ages, the Dutch have built dikes (large barriers of earth and stone) to hold back water and reclaim land from the sea. These reclaimed lands, called **polders,** once were drained and kept dry by power generated bywindmills. Today other sources of power run the pumps that keep the polders dry.

• The **Alps** are a mountain range dividing southern Europe from northern Europe. The **Ural** and **Caucasus** mountains form a border with Asia.

• Italy has Europe's only active volcanoes: **Mount Etna** (on the island of Sicily) and **Mount Vesuvius.**

• **Russia, Turkey, Georgia,** and **Kazakhstan** are all countries that are partly in Europe and partly in Asia.

• Europe is important to the rest of the world because the European Union (EU) represents the largest and most diverse economy of the world. The member nations of the EU are able to keep their own identities, cultures, laws, and governments but cooperate with the other nations when it comes to trade and financial matters. They share the same currency, called the euro. Europe is also the world's biggest contributor of money to help developing countries.

DOWN UNDER
AUSTRALIA/OCEANIA

Is Australia a country, an island, or a continent? Most geographers these days consider the *country* of Australia to be part of a larger *continent* that includes New Zealand and thousands of Pacific islands and coral atolls, or reefs that surround lagoons. Some say the most accurate name is Australia/Oceania; others call it Australasia. Australia/Oceania is located in the Southern Hemisphere, southeast of Asia, and surrounded by the Indian and Pacific oceans. It is the smallest continent in terms of size and the second smallest in population. It may be "small" in terms of dry land; however, it is spread over 3.3 million square miles (8.5 million km^2) of ocean.

What Else Is Special about the Land Down Under?

Although Australia/Oceania does not have a lot of land, it can boast about many other things. Here are just a few of this continent's important facts.

• The largest country in Australia/Oceania is Australia. Australia is the driest inhabited continent, the flattest, and has the least fertile soils.

• There are more sheep in Australia/Oceania than people.

- About 70 percent of all Australians live in a city.

- **Aborigines**, the indigenous people of Australia, traditionally live in the dry and dusty **Outback** in the center of Australia.

- Australia has the greatest number of reptiles of any country in the world, with about 755 species.

- **The Great Barrier Reef** is the largest coral reef in the world and lies a short distance off the coast of Australia. It is considered one of the wonders of the natural world, and it is home to some 1,500 species of fish, 400 types of coral, 500 species of seaweed, 16 species of sea snake, and six species of sea turtle. It is also an important breeding ground for humpback whales.

- **Tasmania** is an island off the southern coast of Australia. It is home to the fierce little Tasmanian devil as well as several other animal species that are now extinct on mainland Australia.

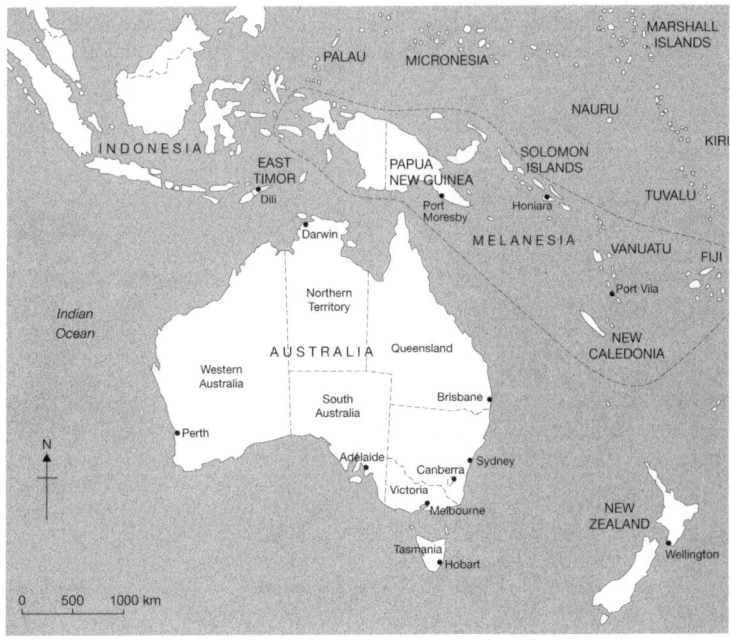

Home, Sweet . . . Pouch?

Many marsupials, such as kangaroos, live only in Australia. Marsupials are animals that grow their young in external pouches instead of inside their bodies. Other marsupials include the platypus, koala bear, wombat, and kookaburra.

But why don't people in Europe look into the trees and see koala bears? Conditions on Australia/Oceania led to the development of these mammals. When the continent broke away from Antarctica about 140 million years ago, it drifted north into warm waters, and the land became isolated from the other continents. Unlike other areas of the world, Australia never experienced an ice age, which means the environment remained relatively stable over the course of 40 million years or so when other continents went through major periods of animal extinctions. And so Australia is home to the koala bear—and to the kangaroo. In fact, more than 80 percent of the country's flowering plants, mammals, reptiles, and frogs live only in Australia. And most of Australia's freshwater fish and almost half of its birds can only be found on this one special place on earth, too.

• **New Zealand, Papua New Guinea** (considered part of Asia), and the **Solomon Islands** are part of the Pacific Ring of Fire (see page 30).

• New Zealanders are called **Kiwis**, an affectionate term that refers to the flightless kiwi bird—and not the fruit with the brown, fuzzy skin.

• Earthquakes and volcanoes are common on New Zealand because the land is split between the Australian plate and the Pacific plate. When New Zealand separated from Australia about 100 million years ago, mammals were just emerging. Because of this timing, New Zealand had few mammals until humans spread across the globe about 80 million years later. There were, however, plenty of flightless—and wingless—birds.

• Australia is home to the greatest number of **marsupial species**, such as koalas and kangaroos, in the world. Marsupial moms usually carry their babies in a pouch as the babies grow.

• Many of the **Pacific Islands** are **volcanic islands** that rose from the sea floor through hot spots in the Pacific Ocean

Where in the World Are the Seven Wonders?

In the fifth century B.C., a historian by the name of Herodotus sat down and wrote a list of the seven wonders of the world. People have been arguing over the list ever since—what he included, what he didn't include. The list itself didn't survive, but scholars think the seven wonders of the ancient world included:

• Great Pyramid of Giza
• Hanging Gardens of Babylon
• Statue of Zeus at Olympia
• Temple of Artemis at Ephesus
• Mausoleum of Maussollos at Halicarnassus
• Colossus of Rhodes
• Lighthouse of Alexandria

Don't be surprised if you've never heard of all these wonders— or visited any of them. Most of them are long gone. Some historians don't think the hanging gardens ever existed. The only wonder you can still visit is the Great Pyramid of Giza, which is located in Egypt.

Basin. Most of these volcanic islands, such as **Fiji** and the **Solomon Islands,** are very small and have tall mountain ranges.

• About 15 million people live on the islands of Australia/Oceania.

• Australia/Oceania is important to the rest of the world as a vacation spot. The country of Australia, and the continent to a lesser extent, is rich in mineral resources, including coal, diamonds, gold, iron ore, natural gas, nickel, petroleum, and uranium.

ISLAND HOPPING

THE WORLD'S BIGGEST ISLAND

A tropical island paradise is a good spot for a vacation. But which one? Planet Earth has more than 100,000 islands, so there are plenty to choose from. The difference between an island and a continent is a matter of size. It seems like finding the world's biggest island would be easy as looking at a map or a globe and picking out the largest area of land that's totally surrounded by water.

Well, it's not that simple. You could be fooled into thinking that the world's biggest island is Australia. After all, it is surrounded by ocean and is more than three times the size of its nearest rival, **Greenland.** However, geographers have decided that there has to be a cutoff point between islands and continents. Australia is often classed as a continent, bouncing it out of the top spot for biggest island. In this book, it is included as part of Australia/Oceania (see pages 84 to 88). This leaves Greenland as the second biggest island. It is part of the North American continent and a protectorate of the European country of Denmark, which just means that Denmark takes care of Greenland politically and financially.

Barrier Islands

A barrier island is a long, thin, sandy piece of land parallel to the mainland coast. It makes a barrier between the mainland and raging ocean storms, protecting the coast from the full force of powerful storm waves. In the United States, barrier islands occur off the Atlantic and Gulf of Mexico coasts, where there are gently sloping sandy coastlines, as opposed to rocky coastlines. **Padre Island,** off the coast of Texas, is the longest barrier island in the world. **Assateague Island** near Maryland is a barrier island and is most famous as a home of wild ponies.

MAKING ISLANDS

Greenland was once connected to North America, so how did it become an island? There are two types of islands: continental and oceanic. Greenland is a continental island.

Continental Islands. These islands are part of a continent that has been flooded so much that only the highest points lie above sea level, creating islands. Most continental islands were formed at the end of the last ice age, when the huge glaciers covering the land melted. Vast amounts of **meltwater** flowed into the oceans and made sea levels rise. Those higher sea levels flooded low-lying areas at the edges of the land. In addition to creating the island of Greenland, the meltwater created more than 3,000 islands along Norway's rugged coast in Europe. The **British Isles** off the coast of mainland Europe are also continental islands. If sea levels fell far enough, the United Kingdom would be reconnected with Europe.

Oceanic Islands. The earth's crust is a jigsaw puzzle of moving pieces called tectonic plates (see page 26). Oceanic islands are formed by volcanic activity along the edges of these plates on the ocean floor. Where plates move

The World's Most Endangered Country

The Maldive Islands are the flattest country on earth. At their highest point, they only reach an altitude of about eight feet (2.4 m) above sea level. About 1,200 islands and atolls in the Indian Ocean make up this country, anchored just north of the equator. Only 200 of the islands are inhabited, but the absolute number and identity of the islands varies because old islands are constantly becoming submerged underwater and new ones are constantly created. White sandy beaches, deep-blue lagoons, and coral reefs are part of the beauty of this nation, but a rise in sea levels threatens its survival. If sea levels continue to rise at current rates, it is expected that the islands will be uninhabitable in about 100 years.

apart from each other, the earth's crust cracks, allowing hot, melted rock known as magma, to bubble up, forming an undersea volcano. The magma cools and solidifies. Eventually, the volcano grows so high that it rises above sea level, forming an island. **Easter Island** in the Pacific Ocean was formed this way.

Oceanic islands are also formed where one tectonic plate slips underneath the other. As the earth's crust pushes into the mantle, it melts and turns into magma. This erupts to form a chain of islands, known as an island arc. This is how the **Aleutian Islands,** located between Russia and Alaska at the northern edge of the Pacific Ocean, were created.

Hot spots also create islands. These superheated places deep inside the earth are so hot that they can melt the earth's crust, allowing lava to burst through to form volcanoes. This lava builds over time until the volcano is tall enough to break through the surface of the sea. Surtsey island off the coast of

Iceland in the Atlantic Ocean is an example of this kind of oceanic island. It formed right in front of Icelanders' eyes in 1963!

Hot spots build islands hundreds of miles away from tectonic plate boundaries. Over millions of years, a single hot spot can build a whole chain of islands. This is because a hot spot stays put as the tectonic plate above slowly moves over it. As the plate moves, the hot spot melts new holes in the crust, creating new volcanoes and new islands.

The **Hawaiian Island chain** was created in this way. There are 132 Hawaiian islands, and the newest is being built right now at the bottom of the Pacific Ocean. But don't plan a vacation there just yet—it will take tens of thousands of years for that little lump of lava to rise above the ocean's surface.

WE'RE NOT AN ISLAND *ATOLL*

Once a new volcanic island has drifted away from the hot spot that created it, the island starts to sink. Rain, wind, and waves wear the island away until it disappears below the surface of the ocean forever. When this

Hurricane Capital of the World

Vacationers love the Cayman Islands, located 150 miles south of Cuba in the western Caribbean. Pristine beaches, coral reefs perfect for diving, and high-end resorts attract people from all over North America. This British territory is also the hurricane capital of the world. Grand Cayman, the largest of the three Cayman isles, is hit or affected by at least one hurricane every two years, more than any other spot in the Atlantic.

happens, that island needs a new name. For example, the oldest and most remote Hawaiian island is not an island at all. It used to be, but now it's just an **atoll**. An atoll is formed when a coral reef grows around a volcanic island. As the coral reef grows, the volcanic island is slowly destroyed and eventually all that is left is a ring of coral with shallow water or a **lagoon** in the middle.

MAKING MOUNTAINS

HOW DO MOUNTAINS CLIMB?

Planet Earth's mountain ranges are jagged towers of rock that rise high into the skies. How did they get there? Why are they all so different in size and shape? Mountains form through processes that begin deep below the surface of the earth. It takes a long time to make a mountain. Scientists have found 18,000-year-old seashells in rock samples from the Himalayan and Andes mountains—far, far away from any beach. This suggests that these mountains were once below sea level. So how do you go from ocean floor to top of the world?

Folds. Mountains form when two continental tectonic plates (see page 26) crash into one another, causing the crust to crumple and pushing the land up. This is the most common way for mountains to form— the Himalayas in Asia were created in this way. And that pushing? It's still happening. Scientists have evidence that the world's highest mountain, Mount Everest, is still growing and moving.

The Most Famous Dome Mountain

Parícutin volcano in the Mexican state of Michoacán is one of the natural wonders of the world because it grew right before the eyes of the farmers who lived nearby. This dome-shaped mountain began as a cornfield and ended up as a mountain in just eight short years. When this volcano first erupted in 1943, it grew so fast that it measured five stories tall in one week. Over the course of its first year, it rose 1,110 feet (336 m) into the air. It continued to erupt until it went dormant in 1952, at the height of 1,390 feet (424 m).

Eruptions. Repeated volcanic eruptions that happen where the continental plates meet can cause molten rock and ash to spew out from inside the Earth. The ash and rock build up over time—a long, long time—to make mountains out of flatland. **Mount Fuji** in Japan and

Mount Rainier in Washington State are examples of this kind of mountain.

Faults. Sometimes when two tectonic plates push together, they crack instead of folding, and a huge chunk of rock is pushed upward to create what is known as a **block mountain**. The **Sierra Nevada Mountains** in California are examples of block mountains.

Domes. Dome mountains form when magma, or molten rock, in the mantle increases in pressure, pushing the earth's crust up from below. This process makes rounded, dome-shaped mountains. The **Black Hills** of South Dakota and the **Adirondack Mountains** of New York State are examples of dome mountains.

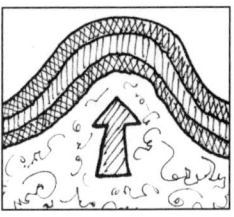

WEAR AND TEAR

If mountains are still growing, why are some so small? Before a mountain has finished growing, wind, water, and ice set to work, wearing it down in a process called **erosion**. Erosion causes the wide variety of mountain shapes you can see today. Ice in the form of **glaciers** creates some of the most eye-catching mountain features by carving deep into the rock and bulldozing away rock and soil. In fact, glaciers in the last ice age acted like giant scouring pads, scrubbing away the tops of mountains. The older the mountains, the more wear and tear from erosion.

THE YOUNG HIMALAYAS

The highest and largest mountain range in the world, the Himalayas stretch about 1,860 miles (3,000 km) across Asia. This mountain range contains the 15 highest peaks in the world, including Mount Everest. When the Himalayas formed, they physically separated South Asia and the Indian

What Is a Glacier?

A glacier is a very, very big sheet of ice formed over years and years as snow falls and never melts. As the snow piles up, its weight increases and causes the snow crystals below the surface to compact into ice crystals. These ice crystals join together to form a "river" of ice that can measure 300 to 10,000 feet (91 to 3,050 m) in thickness—that's quite thick when you remember that there are 5,280 feet in a mile! Ice, as we all know, is slippery. When a glacier becomes very dense and heavy, the ice crystals deep inside it begin to slide over each other, and the glacier starts to move. Because of gravity, the movement is downward, either down a mountain or to the sea. As glaciers move, they pick up soil and rocks and deposit them elsewhere as **sediment**.

subcontinent from the rest of Asia, causing differences in climate and the development of distinctively different cultures.

Plate tectonics created this great mountain range (see page 26) about 70 million years ago—when the Indian plate collided with Eurasian plate. The Himalayas are the youngest mountains in the world, a fact that accounts in part for their great height—there hasn't been as much time for erosion to wear them down as for other, older mountains. At present they are still growing; the Indian plate pushes into the Asian continent at the rate of about $2\frac{1}{3}$ inches (6 cm) annually, slowly but surely folding and lifting up the crust of the earth as it goes.

The Himalayas play a major role in India's climate because they block the flow of cool air from the north. As a result, India's climate is very hot. The mountains also block moist air coming off the Indian Ocean from reaching Central Asia, which is why much of the interior of China is a desert region.

The Himalayas are the source of many of the world's major rivers: the Brahmaputra, Chao Phraya, Ganges, Indus, Irrawaddy, Mekong, Yangtze, and Yellow rivers (among others) start in the Himalayas. As they flow out to the sea, these rivers provide fresh water for about 3 billion people (almost half of earth's population) in Afghanistan, Bangladesh, Bhutan, China, India, Nepal, Burma, Cambodia, Tajikistan, Uzbekistan, Turkmenistan, Kazakhstan, Kyrgyzstan, Thailand, Laos, Vietnam, Malaysia, and Pakistan.

THE OLD APPALACHIANS

The Appalachian Mountains in the United States extend from central Alabama up through the New England states and the Canadian provinces of New Brunswick, Newfoundland, and

Mount Everest: A Natural Wonder

Mount Everest, the highest mountain in the world, is considered one of the natural wonders of the world. Every year adventurous climbers attempt to reach the top of this peak, located on the border between Nepal and Tibet. Its summit was first reached in 1953 by Sir Edmund Hillary (1919–2008) of New Zealand and Tenzing Norgay (1914–1986) of Nepal. Norgay knew the mountain as Cho-molungma, the Tibetan name, which means "Mother of the Universe." However, a British surveyor-general called it Mount Everest, not knowing that the mountain had a Nepalese name. Climbing Everest has generated con-troversy in recent years, because nearly 200 people have died climbing the mountain.

Quebec—about 1,500 miles (2,410 km) in all. The mountains have different names in different parts of the country. They are called the Cumberland Mountains in Tennessee, the Blue Ridge Mountains in Virginia, the Alleghenies in Pennsylvania, the Adirondacks in New York, the Green Mountains in Vermont, and the White Mountains in New Hampshire. The highest point is Mount Mitchell in North Carolina at 6,684 feet (2,037 m). The oldest mountains in the world, the ancient Appalachian Mountains were formed about 300 million years ago when the tectonic plate boundaries of North America and Africa collided during the formation of Pangaea, the supercontinent (see page 28). Over the years, erosion has smoothed out the jagged peaks and knocked down the height of the mountains until they appear as mere bumps on the landscape compared to the Himalayas—or even the Rockies, located in the western region of the United States.

A ROCKY HISTORY FOR THE ROCKY MOUNTAINS

The Rocky Mountains stretch from Canada down to the southwestern United States in North America. These ancient mountains formed along fault lines as the Pacific tectonic plate pushed against the North American tectonic plate. At one point, a vast ocean covered the land and deposited a lot of sand that eventually formed a **sandstone** layer in the rock. At various times the mountains were worn down by glaciers and erosion and built up again by volcanic and plate tectonic action. Like the Himalayas, the Rocky Mountains are still growing even today because the Pacific plate continues to push against North America.

The mountains form the **Continental Divide** for North America, separating the rivers that drain into the Atlantic Ocean from those that drain into the Pacific Ocean. The major rivers that flow to the Atlantic are the Arkansas, Missouri, Platte, Rio Grande, Saskatchewan, and Yellowstone rivers. Those draining to the Pacific Ocean are the Colorado, Columbia, Fraser, Snake, and Yukon rivers.

THE LONG ANDES

This very long mountain range of rugged high peaks extends along the western part of South America, from the northern end all the way south to the islands off the southern tip of the mainland called **Tierra del Fuego** (Land of Fire). The Andes rise to a highest point of 22,835 feet (6,960 m) above sea level at the peak of **Mount Aconcagua** in Argentina.

The Andes are fold mountains, formed when Pangaea broke up and the pieces began to float away from each other (see page 28). The Pacific Ocean tectonic plate began to squeeze under the South America plate, pushing up the Andes.

The Amazon and most of the other major rivers on the South American continent originate in the Andes, which is where the continental divide for this area is located. The Andes are also home to 204 volcanoes, many of them active, including some of the planet's largest. In the far south, along the coast of Chile, large glaciers are common. And when you combine volcanoes with glaciers, you get eruptions that cause major mudslides, which can be deadly.

Mountain Dwellers

Plants and animals that thrive on high-elevation mountains must be adapted to the cold, the lack of oxygen (air is "thinner," or holds fewer molecules as elevation increases), and the rugged landscape. The animals— like mountain goat, ibex (wild goat), sheep, mountain lion, puma, and yak—must be agile and light on their feet so they can travel easily on the steep, rocky mountain sides. Types of plants vary depending on geographic location and altitude. Lower elevations are commonly covered by forests, while very high elevations are usually treeless. Quinoa (pronounced *keen-wah*) is a grain that is specially adapted to growing in the Andes. The Incas relied on it as their staple grain—the way that traditionally people in Europe relied on wheat and people in Asia relied on rice.

Location, north or south along the mountain range (the latitude, see page 59), plays a defining role in the climates of this lengthy mountain range. In the northern region, the climate is warm and wet because those mountains are closest to the equator. Still, the high mountains are snowcapped—like **Mount Cotopaxi** in Ecuador, which is just 30 miles (48 km) from the equator. In the southern region, the mountains are relatively close to the Antarctic, and the climate is far colder.

THE ALPS OF EUROPE

The Alps are a mountain range that curves across Europe from the Mediterranean coast, across southeastern France and northern Italy, through most of Switzerland, Austria, and Liechtenstein, and into southern Germany and Slovenia.

These fold mountains were formed 23 to 34 million years ago, when the African tectonic plate pushed toward the European tectonic plate at a rate of about 3½ inches (9 cm) a year. The shape of these mountains was greatly altered during the last ice age, when the Alps were covered by glaciers. Remnants of these glaciers can still be found at high elevations that allow mountain resorts in the Alps to offer year-round skiing. Ice Age glaciers scooped out broad valleys and formed large, deep lakes, like **Lake Geneva** and **Lake Lucerne** in Switzerland and **Lake Como** in Italy. Were it not for the bulldozing glaciers, the Alps would be closer in height to the Himalayas.

Three of the largest rivers of Europe—the **Rhine, Rhône,** and **Po**—originate in the Alps, as well as tributaries of the **Danube.**

THE WORLD'S TALLEST MOUNTAIN PEAKS

If you wanted to climb the tallest mountain on every continent, where should you go? That's a question you could ask Jordan Romero, the youngest person ever to climb Mount Everest. He called his mom to say *hello* from the world's highest peak when he was just 13 years old! Use this table to see how the heights of the tallest mountains on each continent stack up.

MOUNTAIN	CONTINENT	HEIGHT ABOVE SEA LEVEL
Everest	Asia	29,029 feet (8,848 m)
Aconcagua	South America	22,841 feet (6,962 m)
McKinley	North America	20,308 feet (6,190 m)
Kilimanjaro	Africa	19,340 (5,895 m)
Elbrus	Europe	18,510 (5,642 m)
Vinson Massif	Antarctica	16,043 (4,890 m)
Puncak Jaya	Australia/Oceania	16,024 (4,884 m)*

*Some scientists argue that Australia/Oceania's highest peak should be Mount Kosciuszco in Australia because Puncak Jaya is in Papua, New Guinea, a country that is part of the Australian continental shelf but is considered a nation of Asia. Some people who want to climb the highest mountains on each continent have ended up climbing both—just to be sure!

WATERSHEDS, RIVERS, AND LAKES

GOING WITH THE FLOW

Unless you are reading this book on an airplane or an ocean liner, you are probably located in the middle of a **watershed.** A watershed is the area of land where all of the water that is under it or drains off of it goes into the same place. According to the U.S. Environmental Protection Agency (EPA), there are 2,267 watersheds in the United States, including Hawaii, Alaska, and the territory of Puerto Rico.

Water falls to the ground as precipitation (such as rain or snow) and is absorbed into the soil—becoming **groundwater**—or it drains from the surface of the land into the nearest creek or stream. Streams join other streams and flow into rivers that, in turn, are fed by the groundwater through underwater springs. All of the area that drains into each creek, stream, or river is called its watershed.

If you imagine the earth as a human body, the rivers would be the veins and the arteries that carry essential supplies from place to place. Rivers provide water for drinking, cooking, washing, farming, and transportation—the big, wet roads along which people can transport themselves and their goods. Throughout history, rivers have attracted the first settlers to a new territory.

Cradles of Civilization

A **cradle of civilization** is a place where early people are thought to have first settled down and started farming and developing cities. Asia contains two such cradles: in China along the **Yellow River** and in the Middle East, along the **Tigris-Euphrates** river system in what is now Iraq. Rivers help start civilizations because the land nearby floods frequently, which makes the soil fertile and good for farming. When people figured out how to use the rivers for irrigation (water for crops), they were able to grow a lot more food. This allowed some people to work at jobs other than farming or hunting, like making pottery and clothing, metalworking, and trade. Soon enough, whole civilizations developed.

WHERE DO RIVERS START?

Rivers all flow downhill, thanks to gravity. A river's **source,** or starting point, is high up, sometimes on a mountain. Water from melting snow and rain trickles downward, meeting other trickles, which gather together as the water flows, until

The Very Grand, Grand Canyon

Many people call the Grand Canyon one of the seven natural wonders of the world. It is pretty amazing because of its size, because of what it reveals about the geology and history of the area, and because of its amazing beauty.

Located in northern Arizona State, the Grand Canyon was cut by the Colorado River over centuries. The river carried away rock and more rock as it traveled to the Gulf of California in the Pacific Ocean until a deep canyon was formed. It is 277 miles (446 km) long and up to 18 miles (29 km) wide. It is more than 1 mile (1.6 km) deep at its deepest point.

If you look in the canyon, you can see many layers of rock, some that are at least two billion years old. There is evidence that the Grand Canyon was once part of a large sea, because in some layers of rock, you can find fossils of trilobites, tiny sea creatures that lived in the sea about 500 million years ago. There is also evidence of volcanic ash and lava. All of that history on view through the layers and layers of rock make the Grand Canyon a geologist's paradise.

all of those trickles form a stream. As streams flow quickly downhill, they join other streams to become rivers. Where the land flattens out away from the hills and mountains, rivers usually flow at a slower pace. The place where a river ends and flows out into a lake or ocean is called the **mouth,** and water usually picks up speed as it moves toward the mouth.

EARTH-MOVING MACHINES

Rivers don't just move water and people—they are also the planet's very own earth-moving machines. Day and night, rivers carve out and smooth the landscape. **Canyons** and **gorges** are deep, steep-sided valleys formed by young rivers cutting mainly downward through the land. One of the largest is the **Grand Canyon** of the **Colorado River** in Arizona

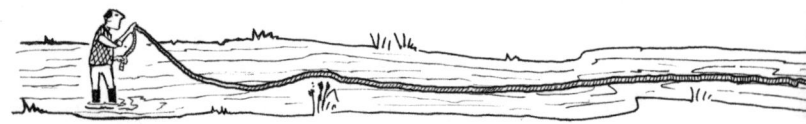

State. Each year, rivers erode and transport vast quantities of sediment, or soil. When sediment builds up at the mouth of a river, it forms new land, often triangular in shape, called a **delta.** The most famous delta is that of the **Nile River** in Egypt, and it is famous because each year the river deposits a new layer of sediment, making the delta even more fertile. The **Ganges** and **Brahmaputra** rivers empty into the Bay of Bengal in the Indian Ocean, making a delta that spans most of Bangladesh and West Bengal, India; it is the world's largest delta. The **Mississippi River** makes a large delta in Louisiana State as it empties into the Gulf of Mexico.

THE WORLD'S LONGEST RIVERS

For centuries, geographers have argued over the length of the world's rivers. You might imagine that it would be a simple process to take a measuring tape and measure from the start of a river to its finish. In reality, the length of a river is hard to calculate. This is because experts don't agree on the precise point where some rivers start or where exactly rivers finish and meet a lake or sea. As a result, the exact lengths of many rivers are hotly debated. Here's a table of the longest rivers on each continent.

RIVER	CONTINENT	LENGTH
Nile	Africa	4,159 miles (6,693 km)
Amazon	South America	3,999 miles (6,436 km)
Yangtze	Asia	3,915 miles (6,300 km)
Mississippi	North America	3,889 miles (6,275 km)
Volga	Europe	2,265 miles (3,645 km)
Murray	Australia/Oceania	1,476 miles (2,375 km)

A river delta

... ER WHERE DO I MEASURE TO?

The Nile: The Longest River in the World

European explorers spent much of the 1800s trying to find the source of this mysterious river that snakes its way through one of the harshest deserts in the world and into the Mediterranean Sea. Today it is often agreed that the Nile begins at Ripon Falls in the African country of Burundi. Along its meandering south to north route, two main **tributaries** (smaller streams or rivers that feed into larger bodies of water) pump water into the Nile. The White Nile travels through Burundi, Tanzania, Lake Victoria in Uganda, and South Sudan. The Blue Nile starts at Lake Tana in Ethiopia and flows into Sudan from the southeast.

The two rivers meet near the Sudanese capital of Khartoum and continue northward to Egypt. The Nile River provided the foundation for one of the oldest and richest civilizations in the world: ancient Egypt. Although you won't find any

On the Nile with the Crocodiles

Crocodiles are probably the most famous inhabitants of the Nile River, though they also live in rivers throughout Africa. A living relic of the age of dinosaurs, crocodiles have been around for about 200 million years, snacking on fish, waterfowl, antelope, wildebeests, zebras, young elephants, and even big cats such as leopards and lions. When given the chance, they are known to prey upon domestic animals like chickens, goats, sheep, and cattle, as well as humans. Crocodiles will leave the water to hunt, if necessary, and they are surprisingly speedy on land, even though their legs are very short. A person cannot outrun an attacking crocodile.

The male crocodile usually measures 12 to 16 feet (3.5 to 5 m) long, but very old, mature crocs can grow to 18 feet (5.5 m) or more. Crocodiles can hold their breath under water for up to 2 hours.

pharaohs ruling over Egypt today, the Nile continues to support life along its banks, providing water and restoring the soil of Egypt's agricultural lands. Every year, snow melts in the mountains of East Africa, sending so much water into the river that the Nile overflows its banks, depositing a black silt, or sediment, that makes excellent **topsoil**.

The Astounding Amazon

North Americans talk about "the mighty Mississippi," but mighty doesn't even begin to describe the Amazon River, which carries the volume of water of 10 Mississippi Rivers. Combined with its 1,100 tributaries, the Amazon carries the greatest volume of water of any river in the world.

The river starts as a glacial stream high in the Andes and flows more than 4,000 miles (6,436 km) across the South American continent. In places, the river can be as wide as 1 to 6 miles (1.6 to 10 km) during the dry season and 30 miles (48 km) or more across during the wet season. The force of the current, from sheer water volume alone—and the fact that salt water is heavier than freshwater—causes the river water to continue flowing about 125 miles out to sea before fully mixing with the Atlantic Ocean's salt water.

The Yangtze Is Number Three

The **Yangtze River** in southern China flows for 3,925 miles (6,300 km). It is the longest river in China and the third longest in the world. It originates in the glaciers of Tibet, plunges through limestone gorges, and finally flows into the East China Sea in Shanghai. Every year the Yangtze floods and deposits massive amounts of silt that create fertile plains for farming, especially rice farming. China accounts for 35 percent of the world's rice production, which is a good thing since rice is the staple food for more than a third of the world's population. For thousands of years, the Yangtze has provided transportation and water for manufacturing, irrigation, and household uses, and today a large percentage of China's population lives in the eastern portion of the basin. Uncontrolled flooding, pollution, and destruction of wetlands are all threats facing the river and the people who live along its basin.

The Mighty Mississippi River

The mighty Mississippi is the centerpiece of the second largest watershed in the world (the Amazon basin is the largest). The Mississippi River begins as a tiny brook, but 2,350 miles

Wonderful Waterfalls

Waterfalls form when a river flows over layers of hard rock with softer rock underneath. Over hundreds of years, the water erodes the softer rock faster than the hard rock, forming a vertical cliff with a plunge pool at the bottom.

One of the natural wonders of the world, the **Victoria Falls,** also know as Mosi-o-Tunya (the Smoke that Thunders) is located in southern Africa on the Zambezi River between the countries of Zambia and Zimbabwe. The falls are the largest, though not the highest, in the world with a width of 5,604 feet (1,708 m)—that's wider than a mile! It is, alas, a mere 354 feet (108 m) in height.

The honor of being the highest waterfall goes to **Angel Falls** in Venezuela, with a height of 3,212 feet (979 m). The waterfall drops over the edge of the Auyantepui Mountain, and while it doesn't have the official title as one of the "natural wonders" of the world, it is a UNESCO (United Nations Educational, Scientific, and Cultural Organization) World Heritage site—which definitely puts it into the "must visit" category. The height of this waterfall is so great that most of the falling water evaporates into mist or is carried away by winds before it hits the ground.

(3,782 km) later it empties into the Gulf of Mexico, having drained the water from more than 1.2 million square miles (3.1 million km²), including tributary rivers from thirty-three states and two Canadian provinces. One of those tributaries is the Missouri River, which at 2,540 miles (4,087.7 km) in length is actually longer than the Mississippi.

Glaciers formed the Mississippi River basin. The glaciers moved and melted millions of years ago, creating vast **floodplains** in the river valley. These floodplains are still prone to flooding and when that happens, the rising water destroys towns, roads, farms, and anything else that might stand in its way.

The Holy Ganges

The Ganges River in India is considered a holy river by Hindus. The river begins in the Himalayas and travels through Nepal, India, and Bangladesh on its 1,560-mile (2,510-km) trip to the Indian Ocean. It is the official "national river" of India because of its importance for irrigation, transportation, hydroelectric power, and, especially, its religious significance. Because the Ganges is a special place for those of the Hindu faith, the major religion of India, holy men, widows, and others who have dedicated

themselves to a thoughtful, spiritual life make their homes at the sacred places along the Ganges. They, in turn, attract millions of people who congregate at periodic festivals and fairs.

People who live near the river cremate (burn) the remains of their loved ones on funeral pyres, or flammable objects that are set afloat, burning, on the river. The dying come to the Ganges for a drink from its waters. It is believed that drinking from the Ganges with one's last breath will take the soul to heaven, and that dying by the river can help a person achieve salvation. Some people travel from distant places to immerse the ashes of a loved one in the waters of the Ganges.

But the Ganges is also a river for the living; it is thought that the waters can wash away sin and that a person must dip into the water at least once in a lifetime. With all that dipping, burning, and ash dumping, it is not a surprise that the Ganges River is one of the most polluted and threatened rivers in the world. Inadequate cremation procedures sometimes result in partially burnt corpses of humans and cows, which are sacred animals to Hindus, floating in the river. Less sacred acts also pollute, however. India's

Flowing Backward

The Tonle Sap River in Cambodia reverses direction every year. Normally, the Tonle Sap flows south, draining into the Mekong River. But when the monsoons (seasonal rains) come, they pour so much water into the Mekong River that it briefly forces the Tonle Sap River to flow backward. The river backs into the Tonle Sap Lake in western Cambodia, which makes the lake grow to more than five times its normal size.

leather industry releases toxic chemicals; millions of gallons of untreated sewage enter the river every day; and dams and irrigation threaten the flow of the river in certain areas. Drinking water from the Ganges has become very risky, although not *too* risky for those drawing their last breath.

Mother Volga

The Russians call the Volga River "Mother Volga" because of its importance as a source of irrigation, transportation, and

hydroelectric power. At 3,692 miles (2,293 km) in length, the Volga is the longest river in Europe and, impressively, lies entirely within the boundaries of Russia. (There is some debate as to whether Russia should be classified as part of Europe or Asia; see page 68 for more information). More than 40 percent of Russia's people, including half of the country's farmers, live near the Volga and its tributaries.

AMAZING DAMS

For centuries, humans have built dams on rivers. Dams control water flow to prevent flooding downstream and create reservoirs for water storage.

More recently dams have been built for **hydropower.** The force of the flowing river turns turbines, which generate electricity. The largest hydroelectric dam in the world is the **Three Gorges Dam** on the Yangtze River in China. The Three Gorges Dam is huge: 1½ miles (2.4 km) wide and 610 feet (186 m) tall. The dam creates a reservoir that is hundreds of feet deep and about 400 miles long, big enough to allow freighters to easily navigate the Yangztze. As the world's largest hydroelectric power plant, the dam's turbines can create the equivalent electricity of 18 nuclear power plants. By contrast, the Grand Coulee Dam on the **Columbia River** in Washington State is the largest hydroelectric dam in the United States. It is 5,223 feet (1,592 m) long—less than 1 mile—and 550 feet (168 m) tall.

Hydropower is considered a renewable energy resource, but building dams is not without controversy. For example, creation of the Grand Coulee Dam forced the relocation of more than 3,000 people, including Native Americans whose ancestral lands were partially flooded. The dam also has blocked the migration of salmon and other fish that try to swim upstream to spawn (lay and fertilize eggs). Dams also stop sediment from being carried downstream to create new land.

The Three Gorges Dam brings additional oversize problems. One of the greatest fears is that the weight of the dam may trigger severe earthquakes; the reservoir sits on two major faults.

FLOODS

Low-lying valleys are great places to live—most of the time—thanks to the lush, fertile soil and the rivers that run through them, providing drinking water, irrigation, and travel. The problem is, river valleys flood. This happens when a river overflows its banks because of a heavy rainfall or rapid melting of snow, or even the collapse of a man-made dam. In addition, humans have covered huge areas of land with concrete, which channels rain into sewers and drains, rather than letting it soak into the ground. This means that water is washed more quickly into rivers.

Where on Earth Does It Flood?

Your chances of being flooded depend a lot on where you live. Historically, the worst place on earth for flood risk is China. In the last 150 years more than 5 million people have been killed by floods in China. As the polar ice caps melt, higher sea levels and more rain may cause flooding across larger areas and in parts of the world that don't typically flood today.

Why Are Floods So Dangerous?

You've probably seen images of floods on television. These natural disasters can be very costly, not to mention danger-ous. A powerful flood can sweep

everything away, from rocks and trees to cars and houses. Foul-smelling water sweeps into buildings and damages properties. On a bigger scale, everything from roads to crops and electricity lines may be destroyed. Although there's plenty of water around, you wouldn't want to drink it, because it's often contaminated with sewage and could make you very sick. Finding food and clean water after a flood can be a real problem—assuming you can get somewhere safe and dry. Even when floodwater drains away, it can be months or even years before an area recovers.

LOVELY LAKES

Lakes are found where rivers flow into hollows in the land. Not only are they lovely places to fish and swim, they also store 87 percent of the world's freshwater found aboveground. On a planet where 97 percent of the water on the surface is salty and undrinkable, what's not to like about lakes?

WHEN WILL THE LAKE BE READY, MOM?

How Lakes Are Formed

Several processes are responsible for creating holes in the ground in which water can collect. Some form in craters made by volcanic explosions (such as **Crater Lake** in Oregon State) or by meteorites striking the earth (such as **Clearwater Lakes** in Canada), but most lakes are formed by the action of glaciers moving on the land.

Glaciation. Glaciers are huge blocks of ice and snow that have built up over time. They creep very slowly down steep hills and mountains. As the glacier moves, inch by inch, it scrapes across the earth's surface like an earth-moving machine, digging out boulders and carving into the **bedrock,** or solid rock, that lies beneath the soil.

Around 18,000 years ago, the earth was much colder than it is today, and glaciers covered most of the land. They were continuously growing and moving, gouging holes in loose soil or soft bedrock, depositing material across stream beds, and burying chunks of ice. Later, as the earth grew warmer and the Ice Age ended, the big rivers of ice that had dominated the land began to melt. Over time, the glaciers' meltwaters filled the basins they had carved out, creating lakes.

Glaciers created the world's largest freshwater lake system, North America's **Great Lakes.** The largest of these lakes is **Lake Superior,** on the border between the United States and Canada. It covers 31,700 square miles (82,100 km^2)—which is about the same size as the state of Maine. Minnesota, in the northern United States, is known as the "land of 10,000 lakes," but it actually has 12,034 glacial lakes. The Finger Lakes of New York State are also glacial lakes.

Tectonic Activity. This describes movements in the plates that make up the earth's crust (see page 13). Tectonic activity can cause the crust of the earth to break into pieces and move apart, forming large holes in the ground called **rift valleys.** When these holes fill with freshwater they form lakes. **Lake Baikal** in Siberia, Russia, was formed in this way 20 to 25 million years ago, making it the **oldest lake** in the world. It is also the world's **deepest lake** at 5,370 feet (1,637 m) deep and contains the largest volume of freshwater on Earth, holding enough water to fill all five of North America's Great Lakes.

Lake Tanganyika in Africa is another rift valley lake and can claim the title of longest freshwater lake in the world.

Man-Made Lakes. People have built many artificial lakes, or reservoirs. **Lake Volta,** in Ghana, has the largest surface area of any man-made lake. It is roughly the same size as the island of Corsica in France.

The Great Lakes of North America

Located on the border between Canada and the United States, the Great Lakes system includes five freshwater lakes: Lake Superior, Lake Michigan, Lake Huron, Lake Erie, and Lake Ontario. Their shores are home to more than 33 million people. Together, the Great Lakes hold more than 21 percent of the world's freshwater. In fact, if you were to pour out the water held in these lakes across the 48 states of mainland America, you'd create a gigantic swimming pool more than 8 feet (2.5 m) deep.

WHAT MAKES A LAKE A SEA?

Some lakes are even saltier than the ocean. These saltwater lakes form in the same way as freshwater lakes but are missing one key thing—there is no way for water to flow out.

Bleach-Filled Lakes

One of the strangest lakes in the world can be found in Antarctica. **Lake Untersee** is Antarctica's largest freshwater lake, but its water isn't the kind anyone would want to drink. Thanks to some unusual chemical processes, the water is more like the bleach used to whiten laundry and kill germs in a bathroom than like the water coming out of your faucet. The freezing water of Lake Untersee is permanently covered with ice and is brimming with a gas called methane.

Scientists have recently made an important discovery in Lake Untersee. Although it appeared that nothing could live in the bleachlike waters, they have found a group of tiny, tiny organisms living there. Organisms that live in conditions too extreme for most forms of life are known as **extremophiles.** They thrive in conditions too difficult for most other creatures. If species can exist in Lake Untersee's environment, could there be life on Mars or on the moons of Jupiter and Saturn, which contain similar combinations of ice and methane?

This means that the only way that water can escape is by evaporating into the atmosphere as water vapor. When the water evaporates, it leaves salts and other minerals behind. As time goes on, the amount of salt in these lakes builds up.

Saltwater lakes can be surrounded by land, so why are some of them known as seas? Back in the days of ancient Rome, people decided that all large bodies of salt water should be called seas. So the world's largest saltwater *lake* is called the **Caspian Sea,** even though it is completely surrounded by land. Russia, Iran, Azerbaijan, Turkmenistan, and Kazakhstan all share its shores.

Some lakes are really salty. The saltiest lake in the world is the **Dead Sea** in Israel. It's so salty that almost nothing can live in the Dead Sea's water, which is where the name comes from. However, an astonishing effect of all that extra salt is that you can float effortlessly in its waters!

ECOLOGICAL COMMUNITIES

BIO-*MAZING*

When geographers study life on planet Earth, they divide the world into **biomes.** A biome describes a region with a specific type of climate and the plants and animals that thrive there. Obviously the climate, and especially the amount of rain that falls on an area, has a big influence on which plants will survive in a particular biome. And which plants grow in an area affects which plant-eating animals (**herbivores**) will thrive. In turn, this influences which **carnivorous** (meat-eating) predators will thrive.

There are five major types of biomes in the world: aquatic, desert, forest, grassland, and tundra. You can further divide these biomes into subcategories. Among aquatic (water) biomes, for example, there is a big difference between marine (ocean) biomes and freshwater biomes. Since life began in the ocean with one-celled organisms, let's start there.

Aquatic Biomes

The **marine biome** is the biggest biome in the world. We are talking about the ocean here, and it covers about 70 percent of the surface of the earth. No one knows how many different plants and animals live in the ocean, but all are dependent on tiny plants like algae and plankton to take in huge amounts of carbon dioxide, release oxygen through photosynthesis, and provide nutrients to other creatures. Fish, mollusks, crustaceans, whales, and more live in the salty water of the oceans (see pages 53 to 56).

The place where freshwater and salt water meet is called an **estuary,** a type of aquatic biome. Estuaries typically are full of plants and animals. Many cities have been built on estuaries (New York City, for example), and in many cases pollution and overfishing have decimated the wildlife that once

World's Biggest Flower

The world's largest flower blooms in the rain forests of Indonesia. The gigantic titan arum grows up to 10 feet (3 m) high and 5 feet (1.5 m) across. But this isn't a flower to buy for your mother—the blossom supposedly smells like rotting meat and dead bodies. Yuck!

thrived there. **Freshwater biomes** include lakes, ponds, rivers, and streams. Again, algae and larger plants provide oxygen through photosynthesis and food for animals in this biome.

Wetlands are an important type of freshwater biome. This is a place where groundwater or rain doesn't drain, and the land stays wet all the time—or for a large portion of the year. Wetlands such as swamps, marshes, and bogs support many plants and animals, help clean the water, control floods, and provide food for humans. The **Pantanal** in South America is the largest wetland of any kind. It is a tropical wetland and is 80 percent underwater during the rainy season. It lies mostly within Brazil but extends into portions of Bolivia and Paraguay, sprawling over an area estimated to be between 54,000 and 75,000 square miles (140,000 to 195,000 km^2). That makes it about 10 times larger than the **Everglades,** the largest wetland in the United States. The Pantanal is home to thousands of species of fish, birds, amphibians, reptiles, and mammals, including a healthy population of jaguars, giant anteaters, toucans, tapirs, and capybaras. The Everglades is famous for its bird population, its alligators, and the endangered Florida panther.

Tundra Biomes

The tundra is a dry, cold, and treeless area. There are two types of tundra, alpine and arctic. Alpine tundras exist above the tree line at the very tops of high mountains. Many peaks in the Alps have alpine tundra, which is where this biome got its name. A handful of peaks in the Appalachians and many mountaintops in the Rocky Mountains have zones of alpine tundra.

The arctic tundra is a flat, treeless swampy plain that extends around the Arctic Ocean in the far north, including northern Europe (Lapland and Scandinavia), Asia (Siberia), and North America (Alaska and Canada), as well as most of Greenland.

Underneath the top layer of arctic tundra soil is a layer of permanently frozen subsoil called **permafrost.** Tree and plant roots cannot penetrate this frozen layer of ground. Above the permafrost is a thin layer of topsoil that thaws in summer, creating many pools, lakes, and marshes that make luxury accommodations for mosquitoes, midges, blackflies, and other biting, stinging insects. The abundant bugs attract more than 100 species of migrant birds, which come for the bug feast each summer. Other animals that live in this biome include polar bears, brown bears, wolves, wolverines, caribou, arctic hare, mink, weasels, and lemmings. Low-growing plants and lichen cover the many rocks on the tundra's terrain. Not many humans live on the tundra.

Dry, Dry Desert Biomes

When you mention the word desert, do you think of a scorching hot, sandy place filled with camels and palm trees? Hot, sandy deserts make up only about a quarter of the deserts on planet Earth. The rest are cold deserts. A desert is an area of land that receives less than 10 inches (25 cm) of rain or snow during the year or loses more moisture by evaporation or **transpiration** (the moisture given off by plants) than it receives from the sky. Low moisture in the air allows more sunlight to reach the ground, raising daytime temperatures. Large differences in night and day temperatures are a distinguishing feature of a desert. Despite what deserts have in common, the landscape can be pretty different in each one.

Antarctica. The world's largest, coldest, and driest desert is the continent of Antarctica. Antarctica receives less than 2 inches (5 cm) of precipitation annually—but all that snow just *never* melts. Over the centuries, the snow has accumulated, and 98 percent of the rocky, barren land of Antartica is covered by a permanent ice sheet. Penguins are the only animals that actually live *on* Antarctica.

WELL, THIS CERTAINLY ISN'T THE TYPE OF DESERT WE'RE USED TO, IS IT, GEORGE?

But the ocean surrounding Antarctica bursts with life, and that's where the penguins feed.

Sahara Desert. If you want to find a classic-looking desert, the central part of the Sahara is where you want to go. It has sand dunes 400 feet (122 m) or more in height. The second largest desert in the world, the **Sahara Desert** is the largest *hot* desert. It pretty much covers the northern end of Africa from the Atlantic Ocean in the west to the Red Sea in the east, a distance of some 3,000 miles (4,828 km). In the north, it starts at the Mediterranean Sea and extends 1,200 miles (1,931 km) south, almost into central Africa. It is part of the landscape of the countries of Morocco, Western Sahara, Algeria, Tunisia, Libya, Egypt, Mauritania, Mali, Niger, Chad, and Sudan.

There's no place on earth as consistently hot as the Sahara, which has an average annual temperature of 86°F (30°C). During the hottest months, temperatures can exceed 122°F (50°C). The highest temperature ever recorded in this desert was in Aziziyah, Libya—136°F (58°C).

Best Places to Go to See Cacti

If you've ever seen an old cowboy movie, you know that the American West has vast areas of desert. In North America, there are four major deserts: the **Great Basin,** the **Mojave,** the **Sonoran,** and the **Chihuahuan.** The Great Basin is a cold desert and is entirely in the United States, covering parts of Idaho, Nevada, Oregon, and Utah. The Mojave, Sonoran, and Chihuahuan are hot deserts, stretching over parts of the American Southwest and Mexico. That's where you want to go to see cacti, Joshua trees, sagebrush, and rattlesnakes.

You'd think the Sahara would be a lifeless place, but plenty of long-rooted grasses, cacti, shrubs, and palm trees do survive in parts of the desert. Desert dwellers include camels, of course, as well as antelopes, gazelles, lizards, snakes, and numerous kinds of insects.

Atacama Desert. Talk about dry! In parts of this South American desert, no rain has been recorded in the last 400 years. The desert starts at the border of Chile and Peru and stretches southward for nearly 600 miles (970 km) along the Pacific coast. The coastal areas support more life than the interior regions, where vegetation is scarce. Llamas are the most famous animals from this region; they are members of the camel family.

Arabian Desert. Another hot desert, the Arabian desert, covers Saudi Arabia, Jordan, Iraq, Kuwait, Qatar, United Arab Emirates, Oman, and Yemen. Parts of this desert are so empty and devoid of life that the Arabs call it the Rub'al-Khali (the Empty Quarter). But other parts of the desert have enough vegetation to support camels, ibex (wild goats), and other grazing animals, as well as plenty of insects, scorpions, lizards, and snakes.

Gobi Desert. This barren region of gravel plains and rocky outcroppings is a high-altitude, cold desert in northern China. A portion of the Gobi has just enough vegetation to support camels, wolves, bears, oxen, wild horses, snow leopards, and gazelles. The Gobi also includes areas with no vegetation whatsoever. Overgrazing, soil erosion from wind, and mining activities have all been identified as environmental problems in the region. This desert is expanding, edging ever closer to the capital city of Beijing with mighty dust storms. Desert biomes account for about one-quarter of China's land.

Desert Dwellers

Trying to survive in a hot desert is tough. On a sunny day in a desert such as the Sahara, the temperature can climb above 122°F (50°C) and fall to below 32°F (0°C) at night. With extreme temperatures like these, people, plants, and animals need to have special ways to adapt to the environment. Cacti and other plants called **succulents** adapt to desert life by storing moisture. A few cold-blooded animals, including reptiles (such as snakes and lizards) and amphibians (such as frogs and toads), are also well adapted to the hot desert. The most famous desert animal is probably the camel, which can make water from the fat it stores in its hump.

Grassland Biomes

Grasslands are usually found in the middle of continents. They have hot, dry summers and enough precipitation to grow grass but not enough for most trees. Grasslands are known throughout the world by different names. In the United States they are called **prairies** and extend from the Midwest to the Rocky Mountains. In South Africa, grasslands are called the **veld.** Hot, tropical grasslands called **savannas** are found in South America and Africa. In Europe and Asia, temperate zone grasslands are called **steppes.** In South America, they are called **pampas.**

Grasslands are usually put to use to grow food crops. In the United States, wheat and corn are grown on the prairies, and cattle graze on much of the land. Before settlers converted the grasslands to farmlands and overhunting occurred, buffalo made their home on the prairies. Grazing animals such as rabbits, mice, antelopes, and horses are typical grassland animals. Because grasslands are such open environments, most grassland animals tend to form herds or make burrows in the ground as protection from predators. Today some of the most common grassland animals in North America include prairie dogs, mule deer, coyotes, and wild turkeys. The lion, giraffe, and zebra make their home on African grasslands.

Forest Biomes

Forests can be found on every single continent, except for Antarctica. They grow almost everywhere—from the hot and steamy areas near the equator to the frosty lands of North America, Europe, and Asia. Climate determines what sort of forest grows where.

Temperate Forests. These forests are found in areas where temperatures are fairly moderate and soils rich. **Deciduous trees** such as oak, ash, and maple mostly make up temperate forests. In autumn, deciduous trees shed their leaves, remaining bare during winter. The leaves on the ground decay, and this enriches the soil. Humans have taken advantage of the forest-enriched soil over the centuries, clearing much of the original temperate forests for cropland. Around 5,000 years ago, most of the United Kingdom was covered by forest, but it was

(continued on page 134)

The Rain Forest. This scene shows a typical rain forest with four layers. Trees and plants need light and space to grow.

The Understory Layer. Very little light reaches this layer. Vines called lianas grow around the trees, small ferns, and shrubs. Many insects, spiders, reptiles, and small mammals also call this layer home.

The Forest Floor. A mind-boggling variety of creatures, from spiders to pigs and deer to big cats, live in this damp and dark layer.

The Emergent Layer. In this layer the tops of the tallest trees, such as mahogany, tower above the canopy and experience strong winds and sunlight. Many birds and insects live in this layer.

The Canopy. This tangled layer of dense branches is rich in life, from flowers and fruits to monkeys and birds. It is so thick that it blocks out virtually all light for the vegetation below.

cleared as humans began to use the land to cultivate crops and keep animals. Very little old-growth forest remains in Europe.

In the United States, the deciduous forest is a home for deer, gray squirrels, wood mice, rabbits, and raccoons, to name a few of the critters who live in the temperate forest.

Boreal Forests. These forests are found in the cooler northern areas of North America, Europe, and Asia, where the boreal forest is called a **taiga. Coniferous trees** such as pine and spruce make up boreal forests. These trees produce their seeds in cones. Coniferous trees keep their needlelike leaves all year-round, so they are also known as **evergreens.** Many species grow to record-breaking heights. In California, a coastal redwood named Hyperion stands at a colossal 377 feet (115 m)!

Boreal forests are the source for building lumber and paper. The moose is one of the most famous residents of the boreal forest.

Tropical Rain Forests. These forests are found in tropical areas around the equator in Africa, Asia, South America, and Australia. Rain forests are warm all year-round and receive about 70 inches (178 cm) of rain a year. They are home to about half of the planet's plant and animal species. There is so much competition for light and space in the rain forest that plants have adapted to living in different layers (see pages 132 to 133).

The **Amazon basin,** roughly the size of the continental United States, is the world's largest tropical rain forest, at 2.5 million square miles (6.5 million km^2). It covers about one-third of South America. About 60 percent of this rain forest is within Brazil, another 13 percent lies within the borders of Peru, and smaller areas are located in Colombia, Venezuela, Ecuador, Bolivia, Guyana, Suriname, and French Guiana.

The Amazon is the wettest of the world's rain forests. Heavy rains drench much of the densely forested lowlands throughout the year, but especially between January and June. The vegetation of the rain forest includes a variety of trees, including tropical hardwoods, palms, tree ferns, and bamboos. The trees grow so closely together that their crowns, the parts of the trees that grow above the ground, form a dense canopy. The canopy may soar up to 130 feet (40 m) and is so impenetrable that sunlight seldom reaches the forest floor.

Rain forests sustain vast numbers of different plant and animal species, but the **biodiversity** of the Amazon basin is the greatest of them all, with more species of plants and animals per square mile than anywhere else on the planet. Some of the animals that live in this tropical rain forest are the anteater, jaguar, lemur, orangutan, marmoset, macaw, parrot, sloth, and toucan. Among the many plant species are bamboos, banana trees, rubber trees, and cassavas.

DESTRUCTION OF THE FORESTS AND CLIMATE CHANGE

In the last 50 years, more than a fifth of the Amazon rain forest has been destroyed. In fact, rain forests all over the world are being cut down. People cut the trees to sell the wood for building homes or making furniture. They also burn the trees to clear the land to grow crops and graze cattle. This affects the planet in many ways.

Extinction of Species. About half of all the species of plants and animals on earth live in rain forests. Cutting down the forest means that these species have nowhere to live, so they die out. Scientists believe that the planet is losing up to 50 species each day, many of them from rain forests. If some

animals and plants disappear, others that depend on them to survive will also die out. Humans use many plant species found in the rain forest to make medicines, and the loss of plant species may mean that the chance to find a cure for some diseases may also be lost.

Global Warming. Carbon dioxide is a **greenhouse gas** that builds up in the atmosphere. Cutting down forests speeds up global warming because the earth's forests absorb billions of tons of carbon dioxide gas each year. This includes 30 percent of the carbon dioxide humans put into the air with cars and electrical plants. As forests are destroyed, fewer trees remain to absorb the carbon dioxide, and the more greenhouse gases there are in the atmosphere, the warmer the planet becomes.

Desertification. The trees and plants in forests hold the soil together and prevent it from blowing away or washing away (erosion). Cutting down forests means that more soil is exposed to the wind and rain, which can lead to more areas becoming deserts.

There are ways to conserve the forests and plant new ones. **Conservationists** urge people to treat forests with respect, to try to reduce global warming before it is too late.

BIOGEOGRAPHY

In the mid-1800s, Alfred Russel Wallace (1823–1913), a British biologist, anthropologist, and explorer-adventurer was studying the plants and animals on the islands of Malaysia in Asia. He was struck by the sudden differences in bird families he found when he sailed only 20 or so miles east of the island of Bali and landed on the island of Lombok. On Bali he saw birds that were clearly related to the birds that lived on the larger islands of Java and Sumatra and mainland Malaysia. On the island of Lombok, the birds were clearly related to the birds that lived on the islands of Papua, New Guinea and on Australia. He marked the channel between Bali and Lombok as the divide between two regions of animal habitats. He also suggested that the land on either side of the dividing line might have been joined at some point in history.

His discovery was the start of a field of science known as **biogeography,** which looks at the distribution of plants and animals in terms of both regional differences and historical changes in the environment. That line between the two regions—which is now called the **Wallace Line**—actually marks the edge of the Asian continental shelf, and plate tectonics explains the distribution of the species he studied.

It seems that some of the islands on each of the plates were once connected to each other and to the mainland by land bridges. Animals could freely migrate among them, but no such bridge existed between the two tectonic plates. So on each side of the Wallace Line, different families of birds developed.

Biogeography is a new field of study. There are plenty of discoveries yet to be uncovered about how and when and where different plants and animals came to be.

The World's Most Dangerous Animals

Any animal can be dangerous when cornered, hurt, or protecting its young, but there are animals that are certainly worth avoiding.

Rhinoceros. Rhinos are cranky and easily annoyed. Angry rhinos move surprisingly fast and will trample or gore with their horns anyone who has upset them. Rhinos are responsible for approximately 12 deaths a year in Africa and India, although since they are vegetarians, they don't eat anyone they've run over.

Hippopotamus. Even crankier than rhinos, hippopotamuses don't have horns, but they do have tusks and they know how to use them, especially when protecting their young. Hippos kill several hundred people a year, so stay out of their way in Africa, where they live.

Cape Buffalo. Also known as the African buffalo, this elegantly horned buffalo lives in Africa and kills more humans each year (about 200) than lions do. Another cranky vegetarian, the cape buffalo regards humans as predators and defends itself and its young accordingly, even if the human is armed only with a camera.

Elephants. Watch out for the unpredictable elephant if you happen to find yourself in Africa or India. It kills an estimated 300 to 500 people a year by trampling or goring them with its tusks, often for no obvious reason. Its size—the average elephant weighs more than 6 tons—gives it a huge advantage.

Nile Crocodile. Despite the specific name, the Nile crocodile lives in almost every major river and body of water in Africa. It kills hundreds of people each year. The danger zone is on the riverbank or lake shore, where a fisherman might be sliding in his boat or a woman might be washing clothes or collecting water. A crocodile attacks by dragging its prey underwater and drowning him.

Lion. Who isn't afraid of lions? They kill about 250 people every year. The king of the jungle lives throughout sub-Saharan Africa (except in forests and deserts). Females do almost all of the hunting, working mainly at night and in teams to stalk and ambush prey. Lions live in groups called prides in grassy plains, savannahs, open woodlands, and scrub country—anywhere where they can hide in the vegetation for a surprise attack. The crocodile is the lion's only predator (besides man).

Scorpion. Related to spiders, the scorpion is small but venomous. It looks like a miniature crab but has four pairs of legs, a pair of pincers, and a long, segmented tail with a stinger on the end that curls up over its back. Only one type of scorpion that lives in the United States is deadly, but all scorpion stings hurt. Scorpions cause more than 5,000 deaths every year.

Snake. Not all snakes bite, but many do and can cause real harm. Snakes cause more than 100,000 deaths every year. Coral snakes, pit vipers, cottonmouths, and rattlers are North American snakes that should be avoided. King cobras are the largest venomous snakes and can be found mainly in southern Asia, northern Africa, and the Philippines. Other species of cobras live in Australia; Papua, New Guinea; and in most of the Eastern Hemisphere.

Mosquito. It is hard to avoid mosquitos because they are found on every continent except Antarctica. In terms of the number of deaths caused, the mosquito is number one on any list of most dangerous animals. Mosquitoes in Africa transmit malaria, which results in about 2 million deaths a year. They also transmit viruses such as dengue, encephalitis, and yellow fever. Mosquito bites in North America are very annoying but are mostly harmless.

INDEX

crust of the earth, 13, 26–28, 36–67. *See also* tectonic plates

currents, ocean, 17–18, 47–48, 49–50

Cyclone Alley, 46–47

D

dams, 115–16

Dead Sea, 54, 122

deserts, 76, 78, 126–30, 136

E

Earth, 12–24
 changes in, 25–40
 tectonic plates, 26–31

earthquakes, 30–34, 44, 73, 74, 86–87

East Africa Rift, 32–33

ecological communities, 124–36

elevation, 22, 79

equator, 16, 60, 66, 71, 134

erosion, 97–98, 100

Europe, 64, 81–84, 103

extinction of species, 135–36

F

faults, 30–31, 73, 97

flooding, 36, 39–40, 91, 113, 117–18

flower, world's biggest, 125

forest biomes, 131–35

G

Galápagos Islands, 77

Ganges River, 108, 113–15

geocaching, 61–62

Georgia, 83

glaciers, 38–39, 79, 80, 97–98, 102, 113. *See also* ice lakes and, 103, 119

global warming, 38–40, 136

Gobi Desert, 130

GPS (Global Positioning System), 60–61

Grand Canyon, 107, 108

grassland, 76, 130–31

Great Barrier Reef, 55, 85–86

Great Lakes, 119, 120

Great Rift Valley, 69–70

Greenland, 46, 72, 74, 90

H

Himalayas, 67, 98–99

history of Earth, 23

hot spots, 37, 92–93

hot springs, 70

hurricanes, 45, 94

I

ice, 19, 21, 40, 7, 79, 80. *See also* glaciers

ice ages, 38

Iceland, 82

India, 65, 66, 99, 113–15

Indian Ocean, 43, 46–47, 68

Indonesia, 65

Indus River, 67

islands, 87–88, 90–94. *See also* specific ones

Isthmus of Panama, 74

Reader's Digest Books for Young Readers

Write (Or Is That "Right"?) Every Time

Divided into bite-size chunks that include Goodness Gracious Grammar, Spelling Made Simple, and Punctuation Perfection, this book provides quick-and-easy tips and tricks to overcome every grammar challenge.

LOTTIE STRIDE

978-1-60652-341-4

i before e (except after c)
The Young Readers Edition

Full of hundreds of fascinating tidbits, presented in a fun and accessible way, this lighthearted book offers kids many helpful mnemonics that make learning easy and fun.

SUSAN RANDOL

978-1-60652-348-3

I Wish I Knew That

This fun and engaging book will give young readers a jump start on everything from art, music, literature, and ancient myths to history, geography, science, and math.

STEVE MARTIN

DR. MIKE GOLDSMITH

MARIANNE TAYLOR

978-1-60652-340-7

COUTURE
CUPCAKES

ERIC LANLARD & PATRICK COX

MITCHELL BEAZLEY

An Hachette UK Company
www.hachette.co.uk

First published as *Cox Cookies & Cake*
in Great Britain in 2011 by Mitchell Beazley,
an imprint of Octopus Publishing Group Ltd,
Endeavour House, 189 Shaftesbury Avenue,
London WC2H 8JY
www.octopusbooks.co.uk

This abridged edition published in 2014

Distributed in the US by Hachette Book Group USA
237 Park Avenue, New York, NY 10017 USA
www.octopusbooksusa.com

Distributed in Canada by Canadian Manda Group
165 Dufferin Street, Toronto, Ontario, Canada M6K 3H6

Commissioning editor Becca Spry
Senior editor Sybella Stephens
Home economist Rachel Wood
Art director Jonathan Christie
Senior art editor Juliette Norsworthy
Designer Jaz Bahra
Photography Patrick Llewelyn-Davies
Production controller Allison Gonsalves

ISBN: 978 1 84533 955 5
Printed and bound in China

Muffin-size cupcake pans and standard paper
baking cups should be used for all cupcake recipes,
unless otherwise stated. Medium eggs and whole milk
should be used, unless otherwise stated.

CONTENTS

I'm a designer. It's in my blood. It's who I am. It affects how I look at everything in the world. I see everyday objects, such as shoes, bags, or cakes, and I want to make them sexier, inject them with glamor, and make them shine! For me life is the triumph of the fantastic over the dull, and when I saw the pastel-shaded world of cupcakes, I wanted to shake it up, sex it up, and create something breathtakingly new.

The result was our Cox Cookies & Cake project—a bakery we opened in Soho, London. The location was a former sex shop in the heart of London's historic red light district; with an original Tracey Emin neon artwork on the wall; staff in leather-studded aprons; mirrored ceilings and a polished black floor—it all set the scene for the most dangerous thing to hit the world of cupcakes since self-rising flour.

However, when it came to the cakes themselves, I faced my limitations as a designer. I needed a skilled pâtissier and business partner to make sure the cakes tasted every bit as good as they looked, with all the quality that one associates with the Patrick Cox name. Fortunately Elizabeth Hurley introduced me to world-renowned and fabulous Eric Lanlard (he made Elizabeth's wedding cake) and as soon as we met I knew instantly we could work together. We created cakes that were sexy, unbelievably tasty, and fun. Each cake was like a work of art.

This book takes that accessibility further. I want people to enjoy the design process themselves and have fun creating these cakes at home. So turn on the music, crank up the volume, and get baking!

Patrick Cox

I'm a pâtissier. It's in my blood and who I am, or at least who I have been since I was a little boy staring in the windows of my local pâtisserie. In times where form often triumphs over substance and where looks too often succeed over taste, it has always been my mission to make cakes that taste as good as they look; cakes where the feasting of the eyes is not followed by a bite of disappointment, but by a feasting of the taste buds. I have been putting this philosophy into practice within my own business over the past 18 years.

Before having the pleasure of meeting Patrick, glamor was always very much part of my world, reflected in the title of my first UK book *Glamour Cakes* and my first two TV series' *Glamour Puds*. As an artisan I've always used cake design as my creative outlet. However, the excitement I felt on first hearing about Patrick's vision, pushed my boundaries way beyond anything I would have dared to do myself.

The results of our efforts speak for themselves in this book. I hope these recipes enable you to bake a little excitement in your own home and put happy faces on your friends and family alike.

Eric Lanlard

NUTTY
& CHOCOLATEY
CUPCAKES

COLA CUPCAKES

Put some fizz into your cupcakes! These little miracles will delight kids and adults, too. The cola makes the cake light and airy, and the addition of the popping candy topping makes them a truly fun experience.

MAKES 12 CUPCAKES

1¾ sticks unsalted butter
1 cup cola (I prefer to use the old-fashioned original one because it has more flavor)
2 cups self-rising flour
1 tsp baking powder
1 tbsp unsweetened cocoa powder
1 cup superfine sugar
2 eggs, beaten
⅔ cup milk

For the cola frosting
7 tbsp unsalted butter, softened
¼ cup unsweetened cocoa powder
3¾ cups confectioner's sugar
scant ½ cup cola
1 tsp vanilla extract
cola-flavored popping candy or fizzy cola bottles, to decorate

Preheat the oven to 400°F, and line a cupcake pan with paper baking cups.

In a saucepan, gently heat the butter and cola until the butter has melted. Remove from the heat and leave to cool.

Sift the flour, baking powder, and cocoa powder together. Add the cooled cola and butter mixture, followed by the sugar and eggs. Mix together then add just enough milk a little at a time until the mixture is smooth.

Divide the batter between the baking cups. Bake for 25–30 minutes, or until a skewer inserted into the center of a cupcake comes out clean. Leave to cool in the pan for 5 minutes then transfer to a wire rack and allow to cool completely before frosting.

To make the Cola Frosting: Cream the butter in a bowl. Sift the cocoa and confectioner's sugar together and mix into the butter a little at a time, alternating with additions of the cola. Beat to give a nice smooth frosting. (You may need to add more cola if the frosting is too stiff). Beat in the vanilla extract.

Pipe the frosting onto the cooled cupcakes and decorate with either popping candy or fizzy cola bottles.

RED VELVET CUPCAKES

This now-celebrated cupcake is usually made as a large cake and there are many variations, including some that use beet juice to give the rich red color. In this recipe I use a combination of pure unsweetened cocoa powder, vinegar, and red food coloring to achieve a vibrant tone.

MAKES 12 CUPCAKES

¼ cup + 1 tbsp unsweetened
  cocoa powder
1 tsp vanilla extract
5 tbsp unsalted butter, softened
  heaped ¾ cup superfine sugar
2 egg yolks
pinch of salt
⅔ cup buttermilk
1¼ cups all-purpose flour, sifted
½ tsp baking soda
½ tsp white wine vinegar
1 tsp red food coloring

For the frosting
½ cup milk
1½ tbsp all-purpose flour
pinch of salt
7 tbsp unsalted butter, softened
1½ cups confectioner's sugar,
  plus extra for dusting
3½oz white chocolate,
  melted and cooled
½ tsp vanilla extract

Preheat the oven to 400°C, and line a cupcake pan with paper baking cups.

In a small bowl, combine the cocoa powder and vanilla extract. Set aside.

In a large bowl, beat the butter and sugar together using a stand mixer or an electric hand mixer on medium-high speed. Add the yolks. Beat for another minute then add the cocoa mixture.

Stir the salt into the buttermilk. Mix one third into the butter mixture, followed by one-third of the flour. Repeat with two further batches of each until all are mixed in.

Mix the baking soda with the vinegar and blend this, along with the food coloring, into the batter. Divide the batter between the baking cups. Bake for 20–25 minutes, or until a skewer inserted into the center of a cupcake comes out clean.

Allow the cupcakes to cool in the pan for 10 minutes, then remove them from the pan and allow to cool completely before frosting.

To make the frosting: In a small saucepan, whisk the milk, flour, and salt over medium heat for 1 or 2 minutes until the mixture thickens and begins to bubble. Transfer to a small bowl and leave to cool.

Beat the butter and confectioner's sugar together until light and fluffy. Stir in the cooled chocolate, the milk mixture, and the vanilla extract, and mix until smooth and fluffy.

Spread or pipe the frosting onto the cooled cupcakes. Crumble some baked red sponge cake on top (you may have to sacrifice one of your cupcakes). Dust with confectioner's sugar to finish.

TRIPLE CHOCOLATE CUPCAKES

Here's one for the chocoholics! There's cocoa powder, melted chocolate, and chocolate chips in this beautiful moist cupcake. Then, for a rich finish, it's covered with chocolate frosting and a coating of chocolate sprinkles. Heaven!

MAKES 12 CUPCAKES

3oz semisweet chocolate,
  broken into pieces
1¾ sticks unsalted butter
1 heaped cup superfine sugar
3 eggs
½ tsp baking powder
1⅓ cups all-purpose flour
¼ cup unsweetened cocoa
  powder
heaped ¼ cup semisweet
  chocolate chips
1 quantity Chocolate Frosting
  (see page 87)
mixture of mini white, milk,
  and dark chocolate sprinkles,
  to decorate

Preheat the oven to 400°F, and line a cupcake pan with paper baking cups.

In a large saucepan, melt the chocolate and butter over medium heat, stirring to prevent if from burning. Allow this to cool for a few minutes.

Stir in the sugar until well mixed. Add the eggs, one at a time, until you have a smooth batter. Sift the baking powder, flour, and cocoa powder into the batter and mix until smooth. Then fold in the chocolate chips.

Divide the batter between the paper baking cups to just about three-quarters full—don't overfill them. Bake for 20–25 minutes, or until a skewer inserted into the center of a cupcake comes out clean.

Leave to cool in the pan for 5 minutes then transfer to a wire rack and allow to cool completely before frosting. I like to spread Chocolate Frosting on top of the cupcakes and then cover them with mini chocolate sprinkles to decorate.

IRISH CREAM & CHOCOLATE CUPCAKES

We call this classic the Irish cupcake because of the addition of Irish cream liqueur, which works perfectly with the chocolate base. Kids should be kept well away from these!

MAKES 12 CUPCAKES

3oz semisweet chocolate, plus extra for decorating
1¾ sticks unsalted butter
1 heaped cup superfine sugar
1 tsp vanilla extract
1 tbsp of Irish cream liqueur
3 eggs
¼ cup unsweetened cocoa powder
1⅓ cups all-purpose flour
½ tsp baking powder
chocolate curls, to decorate

For the frosting
2 sticks unsalted butter
3oz semisweet chocolate, melted and cooled
4½ cups confectioner's sugar
3 tbsp Irish cream liqueur

Preheat the oven to 400°F, and line a cupcake pan with paper baking cups.

Add the chocolate and butter to a large heatproof bowl and set it over a saucepan of barely simmering water, making sure the bowl does not touch the surface of the water. Stir until completely melted then remove from the heat. Stir in the sugar, vanilla extract, and Irish cream liqueur.

Beat in the eggs one at a time. Sift in the cocoa powder, flour, and baking powder and combine until smooth.

Spoon the mixture into the baking cups, filling each three-quarters full. Bake for 20–25 minutes, or until a skewer inserted into the center of a cupcake comes out clean.

Leave to cool in the pan for 5 minutes then transfer to a wire rack and allow to cool completely before covering with frosting.

To make the frosting: Beat the butter into the melted chocolate until smooth. Gradually beat in the confectioner's sugar and finally add the Irish cream liqueur. Using a small metal spatula, spread the frosting over the cupcakes or pipe it on in spirals. Decorate with chocolate curls.

CHOCOLATE & COCONUT CUPCAKES

If you are a fan of Mounds chocolate bars, these cupcakes are for you. Coated with a rich cinnamon ganache, they have a true taste of paradise.

MAKES 12 CUPCAKES

1 cup superfine sugar
1¾ sticks unsalted butter, softened
3 eggs
3 tbsp milk
1⅓ cups self-rising flour
½ tsp baking powder
   heaped ¾ cup desiccated coconut

For the chocolate ganache
5oz semisweet chocolate (55% cocoa solids), broken into small pieces
⅔ cup heavy cream
3½ tbsp very soft unsalted butter
1 tsp ground cinnamon
toasted desiccated coconut, to decorate

Preheat the oven to 400°F, and line a cupcake pan with paper baking cups.

In a large bowl, cream the sugar and butter together until pale and fluffy using a stand mixer or an electric hand mixer, then stir in the eggs one at a time, followed by the milk. Beat until everything is well incorporated.

Fold the flour and baking powder into butter mixture until smooth and well combined. Finally fold in the coconut.

Divide the batter between the paper baking cups. Bake for 20 minutes or until a skewer inserted into the center of a cupcake comes out clean. Leave to cool in the pan for 5 minutes, then transfer to a wire rack to cool completely.

To make the Chocolate Ganache: Add the chocolate to a medium-sized bowl. Put the cream in a small saucepan over medium heat and, as soon as it reaches boiling point, pour it over the chocolate. Leave this to stand until the chocolate pieces have melted.

Once they have melted, pass the mixture through a sieve into a bowl. Then stir in the softened butter and cinnamon. Leave to cool and set slightly.

As soon as the mixture has set, beat it in a stand mixer or using an electric hand mixer until it has almost doubled in volume.

Spread the ganache over the cooled cupcakes then scatter with toasted desiccated coconut to decorate.

CHOCOLATE & RASPBERRY CUPCAKES

The rich semisweet chocolate batter and the sweetness of the raspberries is a combination made in heaven. Then, with a chocolate frosting and more fresh raspberries on top...yummy!

MAKES 12 CUPCAKES

1⅛ sticks unsalted butter
3oz semisweet chocolate, broken into large pieces
1 tsp instant coffee
1 tsp vanilla extract
¾ cup light soft brown sugar
2 eggs, lightly beaten
1 tsp baking powder
1¾ cups self-rising flour
⅔ cup water
3⅔ cups raspberries, plus extra to decorate
1 quantity Chocolate Frosting (see page 87)

Preheat the oven to 400°F, and line a cupcake pan with paper baking cups..

Melt the butter in a large heatproof bowl placed over a saucepan of barely simmering water, making sure the bowl does not touch the surface of the water. When it is half melted, add the chocolate. When the chocolate has melted completely remove from the heat and stir to blend in any lumps. Allow to cool for a few minutes.

Dissolve the coffee in the vanilla extract, then stir this mixture, along with the brown sugar, into the cooled chocolate and butter. When they are fully blended in, stir in the eggs and combine.

Sift the baking powder and the flour into the mixture and beat until all ingredients are well incorporated and the batter is thick. Then stir in the water a little at a time, making sure the liquid is completely absorbed into the batter.

Divide the batter between the paper baking cups, filling each about half full. Place 3 raspberries on the surface of each—they will sink into the batter. Then fill each cup almost to the top and place another fresh raspberry on top.

Bake for about 25 minutes, or until each cupcake is firm to touch or a skewer inserted into the center of a cupcake comes out clean. Leave to cool in the pan for 10 minutes and then transfer to a wire rack to cool completely. Once cool, pipe Chocolate Frosting in swirls on top of each cupcake and decorate with fresh raspberries.

BLACK FOREST CUPCAKES

Don't be discouraged by the lengthy preparation needed for this recipe—all the effort is well worth it to make these very tasty grown-up cupcakes. I like using Amarena cherries if I can get them—Italian delis often stock them.

MAKES 12 CUPCAKES

14oz jar or can of pitted black cherries in syrup, drained (reserving the syrup)
3½oz semisweet chocolate (50% cocoa solids), broken into pieces
1½ sticks unsalted butter, roughly cubed
1½ cups superfine sugar
4 tbsp cherry brandy
1¼ cups all-purpose flour, sifted
2 tbsp self-rising flour, sifted
2 tbsp unsweetened cocoa powder
1 egg

For the decoration
2 tsp cherry brandy
generous ¾ cup heavy cream
2oz chunk of semisweet chocolate (50% cocoa solids), optional

Preheat the oven to 400°F, and line a cupcake pan with paper baking cups.

Put a generous ⅓ cup of the cherries and ½ cup of their syrup in a food processor and process until it becomes a smooth puree.

Cut the remaining cherries in half and reserve the rest of the syrup.

Place the cherry puree in a saucepan together with the chocolate, butter, sugar, and cherry brandy. Stir over low heat until the chocolate has melted. Pour into a large bowl and allow to cool for 15 minutes.

When cool, whisk in the flours and the cocoa powder, followed by the egg. It will be very runny, but that is OK.

Divide the batter between the paper baking cups. You will probably find that you fill the baking cups close to the top, but do not worry—the cupcakes will not rise a great deal.

Bake for 40–45 minutes, or until firm to touch or a skewer inserted into the center of a cupcake comes out clean. Allow to cool in the pan for 5 minutes then transfer to a wire rack to cool completely.

To decorate, mix the cherry brandy into the remaining cherry halves. Whip the cream to soft peaks, and pipe swirls on top of each cake.

Place some of the brandy-soaked cherry halves onto each cupcake and drizzle the reserved syrup on top. If using, scrape along the side of the chocolate chunk with a vegetable peeler to create curls and use these to decorate the top of each cupcake.

CHOCOLATE & MARSHMALLOW CUPCAKES

For this recipe I use a mixture of mini marshmallows and marshmallow creme to frost a rich and gooey brownie-like cupcake. The marshmallow creme gives these devilish little cupcakes a fun, toasted marshmallow dimension, along with an extra marshmallow hit!

MAKES 12 CUPCAKES

3oz semisweet chocolate, broken into pieces
1¾ sticks unsalted butter
1 heaped cup superfine sugar
3 eggs
½ tsp baking powder
¼ cup unsweetened cocoa powder
1⅓ cups all-purpose flour
confectioner's sugar, to decorate

For the marshmallow buttercream frosting
2¼ sticks unsalted butter, softened
1 heaped cup marshmallow creme, plus extra to decorate
mini marshmallows, to decorate (optional)

Preheat the oven to 400°F, and line a cupcake pan with paper baking cups.

In a large saucepan over medium heat, melt the chocolate and butter, stirring constantly to stop it from burning. Allow to cool for a few minutes, then add the sugar and stir until well mixed.

Add the eggs, one at a time, until you have a smooth mixture. Then sift in the baking powder, flour, and cocoa powder and mix just until smooth.

Divide the batter between the paper baking cups filling them about three-quarters full—don't overfill them. Bake for 20–25 minutes, or until a skewer inserted into the center of a cupcake comes out clean. Leave to cool in the pan for 10 minutes and then transfer to a wire rack to cool completely.

To make the Marshmallow Buttercream Frosting: Beat the butter and marshmallow creme together until smooth. Using a small metal spatula, spread the frosting on top of the cupcakes. If you want to add an extra marshmallow hit, spoon a couple of teaspoons of creme on top of the frosting, add some mini marshmallows, if liked, and dust with confectioner's sugar to finish.

Beware! The marshmallow creme will drip down the frosting, so don't let these cakes hang around for too long (although I love the way they look when this happens).

COCONUT CUPCAKES

This recipe uses very soft coconut sponge cake with an indulgent mascarpone cheese frosting. I like using long strands of dry coconut for the topping. To spoil yourself, try drizzling some melted semisweet chocolate on top of the cupcakes. This recipe can be made very grown-up by the addition of some Malibu coconut liqueur.

MAKES 12 CUPCAKES

1½ sticks unsalted butter, softened
⅔ cup superfine sugar
3 eggs, beaten
3 tbsp unsweetened cocoa powder
heaped ½ cup desiccated coconut
1¼ cups all-purpose flour
1 tsp baking powder
¼ cup milk

For the frosting
1⅓ cup mascarpone cheese
½ cup confectioner's sugar
zest of 1 lime
heaped ½ cup desiccated coconut
⅔ cup thin strands of fresh coconut, toasted

Preheat the oven to 400°F, and line a cupcake pan with paper baking cups.

In a large bowl, cream together the butter and sugar until pale and light. Add the beaten eggs and mix well. Add the cocoa powder and coconut, and mix in well. Sift the flour and baking powder together and then fold it into he butter and egg mixture. Add the milk and mix until smooth.

Divide the batter between the paper baking cups and bake on the middle rack of the oven for 20 minutes, or until the cakes are golden and a skewer inserted into the center of a cupcake comes out clean. Leave to cool in the pan for 5 minutes and then transfer to a wire rack to cool completely.

To make the frosting: beat the mascarpone cheese, confectioner's sugar, and lime zest together until smooth. Add the desiccated coconut and mix in well. When ready, spread an even layer of the frosting on top of each cupcake. Scatter with toasted coconut strands, to finish.

PISTACHIO & ROSEWATER CUPCAKES

Here are all the flavors of the Middle East in a cute little cupcake—the combination of the spices, floral extracts, and nuts works so well. I like to scatter dried organic rose petals on top of mine.

MAKES 12 CUPCAKES

½ cup plain yogurt
⅔ cup milk
¼ cup + 1 tbsp sunflower oil
heaped ¾ cup superfine sugar
1½ tbsp rosewater
1⅓ cups all-purpose flour
2 tbsp cornstarch
½ tsp baking soda
½ tsp baking powder
1 tsp vanilla extract
generous pinch of cardamom
   seeds (the little black seeds
   inside cardamom pods)
scant ½ cup chopped
   pistachio nuts

For the rosewater glaze
1⅔ cups confectioner's sugar
1 tbsp unsalted butter
2–3 tsp milk
½ tsp rosewater

Preheat the oven to 400°F, and line a cupcake pan with paper baking cups.

In a large bowl, beat together the yogurt, milk, oil, sugar, and rosewater. Sift in the flour, cornstarch, baking soda, and baking powder, then stir in the vanilla extract, cardamom seeds, and chopped pistachio nuts.

Divide the mixture between the paper baking cups, but only fill them three-quarters full. Bake for 20–25 minutes, or until a skewer inserted into the center of a cupcake comes out clean.

Leave to cool in the pan for 5 minutes and then transfer to a wire rack to cool completely before covering with the rosewater glaze.

To make the Rosewater Glaze: Cut all of the butter into half of the confectioner's sugar until the mixture resembles fine crumbs, then mix in the milk and rosewater. Finally beat in the remaining confectioner's sugar. Spread the glaze on top of the cupcakes to finish.

PISTACHIO & PRALINE CUPCAKES

These little marvels are so irresistible, with a pistachio sponge cake topped with Italian meringue and nutty praline. They also look very pretty, with the praline shining like jewels.

MAKES 12 CUPCAKES

1⅛ sticks unsalted butter, softened
heaped ¾ cup superfine sugar
seeds from ½ vanilla bean
⅓ cup pistachio nut paste
2 eggs
1½ cups all-purpose flour
1 tsp baking powder
½ cup milk

For the pistachio praline
sunflower oil, for brushing
⅔ cup unsalted pistachio nuts
1 cup superfine sugar
½ cup water

For the meringue topping
¾ cup superfine sugar
3 tbsp water
generous pinch of cream of tartar
2 egg whites
pinch of salt

Preheat the oven to 400°F, and line a cupcake pan with paper baking cups.

Beat together the butter, sugar, vanilla seeds, and pistachio nut paste until light and creamy. Slowy add the eggs and beat again. Sift in the flour and baking powder, and beat until combined. Stir in the milk. Divide the batter between the baking cups. Bake for 15–17 minutes, or until a skewer inserted into the center of a cupcake comes out clean. Remove the cupcakes from the pan and transfer them to a wire rack to cool.

To make the Pistachio Praline: Line a baking pan with foil, brush it with sunflower oil, and scatter the nuts onto the foil. Place the sugar and water in a saucepan over low heat, stirring until the sugar has dissolved. Increase the heat and bring to a boil, brushing any sugar crystals down the inside of the pan with a wet pastry brush. Cook for 8–10 minutes, or until dark golden. Remove from the heat and pour onto the nuts. Leave to cool, then chop into small chunks.

To make the Meringue Topping: Combine the sugar, water, and cream of tartar in a heavy saucepan on medium heat and stir until it boils. Insert a candy thermometer. When the syrup reaches 230°F, whisk the egg whites, ideally in a stand mixer, until stiff. When the syrup reaches 250°F, with the mixer still on, slowly pour the syrup into the egg whites down the side of the bowl avoiding the whisk. Beat until the meringue is thick, glossy, and completely cold, about 10–15 minutes. To decorate, pipe the meringue onto the cupcakes (see page 94 for styling tips). Arrange a few nuggets of pistachio praline on top.

CARROT CAKE CUPCAKES

This all-American classic is such a versatile recipe. It is usually made as a loaf, a round, or baked in a square pan—but now as cupcakes! Using oil instead of butter as a fat gives you a very moist result. The cream cheese frosting is rich and delicious, but make sure you use a very dry cream cheese to get a nice firm texture. These cupcakes will keep very well in a pan, but do not store them in the fridge because they will go hard.

MAKES 12 CUPCAKES

1 cup sunflower or corn oil
1 heaped cup golden superfine sugar
3 eggs
1¾ cups self-rising flour
1 tsp ground cinnamon
1 tsp ground nutmeg
1⅔ cups carrots, coarsely grated
heaped ¾ cup golden raisins, plus extra to decorate
heaped ¾ cup chopped walnuts, plus extra to decorate

For the cream cheese frosting
1 scant cup reduced-fat cream cheese
1 cup unrefined golden confectioner's sugar, sifted
finely grated zest of 1 orange

Preheat the oven to 400°F, and line a cupcake pan with paper baking cups.

Pour the oil into a large bowl, add the superfine sugar, and beat with a large whisk for a few minutes. Then add the eggs one at a time.

Sift the flour, cinnamon, and nutmeg together, and, using a large metal spoon, fold the flour mixture into the egg mixture. Then fold in the carrots, golden raisins, and walnuts.

Divide the batter between the paper baking cups and bake for 20 minutes, or until a skewer inserted into the center of a cupcake comes out clean. Leave to cool in the pan for 5 minutes and then transfer to a wire rack to cool completely.

To make the Cream Cheese Frosting: Gently beat the cream cheese until it is soft and smooth. Then gradually add the confectioner's sugar, followed by the orange zest.

When the cupcakes are cold, use a small metal spatula to spread the frosting on the top of each cake. Decorate each one with few golden raisins and some chopped walnuts.

CHOCOLATE PEANUT BUTTER CUPCAKES

These cupcakes are just so delicious; the combination of the rich chocolate and the salty, crunchy peanut butter works wonderfully.

MAKES 12 CUPCAKES

1½ sticks unsalted butter
¾ cup superfine sugar
¾ cup light brown sugar
2 eggs
2 tsp vanilla extract
1 cup buttermilk
½ cup sour cream
2 tbsp espresso coffee
2 tbsp crunchy peanut butter
2 cups all-purpose flour
1 cup unsweetened cocoa powder
1½ tsp baking powder

For the peanut butter frosting
1¼ cups confectioner's sugar
½ cup smooth peanut butter
3½ tbsp unsalted butter, softened
¾ tsp vanilla extract
2 tbsp heavy cream
chopped salted peanuts, to decorate

Preheat the oven to 400°F, and line a cupcake pan with paper baking cups.

Cream the butter with both sugars, ideally in the bowl of a stand mixer or using an electric hand mixer, on high speed until light and fluffy (about 5 minutes). Lower the speed to medium, and add the eggs one at a time. Then add the vanilla extract and mix in well.

In another bowl, whisk together the buttermilk, sour cream, coffee, and peanut butter.

Into a third bowl, sift together the flour, cocoa powder, and baking powder.

On low speed, add one-third of the buttermilk mixture followed by one-third of the flour mixture to the butter and sugar mixture, beating only until just blended. Repeat until all the buttermilk and flour have been incorporated. Gently fold the batter with a spatula to ensure everything is completely blended. Divide the batter between the baking cups. Bake for 20–25 minutes, or until a skewer inserted into the center of a cupcake comes out clean. Leave to cool in the pan for 5 minutes, then transfer to a wire rack to cool completely.

To make the Peanut Butter Frosting: Mix the confectioner's sugar, peanut butter, butter, and vanilla extract in a stand mixer on medium-low speed (or use an electric hand mixer) until creamy, scraping down the bowl with a spatula as you work. Add the cream and beat on high speed until the mixture is light and smooth. Using a pastry bag fitted with a small round tip, pipe the frosting onto each cupcake (see page 94 for styling tips). Finish by scattering the frosted cupcakes with chopped salted peanuts.

FRUITY CUPCAKES

KEY LIME CUPCAKES

These fresh, zesty cupcakes make great summer treats. You could add some chopped fresh mint to turn them into Mojito cupcakes, and a cup of roasted coconut in the mix works very well, too. Its a good idea to make the crystallized lime zest decoration the day before you want to serve these cupcakes.

MAKES 12 CUPCAKES

1½ sticks unsalted butter, softened
1½ cups superfine sugar
3 eggs
finely grated zest of 1 lime
   and 4 tbsp juice
1 tsp vanilla extract
2½ cups all-purpose flour
1 tsp baking powder
1½ cups buttermilk

For the crystallized lime peel
2 unwaxed limes
½ cup superfine sugar,
   plus extra to coat
scant ½ cup water

For the lime syrup
¼ cup confectioner's sugar
   dissolved in the juice of 1½ limes

For the white chocolate frosting
7oz white chocolate,
   broken into pieces
½ cup heavy cream
1½ sticks unsalted butter, softened
grated zest of 1 lime and juice of ½
3 cups confectioner's sugar

To make the Crystallized Lime Zest: Pare the zest from each lime, then carefully cut it into thin strips. Add the superfine sugar and the water to a pan and bring to a boil, stirring. Once bubbling, add one-third of the lime zest and cook for 3–4 minutes. Remove the zest, roll gently in superfine sugar, and set on waxed paper. (Space the pieces of zest out or they will stick together in clumps.) Repeat with the remaining zest and leave to dry overnight.

Preheat the oven to 400°F, and line a cupcake pan with paper baking cups.

Using a stand mixer or an electric hand mixer, cream the butter and sugar until pale and fluffy. Slowly beat in the eggs, one at the time. Add the lime zest and juice, then the vanilla extract. In another bowl, sift together the flour and baking powder. Gradually add this to the butter mixture with alternate spoonfuls of buttermilk. Divide the batter between the baking cups. Bake for 25–30 minutes, or until a skewer inserted into the center of a cupcake comes out clean. Leave to cool in the pans for 5 minutes then transfer to a wire rack. While warm, use a toothpick to prick small holes into the top of each cupcake. Drizzle a teaspoon of lime syrup over each and allow it to soak and cool before frosting.

To make the frosting: Melt the chocolate with the cream in a heatproof bowl set over a saucepan of simmering water, making sure the bowl does not touch the surface of the water. Allow the chocolate to cool completely. Then whisk in the butter, lime zest, juice, and confectioner's sugar. When smooth, use a pastry bag to pipe the frosting onto each cupcake, and decorate with a few strands of crystallized lime zest.

ZESTY LEMON & WHITE CHOCOLATE CUPCAKES

This light and zesty cupcake carries off the rich white chocolate frosting with serious style, making a great summer dessert. Lemon curd is available by mail order online and in gourmet markets and some supermarkets.

MAKES 12 CUPCAKES

1½ sticks unsalted butter, softened
½ cup superfine sugar
2 eggs
1 scant cup plain yogurt
grated zest of 1 lemon and 2 tsp lemon juice
½ tsp lemon oil
1½ cups all-purpose flour
1 tsp baking powder
2 tsp poppy seeds
½ of an 11oz jar of lemon curd

For the white chocolate frosting
5 tbsp unsalted butter
¼ cup + 1 tbsp cream cheese
1¼ cups confectioner's sugar
3½oz white chocolate, melted, plus extra to decorate

Preheat the oven to 400°F, and line a cupcake pan with paper baking cups.

In a large bowl, cream the butter and sugar together until light and fluffy. Then mix in the eggs, one at a time, followed by the yogurt, lemon zest and juice, and the lemon oil. Sift the flour and baking powder together and stir this into the butter mixture with the poppy seeds until just combined.

Divide the batter between the paper baking cups, but only filling them half-full. Place a heaped teaspoonful of lemon curd onto each cupcake and then fill to the rim with the remaining batter. Bake for about 25–30 minutes, or until a skewer inserted into the side of a cupcake comes out clean. Leave to cool in the pans for 5 minutes then transfer to a wire rack and allow to cool completely before frosting.

To make the White Chocolate Frosting: Cream together the butter, cream cheese, and confectioner's sugar, then add the melted white chocolate. Either spread the frosting using a small metal spatula or pipe the frosting onto the cooled cupcakes. Scatter with white chocolate curls and leave to set.

ORANGE MARMALADE CUPCAKES

This could almost be a breakfast cupcake! When I can get hold of it, I make mine with blood orange marmalade. And if you happen to have it, a homemade marmalade makes these cupcakes even more divine.

MAKES 12 CUPCAKES

1¼ sticks unsalted butter, softened
½ cup golden superfine sugar
2 eggs
finely grated zest of 2 oranges and 2 tbsp juice
3 tbsp Seville orange marmalade, plus extra to decorate
1 tsp vanilla extract
2 cups self-rising flour

For the frosting
1 quantity Vanilla Buttercream Frosting (see page 84)
finely grated zest of 1 orange

Preheat the oven to 400°F, and line a cupcake pan with paper baking cups.

In a large bowl, cream together the butter and sugar. Stir in the eggs one at a time. Mix in the orange zest and juice, the marmalade, and the vanilla extract. Sift the flour into the mixture and combine until smooth.

Divide the batter between the paper baking cups and bake for about 20–25 minutes, or until a skewer inserted into the center of a cupcake comes out clean. Leave to cool in the pan for 5 minutes and then transfer to a wire rack and allow to cool completely before frosting.

Decorate the cupcakes with Vanilla Buttercream Frosting mixed with the orange zest. Finish by placing a teaspoon of marmalade on top.

ORANGE & PUMPKIN CUPCAKES

This is a nice recipe to bake in the fall. It's also perfect for Halloween celebrations.

MAKES 12 CUPCAKES

2½ cups all-purpose flour
1 tbsp baking powder
½ tsp baking soda
½ tsp ground ginger
¾ tsp ground cinnamon
½ tsp ground nutmeg
grated zest of 1 orange
7 tbsp unsalted butter, softened
1 cup superfine sugar
2 eggs
1 cup canned pumpkin
generous 2/3 cup milk

For the mascarpone frosting
1⅓ cups mascarpone cheese
¾ cup confectioner's sugar, sifted
grated zest of 1 orange and 1 tbsp juice

Preheat the oven to 400°F, and line a cupcake pan with paper baking cups.

In a large bowl, sift together the flour, baking powder, baking soda, ginger, cinnamon, and nutmeg. Then stir in the grated orange zest.

In another bowl, cream together the butter and sugar until light and fluffy. Then beat in the eggs, one at a time. Blend the canned pumpkin into this mixture and then stir in the sifted dry ingredients, a little at a time, alternating with some of the milk, blending after each addition until smooth.

Divide the batter between the paper baking cups and bake for 25 minutes, or until a skewer inserted into the center of a cupcake comes out clean. Leave to cool in the pan for 5 minutes then transfer to a wire rack and allow to cool completely before frosting.

To make the Mascarpone Frosting: Beat the mascarpone cheese until light and smooth, and then gradually add the confectioner's sugar, stirring after each addition. Stir in the grated orange zest and juice, and mix until smooth. Using a small metal spatula, spread the frosting onto the top of each cupcake.

LEMON MERINGUE CUPCAKES

The classic lemon meringue pie turned into a delicious cupcake. You could serve these as a dessert and add a few berries for an extra finishing touch. Lemon curd is available by mail order online and in gourmet markets and some supermarkets.

MAKES 12 CUPCAKES

7 tbsp unsalted butter, softened
½ cup superfine sugar
seeds from 1 vanilla bean
2 eggs
¾ cup self-rising flour, sifted
finely grated zest of 1 lemon,
  plus a few strips to decorate
¼ cup lemon curd

For the meringue
2 egg whites
½ cup superfine sugar

Preheat the oven to 400°F, and line a cupcake pan with paper baking cups.

In a large mixing bowl, ideally using an electric hand mixer, cream together the butter, sugar, and vanilla seeds until the mixture is pale, fluffy, and well combined. Crack in the eggs one at a time, and beat them in until both are fully incorporated into the mixture. Fold in the sifted flour and the lemon zest until well combined.

Divide the batter between the paper baking cups and add a teaspoonful of lemon curd to the top of each cupcake. Bake for 15–20 minutes, or until they are pale golden brown and spring back when pressed lightly in the center.

While the cupcakes are baking, make the meringue: whisk the egg whites until they form soft peaks. Gradually add the sugar, whisking continuously, until stiff peaks form again. The mixture should be thick and glossy.

When the cakes have cooked, remove them from the oven to cool. Turn the oven off and preheat the broiler to its highest setting.

Spoon the meringue into a pastry bag fitted with a small tip and pipe it on top of each cupcake. To create a spiked effect, pipe small dots in a circle around the rim, pushing the bag down and up sharply to make a point, then repeat in a spiral until you reach the center.

Place the cupcakes under the hot broiler for 2 minutes to color the meringue (or you can use a kitchen torch).

STRAWBERRY & CREAM CUPCAKES

The great British tradition of strawberries and cream in a sassy little cupcake. These are perfect for an al fresco lunch or picnic.

MAKES 12 CUPCAKES

1½ sticks unsalted butter, softened
heaped ¾ cup superfine sugar
3 eggs, beaten
1 tsp vanilla extract
1⅓ cups self-rising flour, sifted

For the frosting
1¼ cups strawberries, plus 6 extra,
sliced in half, to decorate
1¼ cups regular cream cheese
2¼ cups confectioner's sugar, sifted

Preheat the oven to 400°F, and line a cupcake pan with paper baking cups.

Cream the butter and sugar together until light and fluffy, then gradually beat in the eggs. When the eggs have been incorporated add the vanilla extract and fold in the flour.

Divide the batter between the paper baking cups and bake for about 20 minutes, or until the cupcakes have risen and are golden. Leave to cool in the pan for 5 minutes then transfer to a wire rack and allow to cool completely before frosting.

To make the frosting: Blend or mash the strawberries to a puree, then push them through a fine sieve to remove the seeds. Beat the cream cheese, confectioner's sugar, and strawberry puree together to form a smooth, shiny frosting. Transfer to a pastry bag and pipe the frosting onto the cooled cupcakes (see page 94 for piping tips), then place half a strawberry on top of each cupcake.

BLUEBERRY COMPOTE CUPCAKES

I like to add the berries in the center of these delicious blueberry compote "kiss cakes," in order to enhance the flavor and provide a nice surprise when cutting or biting into the cupcake. I have decorated them with white chocolate lips painted with red edible coloring, but you can put whatever you like on top of yours.

MAKES 12 CUPCAKES

2 eggs
1 cup superfine sugar
½ cup sunflower oil
¼ tsp vanilla extract
2 cups all-purpose flour
pinch of salt
½ tsp baking powder
1 cup sour cream
1 quantity Vanilla Buttercream
  Frosting (see page 84)

For the blueberry compote
1 cup blueberries
¼ cup superfine sugar

First make the Blueberry Compote: Place the blueberries and the sugar in a small saucepan over low heat. Cook them gently, stirring constantly to prevent the sugar from catching. When the fruit starts to pop, remove the pan from the heat and set it aside to cool. If your compote has produced a lot of liquid, strain a little into a bowl to avoid adding too much extra liquid to your cupcake batter. (Any spare juice will come in handy later!)

Preheat the oven to 400°F, and line a cupcake pan with paper baking cups.

In a large bowl, beat the eggs, gradually adding the sugar while beating. Continue beating and slowly pour in the oil. Stir in the vanilla extract. In a separate bowl sift together the flour, salt, and baking powder. Stir these dry ingredients into the egg mixture in small amounts alternating with the sour cream.

Divide the batter between the paper baking cups, but fill them only half full. Then spoon 1½ teaspoons of the compote to each baking cup. Add another spoonful of batter to cover the compote, filling almost to the top of the baking cups.

Bake for 25 minutes, or until a skewer inserted into the side of a cupcake comes out clean. Leave to cool in the pans for 5 minutes then transfer to a wire rack and allow them to cool completely before frosting.

Pipe Vanilla Buttercream Frosting in spirals on top of each cupcake. If you have any excess compote or blueberry juice left over you can drizzle this on top of the frosting before adding a decoration, if using.

RHUBARB CUPCAKES

For this recipe you must get the beautiful stalks of red/pink "champagne" rhubarb usually in season at the beginning of the year. As well as being less fibrous, this gives a lovely color to these cute cupcakes.

MAKES 12 CUPCAKES

2¼ sticks unsalted butter, softened
1 cup soft brown sugar
3 eggs
1¾ cups self-rising flour
2 tsp ground ginger
¾ cup milk
1 quantity Vanilla Buttercream Frosting (see page 84)

For the baked rhubarb strips
2 sticks of pink rhubarb
confectioner's sugar, for dusting

For the rhubarb compote
1 cup trimmed and finely diced rhubarb
2 tbsp superfine sugar
1 tsp ground ginger
1 tbsp water

It is best to make the baked rhubarb strips the day before: preheat the oven to 250°F. With a very sharp knife, cut the rhubarb sticks into 4-inch pieces and then slice each piece very thinly lengthwise. Line a cookie sheet with parchment paper or a silicone baking mat. Arrange the rhubarb strips on the prepared cookie sheet, dust them generously with confectioner's sugar, and bake for 2–3 hours, or until dried out and crisp. Do not overcook them or you will lose the beautiful pink color.

Preheat the oven to 400°F, and line a cupcake pan with paper baking cups.

Cream the butter and sugar until pale and fluffy. Add the eggs, then slowly pour in the milk. Sift in the flour and ginger. Divide the batter between the baking cups. Bake for 18–20 minutes, or until a skewer inserted into the center of a cupcake comes out clean. Leave to cool in the pan for 5 minutes then transfer to a wire rack and allow to cool completely.

To make the Rhubarb Compote: Place all the ingredients in a small pan and heat gently to boiling point (you want the rhubarb to just release its natural juices and turn a beautiful shade of pink). Leave to bubble and reduce for 2–3 minutes. Once the rhubarb has softened and the liquid has turned syrupy, remove the pan from the heat and leave to cool completely.

Use a cutter ¾ inches in width to cut $1/3$ inch deep into the center of each cupcake to make a space for the compote. Spoon the compote into these spaces and then pipe vanilla frosting onto the top. Once the frosting has set, arrange the dried pieces of baked rhubarb decoratively on top of each cupcake.

APPLE CRISP CUPCAKES

With their crumbly topping, these are more of a dessert than a cupcake—you could even serve them hot with runny custard, cream, or ice cream.

MAKES 12 CUPCAKES

2 all-purpose apples, peeled, cored, and diced
1 tsp ground cinnamon
½ tsp baking soda
7 tbsp butter, softened
1 heaped cup soft brown sugar
2 eggs
2¾ cups self-rising flour
confectioner's sugar, for dusting

For the crisp topping
scant ½ cup all-purpose flour
⅓ cup soft brown sugar
½ tsp ground cinnamon
⅓ cup cold unsalted butter

Preheat the oven to 400°F, and line a cupcake pan with paper baking cups.

First make the crisp; add the flour, sugar, and cinnamon to a bowl. Cut the unsalted butter into the flour mixture until it resembles coarse crumbs. Set the crisp aside.

Put the apples in a saucepan with the cinnamon and cook over very low heat until mushy. Leave to cool, then drain through a fine sieve to remove any liquid. Then measure out 1 cup of the drained apple, place it in a bowl, and stir in the baking soda. Set aside.

In a large bowl, cream the butter and sugar together, and then beat in the eggs. Fold the self-rising flour and the apples alternately into the butter and sugar mixture and combine.

Divide the batter between the paper baking cups. Divide the crisp mixture evenly among the tops and bake for 20–25 minutes, or until golden brown on top and a skewer inserted into the center of a cupcake comes out clean.

Leave to cool in the pan for 5 minutes then transfer to a wire rack and allow to cool completely. When cool, finish with a dusting of confectioner's sugar.

MAURITIUS PINEAPPLE CUPCAKES

This recipe is inspired by a fabulous dessert of spit-roasted baby pineapple with Amaretto that I once had in Mauritius. All the luscious flavors are here in these cupcakes.

MAKES 12 CUPCAKES

1⅓ cups all-purpose flour
⅓ cup ground almonds
1 tsp baking powder
1⅛ sticks unsalted butter, softened
1½ cups golden superfine sugar
3 eggs at room temperature
1 tsp pure vanilla extract
½ tsp pure almond extract
½ cup milk
⅓ cup Amaretto
1⅔ cups heavy cream

For the flambéed pineapple
½ cup superfine sugar
1 small pineapple, peeled, cored, and finely diced
scant ½ cup Amaretto
scant ½ cup heavy cream
1 tbsp fresh orange juice
seeds from 1 vanilla bean

Preheat the oven to 400°F, and line a cupcake pan with paper baking cups.

In a bowl, sift together the flour, ground almonds, and baking powder. In another large bowl, cream the butter and sugar until pale and fluffy. Add the eggs, one at a time, beating each one until incorporated. Stir in the vanilla and almond extracts. Add the flour mixture in three batches, alternating with the milk in two additions, and mixing until just combined. If using an electric hand mixer, reduce the speed to low.

Divide the batter between the paper baking cups, to fill each three-quarters full. Bake for 18–20 minutes, or until a skewer inserted into the center of a cupcake comes out clean. Set the pan on a wire rack. Immediately prick holes into the tops of the cupcakes with a toothpick then pour a teaspoon of Amaretto over each one. Leave to cool completely before removing from the pan.

To make the Flambéed Pineapple: in a large pan, heat the sugar over medium heat, stirring, until the sugar dissolves and turns golden brown. Add the diced pineapple and gently toss it in the dissolved sugar. Carefully pour in the Amaretto and ignite the alcohol. If there is a lot of liquid still in the pan once the flames subside and the caramel melts, strain a little away. Then stir in the cream, orange juice, and vanilla seeds. Bring to a boil, stirring occasionally until thickened, for about 5 minutes. Remove from the heat and allow to cool completely. When ready to serve, whip the cream to soft peaks and spread it on top of each cooled cupcake. Place a generous spoonful of Flambéed Pineapple on top of each one.

RICH & SPICY
CUPCAKES

MEXICAN CHOCOLATE CUPCAKES

The rich chocolate and all the lovely exotic spices in these cakes work very well together, and just when you thought you'd tasted everything, a lovely hot sensation hits you as the cayenne chile-flavored frosting works its wonders...another one for adults only!

MAKES 12 CUPCAKES

1⅓ cups all-purpose flour
1 heaped cup superfine sugar
¼ cup unsweetened cocoa
  powder
1 tsp baking soda
1 tsp cinnamon
¼ tsp ground nutmeg
1 tsp vanilla extract
1 tbsp white wine vinegar
¼ cup + 1 tbsp sunflower oil
chile pepper cake decorations,
  to decorate

For the frosting
3½oz semisweet chocolate,
  broken into pieces
1⅜ sticks unsalted butter
1¼ cups confectioner's sugar
¼ tsp ground cayenne pepper

Preheat the oven to 400°F, and line a cupcake pan with paper baking cups.

Sift together the flour, sugar, cocoa powder, baking soda, cinnamon, and nutmeg into a bowl. In a large bowl, blend together the vanilla extract, vinegar, oil, and 1 cup cold water. Mix the dry ingredients into this mixture until well combined and the batter is smooth—a stand mixer or an electric hand mixer will help in doing this.

Divide the batter between the paper baking cups (it will be fairly liquid, so you may want to use a large measuring jug to pour it). Bake for 20–25 minutes, or until a skewer inserted into the center of a cupcake comes out clean. Allow the cupcakes to cool in the pan for 5 minutes, and then transfer them to a wire rack to cool completely.

To make the frosting: Melt the chocolate in a heatproof bowl set over a saucepan of barely simmering water, making sure the bowl does not touch the surface of the water. When melted leave to cool.

Whisk the butter and confectioner's sugar together until pale and fluffy, then whisk in the cooled melted chocolate and the cayenne pepper. Pipe the frosting onto the cooled cupcakes. Set a chile pepper cake decoration on top to finish.

TIRAMISU CUPCAKES

This is my favorite Italian dessert in a cupcake. The light coffee-flavored cupcake covered with a mascarpone and Marsala frosting makes a truly delicious combination. These cupcakes must be eaten on the day they are made.

MAKES 12 CUPCAKES

3½ tbsp unsalted butter
⅔ cup golden superfine sugar
4 eggs
1 cup all-purpose flour
1 level tbsp instant espresso granules dissolved in 2 tsp boiling water

For the frosting
1 cup + 2 tbsp mascarpone cheese
1¼ cups golden confectioner's sugar sifted
1 tbsp Marsala wine
unsweetened cocoa powder, to decorate
confectioner's sugar, to decorate

Preheat the oven to 400°F, and line a cupcake pan with paper baking cups.

Put the butter in a heatproof bowl and melt in the microwave or in a heatproof bowl placed over a saucepan of barely simmering water, making sure the bowl does not touch the surface of the water.

Put the sugar and eggs in another bowl and, ideally using a stand mixer or an electric hand mixer, cream them together until light and frothy and doubled in volume—this will take several minutes.

Sift the flour and gently fold half of it into the mixture. Mix the coffee into the melted butter and pour half of this into the mixture. Add the remaining flour, followed by the rest of the coffee and butter mixture. Work gently as you fold these in.

Divide the batter between the paper baking cups and bake for 25 minutes, or until a skewer inserted into the center of a cupcake comes out clean. Leave to cool in the pan for 5 minutes and then set the individual cupcakes out on a wire rack and allow to cool completely.

To make the frosting: Beat the mascarpone cheese with the golden confectioner's sugar, then add the Marsala and combine. Spread this on top of each cupcake and finish with a generous dusting of unsweetened cocoa powder and confectioner's sugar.

MOCHA CUPCAKES

Dark chocolate and coffee always make a good combination, so I've put these two fabulous flavors together to create the most delicious cupcakes.

MAKES 12 CUPCAKES

1½ sticks unsalted butter, softened
heaped ¾ cup superfine sugar
3 eggs
1 tbsp hot water mixed with 1 tsp instant coffee
1¼ cups all purpose flour
¼ cup unsweetened cocoa powder

For the frosting
7 tbsp unsalted butter, softened
1¼ cups confectioner's sugar
2 tsp fresh coffee, ideally espresso, cooled
2oz melted semisweet chocolate
chocolate coffee beans, to decorate
edible gold paint, to decorate (optional, see page 127 for suppliers)

Preheat the oven to 400°F, and line a cupcake pan with paper baking cups.
....
Cream the butter and sugar together until light and fluffy, then add the eggs one at the time, beating well after each addition until combined and the mixture is smooth. Stir in the coffee mixture. Sift the flour and unsweenetend cocoa powder onto the mixture and fold it in.
....
Divide the batter between the paper baking cups and bake for 20 minutes, or until a skewer inserted into the center of a cupcake comes out clean. Leave to cool in the pan for 5 minutes and then set the individual cupcakes out on a wire rack and allow to cool completely.
....
To make the frosting: Beat the butter and confectioner's sugar together until pale and fluffy. Add the coffee and melted chocolate, and beat until smooth. Pipe or spoon this onto each cupcake and, if using, finish by decorating them with some chocolate coffee beans lightly painted with edible gold paint.

PRESERVED GINGER CUPCAKES

This powerful recipe will give an afternoon tea party a punchy start! The addition of the ginger in syrup makes this little wonder very moist and extremely difficult to resist.

MAKES 18 CUPCAKES

2¼ sticks unsalted butter
1⅓ cups dark brown soft sugar
1⅓ cups molasses
1¼ cups milk
3 eggs, lightly beaten
1 cup ginger in syrup, drained and diced, plus extra to decorate
3¼ cups all-purpose flour
2 tsp baking powder
1 tsp mixed spice
2 tsp ground ginger
1½ quantities Vanilla Buttercream Frosting (see page 84)

Preheat the oven to 400°F, and line a 12-hole and a 6-hole cupcake or muffin pan with paper baking cups.

Put the butter, sugar, and molasses in a saucepan and heat gently for about 5 minutes until the butter and sugar have melted. Stir in the milk and leave to cool before beating in the eggs.

Mix the diced ginger and remaining ingredients together in a large bowl. Pour in the melted mixture and, using a wooden spoon, mix it all together to form a smooth thick batter.

Divide the batter between the paper baking cups and bake for about 25 minutes, or until a skewer inserted into the center of a cupcake comes out clean. Leave to cool in the pans for 5 minutes then transfer to a wire rack. Allow the cupcakes to cool completely before frosting them.

I like to finish mine with Vanilla Buttercream Frosting, and with some more diced ginger scattered on the top.

LADY GREY CUPCAKES

This light and fruity cupcake has just the right balance of the tea flavor. The delicate Italian candied fruits have been soaked in orange liqueur and look like jewels on top, adding a dash of glamor.

MAKES 12 CUPCAKES

⅔ cup mixed candied fruit, finely diced, plus extra to decorate
2–3 tbsp orange liqueur
2 Lady Grey tea bags
1 scant cup water
2 eggs
1 cup golden superfine sugar
½ cup vegetable oil
1 tsp vanilla extract
2 cups all-purpose flour
½ tsp baking powder

For the topping
1 quantity Cream Cheese Frosting (see page 85)
edible gold leaf (see page 127 for suppliers)

The day before you want to bake, mix together the chopped candied fruits and the orange liqueur in a small bowl. Leave it to soak overnight.

Place the tea bags in another small bowl. Bring the water to a boil and pour it onto the tea bags. Leave to infuse to create a strong tea then discard the tea bags and allow the tea to cool.

Preheat the oven to 400°F, and line a cupcake pan with paper baking cups.

In a large bowl, beat the eggs and gradually add the sugar while still beating. Continue beating while slowly pouring in the oil. Stir in the vanilla extract. Sift the flour and baking powder together. Fold these into the mixture a little at a time, alternating with additions of some of the strong tea, until the batter is smooth.

Strain the candied fruits, reserving the orange liqueur. Fold the fruits into the cupcake batter and then divide the batter between the baking cups. Bake for 20 minutes, or until a skewer inserted into the center of a cupcake comes out clean. Once the cupcakes have cooked but while they are still warm, prick several holes into the top of each cupcake using a toothpick. Spoon the reserved orange liqueur onto the cupcakes then leave them to cool in the pan before decorating.

Pipe Cream Cheese Frosting on top of each cupcake and decorate with flecks of edible gold leaf to finish.

LICORICE CUPCAKES

If you enjoy the rich flavor of licorice, this recipe is for you. I like using this batter as my base for Halloween cakes because of the natural dark color of the cupcake and the frosting.

MAKES 16 CUPCAKES

3½oz black licorice laces
¾ cup milk
2¼ sticks unsalted butter, softened
¼ cup Barbados sugar
4 eggs
1½ cups self-rising flour
½ cup all-purpose flour

For the licorice frosting
3½oz black licorice laces, plus some extra laces to decorate
scant ½ cup confectioner's sugar
3½ tbsp unsalted butter, softened

Preheat the oven to 400°F and line a 12-hole and a 4-hole cupcake or muffin pan with paper baking cups.

Place the licorice laces and the milk in a saucepan over low heat. Stir until the licorice has dissolved. Set aside to cool.

Place the butter and sugar in a bowl and cream together until pale and creamy. Add the eggs one at a time, beating well after each addition until well combined and smooth. Sift the flours together and fold them into the mixture together with the cooled licorice milk. Stir until smooth.

Divide the batter between the paper baking cups to fill them three-quarters full. Bake for 20 minutes, or until a skewer inserted into the center of a cupcake comes out clean. Leave to cool in the pans for 5 minutes then transfer to a wire rack and allow to cool completely before frosting.

To make the Licorice Frosting: Add the licorice laces to a heatproof bowl and place over a saucepan of barely simmering water, making sure the bowl does not touch the surface of the water. Heat until completely dissolved, stirring occasionally. Remove from the heat and allow to cool.

Beat the confectioner's sugar and butter together until pale and smooth. Still mixing, add in the dissolved licorice and beat until smooth.

Pipe or spoon the frosting on top of the cooled cupcakes and decorate with black licorice laces.

MADAGASCAN VANILLA CUPCAKES

This is a classic cupcake that could be a reliable base for any topping—and we all have a day when a good simple vanilla cupcake does the trick!

MAKES 12 CUPCAKES

2¼ sticks unsalted butter, softened
1¼ cups superfine sugar
4 eggs
1 tsp vanilla extract, preferably Madagascan
1½ cups self-rising flour
½ cup all-purpose flour
¾ cup milk
1 quantity Vanilla Buttercream Frosting (see page 84) or Cream Cheese Frosting (see page 85)
sugar cake decorations, to decorate

Preheat the oven to 400°F, and line a cupcake pan with paper baking cups.

Place the butter and sugar in a bowl and cream together until pale and creamy. Add the eggs, one at a time, then add the vanilla extract and beat until well combined. Sift the flours together then fold them in, a little at a time, alternating with some of the milk. Stir until smooth.

Divide the mixture between the paper baking cups and bake for 20 minutes, or until a skewer inserted into the center of a cupcake comes out clean. Leave to cool in the pan for 5 minutes, then transfer to a wire rack and allow to cool completely before frosting.

Pipe Vanilla Buttercream Frosting or Cream Cheese Frosting on top, and scatter with sugar decorations to finish.

SALTED BUTTER CARAMEL CUPCAKES

One of the most popular flavors in Brittany, where I come from in France, is salted butter caramel. I grew up eating ice cream, candies, and spreads flavored by this now very fashionable combination. These cupcakes are so decadent with a rich caramel sauce poured over the top.

MAKES 12 CUPCAKES

1⅓ cups self-rising flour
1 tsp baking soda
5 tbsp unsalted butter, softened
½ heaped cup Barbados sugar
2 eggs, lightly beaten
1 tsp vanilla extract
2 tbsp milk
2oz toffee or pieces of fudge,
  cut into small dice

For the caramel sauce
⅔ cup superfine sugar
5 tbsp salted butter
¼ cup + 1 tbsp heavy cream
1 tsp vanilla extract

For the buttercream frosting
1⅜ sticks unsalted butter,
  softened
1¼ cups confectioner's sugar
1 tsp vanilla extract
1 tsp caramel extract (optional)
few flakes of sea salt,
  to decorate

Preheat the oven to 400°F, and line a cupcake pan with paper baking cups.

Sift the flour and baking soda together into a bowl and set aside. Using a stand mixer or an electric hand mixer, cream the butter and sugar together for a good 5 minutes until very light and fluffy. Add the beaten eggs gradually, beating between each addition and adding 1 tablespoon of flour about halfway through to stop the mixture from curdling. Beat in the vanilla extract then fold in the remaining flour, the milk, and the toffee or fudge.

Divide the batter between the paper baking cups and bake for 15–20 minutes, or until the tops spring back when pressed with a finger. Leave to cool in the pan for 5 minutes, then transfer to a wire rack and allow to cool completely.

To make the Caramel Sauce: Dissolve the sugar in ¼ cup water in a small heavy saucepan over very low heat. Increase the heat and simmer. As soon as you have a nice blond-colored caramel remove the pan from the heat. Add the butter—be careful because it may splutter. Continue stirring as you add the cream and vanilla extract. Stir until smooth then leave to cool.

To make the Buttercream Frosting: Cream the butter and confectioner's sugar together for at least 5 minutes then beat in the vanilla and caramel extracts.

Use a small metal spatula to spread Buttercream Frosting onto the cupcakes. Pour a little Caramel Sauce over the top, and scatter each cupcake with a few sea salt flakes to finish.

FUSION CUPCAKES

Since traveling more often to the Far East, I have really begun to appreciate the taste of Asian food. The fusion of sweet and sour flavors works so well in traditional Asian cooking, and in these delicious cupcakes, too.

MAKES 12 CUPCAKES

2-inch piece of fresh ginger root, peeled
2 lemon grass stalks, trimmed and roughly chopped
2 tsp vanilla extract
7 tbsp butter, softened
heaped ¾ cup golden superfine sugar
2 eggs
1½ cups + 1 tbsp self-rising flour
½ cup milk

For the frosting
7 tbsp butter, softened
3 cups confectioner's sugar
3 tbsp milk
1 tsp vanilla extract
3½oz mixed exotic dried fruits (such as mango, coconut, or pineapple), to decorate

Preheat the oven to 400°F, and line a cupcake pan with paper baking cups.

Place the ginger, lemon grass, and vanilla extract in a food processor and process to a fine paste. Push the paste through a sieve to extract the juice. Discard the pulp.

Cream the butter and sugar together until light and fluffy. Add the reserved juice, then add the eggs one at a time, beating slowly until just combined. Add the flour and milk in alternate batches. Stir with a wooden spoon until just combined.

Divide the batter between the paper baking cups and bake for 15–20 minutes, or until a skewer inserted into the center of a cupcake comes out clean. Leave to cool in the pan for 5 minutes, then transfer the individual cupcakes to a wire rack and allow to cool completely before frosting.

To make the frosting: Beat the butter until very pale, then gradually beat in the confectioner's sugar. Add the milk and vanilla extract and beat until well combined.

Use a small metal spatula or pastry bag to decorate the cakes with the frosting. Roughly chop the dried exotic fruit and arrange it on top as decoration.

STICKY TOFFEE CUPCAKES

One of my favorite things about the arrival of "gastropubs" in Britain is the rebirth of traditional English desserts, like Sticky Toffee Pudding. When properly made, traditional English desserts are rich, filling, and so indulgent. To make these cupcakes cute and tiny, bake them in smaller standard cupcake cups and not the larger "muffin" type. Bake for 12 minutes then check to see if they are done.

MAKES 12 STANDARD CUPCAKES

⅔ cup hot water
1 tea bag
3 tbsp dried apricots, roughly chopped
heaped ¼ cup dates, pitted and roughly chopped
1¼ cups self-rising flour
1 tsp baking powder
¼ cup Barbados sugar
1 tbsp light corn syrup
2 large eggs, lightly beaten
3½ tbsp butter, melted

For the toffee sauce
¼ cup superfine sugar
3½ tbsp butter
scant ½ cup heavy cream
light cream, to serve

Preheat the oven to 400°F, and line a cupcake pan with paper baking cups.

Put the hot water, tea bag, apricots, and dates in a saucepan, bring to a boil, then remove from the heat and leave to soak and cool.

Sift the flour and baking powder together into a large mixing bowl. Drain the fruits, then add them to the flour with the Barbados sugar, light corn syrup, eggs, and butter. Mix together until blended.

Divide the batter between the paper baking cups and bake for 25–30 minutes, or until a skewer inserted into the center of a cupcake comes out clean.

Toward the end of the baking time, make the toffee sauce: heat the superfine sugar in a heavy saucepan until you get a dark caramel. Add the butter, stirring well with a wooden spoon. Deglaze the pan by stirring in the heavy cream. When all the caramel has dissolved, pour it through a sieve into a warmed measuring jug.

When the cupcakes are done, carefully remove the paper baking cups and serve immediately, piping hot, with the toffee sauce and lots of light cream.

GUILT-FREE
CUPCAKES

ANGEL FOOD CUPCAKES WITH RASPBERRY FROSTING

This fat-free cupcake is very light and delicate, like an angel, while the raspberry frosting adds a great fruity touch. These cupcakes are absolutely perfect for summer.

MAKES 12 CUPCAKES

1 cup less 1 heaped tbsp
   all-purpose flour
¾ cup confectioner's sugar
1 tsp cream of tartar
8 egg whites
pinch of salt
¾ cup superfine sugar
½ tsp vanilla extract
½ tsp almond extract

For the raspberry frosting
heaped ¾ cup fresh raspberries,
   plus extra to decorate
1⅛ sticks unsalted butter,
   softened slightly and diced
2¼ cups confectioner's sugar,
   sifted, plus more to decorate
   (optional)

Preheat the oven to 400°F, and line a cupcake pan with paper baking cups.

Sift the flour, confectioner's sugar, and cream of tartar into a bowl and set aside. In a large bowl whisk the egg whites until frothy, ideally using a stand mixer or an electric hand mixer. Then add the salt and gradually begin to add the superfine sugar a tablespoonful at a time. Continue whisking until stiff peaks form—this will take several minutes.

Stir in the vanilla and almond extracts, then add the flour and confectioner's sugar. Fold gently with a large metal spoon until combined. Be quick—if the mixture is left to stand, it will collapse and spoil the light consistency of the cakes.

Divide the batter between the paper baking cups and bake for 15–20 minutes, or until a skewer inserted into the center of a cupcake comes out clean. Leave to cool in the pan for 5 minutes, then transfer to a wire rack and allow to cool completely. These cakes will sink a little as they cool.

To make the Raspberry Frosting: Rub the raspberries through a fine sieve to yield about 2 tablespoons of raspberry puree and set aside. Add the butter to a clean bowl and cream until soft. Sift in some of the confectioner's sugar, then beat it in to combine. Repeat this process until all of the sugar has been incorporated into the butter. Beat in the raspberry puree until the frosting has a spreading consistency.

Using a pastry bag fitted with a pastry tip, pipe the frosting (see page 94 for piping hints), and decorate with fresh raspberries. Dust with confectioner's sugar to finish, if using.

LOW-FAT CHOCOLATE CUPCAKES

I think that if I was on a diet, I would miss chocolate the most. But don't worry, you can spoil yourself with this recipe...but not too often!

MAKES 12 CUPCAKES

¾ cup all-purpose flour
¼ cup unsweetened cocoa
  powder
4 large eggs
⅔ cup superfine sugar
2 tbsp chocolate chips

For the topping
heaped ¼ cup low-fat spread
⅔ cup low-fat cream cheese
3½oz unsweetened chocolate,
  melted and cooled
artificial sweetener, to taste

Preheat the oven to 400°F, and line a cupcake pan with paper baking cups.

Sift together the flour and unsweetened cocoa powder. In a large bowl, whisk together the eggs and sugar using an electric hand mixer until the mixture becomes thick and foamy and has doubled in size. This may take up to 10 minutes, but it is worth the effort because the more air that gets in the lighter the sponge will be. Gently fold in the flour and cocoa powder followed by the chocolate chips, being careful to knock out as little air as possible.

Divide the batter between the baking cups and bake for 20 minutes, or until a skewer inserted into the center of a cupcake comes out clean. Leave to cool in the pan for 5 minutes, then transfer the individual cupcakes to a wire rack and allow them to cool completely.

To make the topping: Beat the low-fat spread with the cream cheese, then stir in the cooled melted chocolate. Sweeten the frosting to taste with the artificial sweetener, then frost the cupcakes.

LOW-FAT WHITE CHOCOLATE & BERRY CUPCAKES

As much as I always try not to compromise on ingredients, it is still possible to indulge yourself even if you are following a low-fat diet. Despite being low in fat, these cupcakes are delicious, light, and tasty. They won't make you feel guilty and one of these is much more enjoyable than an apple!

MAKES 12 CUPCAKES

⅓ cup + 2 tbsp low-fat spread
½ cup golden superfine sugar
1⅓ cups self-rising flour, sifted
2 eggs
½ tsp vanilla extract
¼ cup skim milk

For the white chocolate topping
2oz white chocolate, broken
   into pieces
⅔ cup low-fat cream cheese
2 tbsp confectioner's sugar, plus
   extra to decorate
1⅓ cups mixed raspberries,
blueberries, and red currants,
   for decorating
white chocolate curls,
   to decorate

Preheat the oven to 400°F, and line a cupcake pan with paper baking cups.

Add all the cake ingredients to a large mixing bowl and beat for 2–3 minutes, ideally using an electric hand mixer, until pale and fluffy.

Divide the batter between the paper baking cups and bake for 18–20 minutes, or until a skewer inserted into the center of a cupcake comes out clean. Leave to cool in the pan for 5 minutes and then set the individual cupcakes on a wire rack and allow them to cool completely.

To make the White Chocolate Topping: Put the white chocolate in a large heatproof bowl and place over a saucepan of barely simmering water, making sure the bowl does not touch the surface of the water. Heat until completely melted. Allow to cool slightly, then beat in the cream cheese and confectioner's sugar until smooth. Chill in the refrigerator until it firms up a little.

Using a small metal spatula or pastry bag, cover the cupcakes with the topping. Decorate with the berries, dust with confectioner's sugar, and scatter some white chocolate curls on top.

FAT-FREE JASMINE & VIOLET CUPCAKES

Yes, it is possible—these dainty cupcakes are fat-free and delicious, too. The crystallized flowers give them a perfect look for a chic afternoon treat.

MAKES 12 CUPCAKES

For the crystallized flowers
a few violet and jasmine flowers
1 egg white, lightly beaten
2 tbsp granulated sugar
3 eggs
⅓ cup golden superfine sugar
⅔ cup self-rising flour
1 tsp vanilla extract
2 drops of vanilla essence

For the jasmine drizzle
1 jasmine tea bag
3 tbsp boiling water
2 cups confectioner's sugar

First make the crystallized edible flowers: The day before you want to bake, dip the violet and jasmine flowers in the beaten egg white, then set them on a sheet of waxed paper. Dust the flowers generously all over with granulated sugar and leave them to dry overnight.

Preheat the oven to 400°F, and line a cupcake pan with paper baking cups.

In a large bowl beat the eggs and sugar together using an electric hand mixer until light, fluffy, and doubled in volume. Sift the flour and gently fold it into the mixture, followed by the vanilla extract and essence.

Divide the batter between the paper baking cups and bake for 20 minutes, or until a skewer inserted into the center of a cupcake comes out clean. Leave to cool in the pan for 5 minutes, then transfer the individual cupcakes to a wire rack and allow to cool completely.

To make the Jasmine Drizzle: Put the tea bag in a small heatproof bowl and pour the boiling water over it. Leave to infuse until the tea is very strong. Discard the tea bag. Mix the confectioner's sugar into the tea until you get a thick, runny consistency. Drizzle it onto the cooled cupcakes and, before the mixture sets, decorate the cupcakes with the crystallized violet and jasmine flowers.

GLUTEN-FREE PEAR & ALMOND CUPCAKES

These cupcakes are based on my favorite French pear dessert, Tarte Bordaloue. There is, of course, no pastry in this version and, being gluten-free, it is perfect for anyone with a gluten allergy.

MAKES 12 CUPCAKES

3 cups + 1 tbsp ground almonds
1 tbsp gluten-free baking powder
½ cup superfine sugar
7 tbsp butter, melted
2 eggs, beaten
1 cup milk
3 canned baby pears, drained
¼ cup sliced almonds
confectioner's sugar, to decorate

For the poached pears
2 large ripe pears, peeled, cored, and quartered
½ cup superfine sugar
1 scant cup water
1 vanilla bean, split lengthwise

If time allows poach the pears the day before. Put the sugar, water, and vanilla bean in a saucepan. Slowly bring to a boil, stirring continuously until the sugar has dissolved. Add the pear quarters, cover, and simmer over low heat for 15 minutes. Remove from the heat and set aside to cool.

When you are ready to bake, preheat the oven to 400°F, and line a cupcake pan with paper baking cups.

In a large bowl, mix together the ground almonds, baking powder, and sugar. Add the melted butter, eggs, and milk, and mix until creamy. Drain the poached pears, dice them finely, then fold them into the mixture.

Divide the batter between the paper baking cups. Chop each of the canned baby pears into quarters (you should have 12 pieces) and place one baby pear quarter standing upright on top of each cupcake. Scatter with the sliced almonds and bake for 25–30 minutes, or until a skewer inserted into the center of a cupcake comes out clean. Leave to cool in the pan for 5 minutes, then transfer to a wire rack and allow to cool completely. Dust with confectioner's sugar before serving.

GRANOLA & MIXED SPICE CUPCAKES

These energy-packed cupcakes are perfect for kids' lunchbags or for a healthy treat or snack to help keep you going through the day.

MAKES 12 CUPCAKES

1½ cups whole-wheat flour
heaped 1¼ cups granola
2 tsp baking powder
1 tsp mixed spice
1 tbsp poppy seeds
1 cup dried apricots, chopped
½ cup golden raisins
3 tbsp sunflower oil
2 eggs
¾ cup milk
⅓ cup liquid honey

Preheat the oven to 400°F, and line a cupcake pan with paper baking cups.

In a large mixing bowl, mix together the flour, a heaped ¾ cup of the granola, the baking powder, mixed spice, poppy seeds, and dried fruit.

In another bowl, whisk together the oil, eggs, milk, and honey until well blended. Pour the mixture into the dry ingredients and quickly stir.

Divide the batter between the paper baking cups and scatter the remaining ½ cup of granola evenly over the tops. Bake for 25 minutes, or until a skewer inserted into the center of a cupcake comes out clean. Leave to cool in the pan for 5 minutes, then transfer to a wire rack and allow to cool completely. They will keep in the fridge for 2–3 days, or can be frozen.

GLUTEN-FREE PROVENÇAL ORANGE CUPCAKES

These flour-free cupcakes are perfect for people who have a gluten allergy. The decadent addition of ground almonds makes them very moist, while the final drizzle of spicy syrup adds to their great taste.

MAKES 12 CUPCAKES

1¾ cups ground almonds
¾ cup superfine sugar
2 tsp gluten-free baking powder
4 eggs, beaten
1 cup less 2 tbsp sunflower oil
finely grated zest of 1 lemon
finely grated zest of 2 oranges, ideally Seville, plus a few extra strands of zest to decorate

For the syrup
juice of 1 lemon
juice of 2 oranges, ideally Seville
½ cup superfine sugar
pinch of ground cloves
2 tsp ground cinnamon

Preheat the oven to 400°F, and line a cupcake pan with paper baking cups.

In a mixing bowl, combine the ground almonds, superfine sugar, and baking powder. Add the eggs and oil, and mix gently together. Stir the lemon and orange zest into the mixture.

Divide the batter between the paper baking cups and bake for 30 minutes, or until a skewer inserted into the center of a cupcake comes out clean. Leave to cool in the pan for 5 minutes, then transfer the individual cupcakes to a wire rack to cool slightly.

To make the syrup: pour the lemon and orange juices into a small saucepan. Add the sugar, cloves, and cinnamon. Bring to a boil, then reduce the heat and simmer for 3 minutes.

While the cupcakes are still warm, pierce the tops several times with a toothpick. Spoon the syrup onto the cupcakes and allow it to soak in a little while they cool. Decorate with strands of orange zest to finish.

ZUCCHINI CUPCAKES

These breakfast cupcakes make a delicious, nourishing kickstart to any day. I like to eat mine straight from the oven with honey, because you get all the hearty flavor.

MAKES 12 CUPCAKES

1⅔ cups whole-wheat flour
2 tsp baking powder
1 tsp mixed spices
⅔ cup mixed seeds
  (such as pumpkin, sesame,
  and sunflower seeds)
2 eggs
1 cup less 2 tbsp milk
4 tsp vegetable oil
4 tsp liquid honey
5oz zucchini, trimmed
  and then grated
liquid honey and Greek-style
  yogurt, to serve (optional)

Preheat the oven to 400°F, and line a cupcake pan with paper baking cups.

In a large bowl, thoroughly mix together all the dry ingredients (but do not sift the flour—you want to keep all the goodness from the whole wheat). Stir in all of the liquid ingredients and combine until smooth. Gently fold in the grated zucchini.

Divide the batter between the paper baking cups and bake for 25 minutes or until a skewer inserted into the center of a cupcake comes out clean. Leave to cool in the pan for 5 minutes, then transfer the individual cupcakes to a wire rack and allow to cool completely.

To serve, drizzle with honey and some Greek-syle yogurt, if liked.

STYLING CUPCAKES

VANILLA BUTTERCREAM FROSTING

This frosting can be tinted using natural food coloring. I prefer to use an edible paste coloring rather than a liquid because it doesn't affect the consistency of the frosting.

FOR 12 CUPCAKES

2¼ sticks unsalted butter, softened
5 cups confectioner's sugar
2 tbsp milk
1 tsp vanilla extract

In a large bowl, cream the butter, ideally using an electric hand mixer on medium speed. Blend in the sugar, one-quarter of it at a time, beating well after each addition. Beat in the milk and vanilla extract, and continue mixing until light and fluffy.

Keep the frosting covered until you are ready to use it.

Smooth the frosting onto the cupcakes using a small metal spatula. You can also create small spikes by quickly touching the frosting with the flat blade of the metal spatula.

CREAM CHEESE FROSTING

Be careful when melting white chocolate because it is much more temperamental than semisweet.

FOR 12 CUPCAKES

2oz white chocolate, broken into pieces
heaped ¾ cup cream cheese, softened
7 tbsp unsalted butter, softened
1 tsp vanilla extract
4¼ cups confectioner's sugar

Add the white chocolate pieces to a heatproof bowl and place over a saucepan of barely simmering water making sure the bowl does not touch the surface of the water. Stir until the chocolate melts and is smooth. Remove the bowl from the heat and leave to cool to room temperature.

In another bowl, using a wooden spoon or an electric hand mixer, beat together the cream cheese and butter until smooth. Then stir in the melted white chocolate and the vanilla extract. Gradually beat in the confectioner's sugar until the mixture is fluffy.

Smooth the frosting onto the cupcakes using a small metal spatula. You can also create small spikes by quickly touching the frosting with the flat blade of the metal spatula.

ROYAL ICING

This recipe calls for raw egg whites. If you are worried about using raw eggs, you can buy reconstituted albumen powder instead.

MAKES 1LB 2OZ

2 egg whites
1 tsp lemon juice
about 5 cups confectioner's sugar, sifted
edible food coloring paste (see page 127 for suppliers)

Add the egg whites to a bowl and stir in the lemon juice. Gradually add the sifted confectioner's sugar, mixing well after each addition.

Continue adding small amounts of confectioner's sugar until you achieve the desired consistency. For piping, the icing should be fairly stiff.

Edible food coloring paste is highly concentrated so only use a tiny amount. Dip a toothpick into the coloring paste. Mix well into the icing before adding more coloring paste to avoid streaks.

CHOCOLATE FROSTING

Use high-quality semisweet chocolate to make this rich chocolate buttercream frosting. It makes a great frosting for chocolate cupcakes or cakes.

FOR 12 CUPCAKES

1 cup less 2 tbsp light cream
8oz semisweet chocolate, finely chopped
3½ tbsp unsalted butter, softened

Heat the cream in a small saucepan, but do not allow it to boil.

Put the chocolate into a heatproof bowl and pour the hot cream through a fine sieve onto the chocolate. Gently stir the cream into the chocolate until the mixture is glossy. Carefully stir in the softened butter and leave the mixture to cool completely.

Once it is cool, beat until fluffy, ideally using an electric hand mixer.

Use this frosting as a filling for cupcakes or cakes, or for spreading on top. To achieve a dark glossy chocolate coating, you can use this without the final whipping.

VALENTINE'S DAY ROSE CUPCAKES

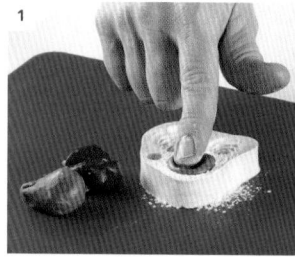

FOR 12 MINI CUPCAKES

You will need:
rose mold, approximately the same diameter as your cupcakes (see page 127 for suppliers)
cornstarch, for dusting
chocolate paste or "plastic," colored with red and pink edible food coloring paste (see page 127 for suppliers)
small paintbrush
boiled water, cooled
edible glitter in "disco red" and "plum perfection" (see page 127 for suppliers)
pastry bag fitted with a star tip
½ quantity Vanilla Buttercream or Cream Cheese Frosting (see pages 84–5), colored with red or pink edible food coloring pastes
12 mini cupcakes

1. Dust the inside of the mold with a little cornstarch to stop the chocolate "plastic" from sticking.

2. Coat your fingertips with cornstarch, take a small ball of chocolate "plastic," and press it tightly into the mold. Pop out the rose shape —it will not set hard so there is no need to leave it to dry.

3. Using a small dry paintbrush, brush the excess cornstarch off of the rose shapes, then lightly brush the surface with the cooled boiled water.

4. Dust generously with red or pink edible glitter. Shake off the excess, and leave to dry. Using a pastry bag fitted with a star tip, pipe spirals of frosting onto each cupcake and place a glittery rose on top to finish.

BUNNY CUPCAKES

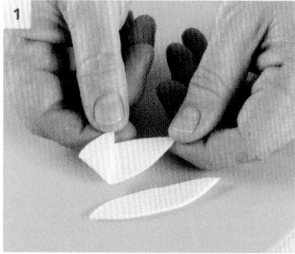 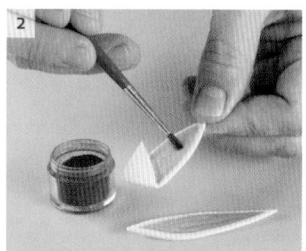

FOR 12 CUPCAKES

You will need:
cornstarch, for dusting
small rolling pin
2oz white ready-made gum
  paste (see page 127 for
  suppliers)
small dry paintbrush
edible rainbow dust in
  "Christmas red" (see page
  127 for suppliers)
boiled water, cooled
1 heaped cup desiccated
  coconut
small metal spatula
1 quantity Vanilla Buttercream
  or Cream Cheese Frosting
  (see pages 84–5), colored
  with green edible food
  coloring paste
12 chocolate or vanilla cupcake
  bases (see pages 14 and 62)

1. Dust a little cornstarch onto your work surface and roll out the gum paste very thinly, about ⅛ inch thick. To make the ears, cut out 24 petal shapes, each 3½ inches long and ¾ inch at the widest part. (You may want to make a paper template to cut around.) Leave to dry in the refrigerator for several hours, or ideally overnight, until hard.

2. Using a small dry paintbrush, stain one side of each ear with red edible rainbow dust, leaving a white border.

3. Lightly paint the white areas only of each ear on both sides with cooled boiled water and immediately dip into the desiccated coconut to coat. Leave to dry for a few minutes.

4. Using a small metal spatula, spread the frosting onto each cupcake. You can create a spiky grass effect by tapping the flat blade of the metal spatula onto the frosting. Poke 2 ears into each cupcake to finish.

CROWN CUPCAKES

 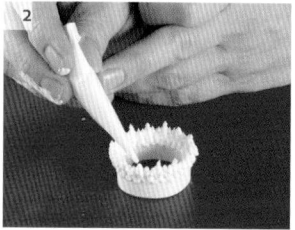 

1. Dust a little cornstarch onto your work surface to stop the gum paste from sticking to it. Roll out the gum paste to ¼ inch thick. Cut 12 strips, each 6 inches long and ½ inch wide. Press the two ends together to make a circle. Leave to dry in the refrigerator for a few hours, or ideally overnight, until hard.

2. Make a miniature pastry bag with the waxed paper by rolling it into a cone and folding the edges over. Fill with royal icing and snip off the tip. Pipe a row of small dots on top of the rim of the crown, holding the bag vertically with the tip close to the surface. Squeeze a little icing out, then push down and up sharply to finish. Pipe a second row of dots on top of the first row in between the gaps, then more dots to build up the tips of the crown. Leave to dry for a few minutes.

3. Lightly brush the crown all over with the cooled boiled water and sprinkle with gold edible glitter. Use a small paintbrush to paint on additional colors as desired. Repeat with the remaining crowns and set aside. Using a small metal spatula, spread the frosting on top of each cupcake. (If your frosting seems a little too thick, dip your metal spatula in hot water and this will make spreading easier.) Arrange a glittering crown on top of each frosted cupcake to finish.

FOR 12 CUPCAKES

You will need:
cornstarch, for dusting
small rolling pin
1½oz white ready-made gum paste (see page 127 for suppliers)
6-inch square piece of waxed paper
½ cup Royal Icing (see page 86)
small paintbrush
boiled water, cooled
edible glitter in gold, blue, and red (see page 127 for suppliers)
small metal spatula
1 quantity Vanilla Buttercream or Cream Cheese Frosting (see pages 84–5), colored with violet edible food coloring paste (see page 127 for suppliers)
12 chocolate or vanilla cupcake bases (see pages 14 and 62)

BLING CUPCAKES

FOR 12 CUPCAKES

You will need:
1 quantity Vanilla Buttercream or Cream Cheese Frosting (see pages 84–5), colored with peach edible food coloring paste
pastry bag fitted with a plain round tip
12 chocolate or vanilla cupcake bases (see pages 14 and 62)
edible diamonds, edible gold balls, sugar flowers, and edible glitter in gold, to decorate
tweezers

1. Your frosting needs to flow freely and not be too stiff. Fill the pastry bag with frosting, twist the end tightly, and squeeze gently until the frosting starts to come through. Starting at the rim farthest away from you, hold the pastry bag at a 45° angle, pipe a dot, and stop squeezing, tipping the bag vertically toward the center of the cake.

2. Repeat around three-quarters of the rim, then create a second row in between the gaps, and keep repeating until you reach the middle.

3. Continue piping dots down the back of the cupcake to the rim. Repeat for the remaining cupcakes.

4. Use tweezers to arrange your chosen bling decorations carefully on top of the frosting then dust lightly with edible glitter in gold to finish. Repeat with the remaining cupcakes.

PORCUPINE CUPCAKES

FOR 12 CUPCAKES

You will need:
6-inch square piece of waxed
  paper
½ quantity Vanilla Buttercream
  or Cream Cheese Frosting,
  (see pages 84–5), leaving
  some white (for the noses),
  with half the remainder
  colored with beige edible
  food paste and the rest
  colored brown
12 chocolate or vanilla cupcake
  bases (see pages 14 and 62)
2 pastry bags fitted with plain
  round tips
24 chocolate "eyes" (see page
  127 for suppliers)
6 miniature marshmallows

1. Make a miniature pastry bag with the waxed
paper by rolling it into a cone shape and folding
the edges over. Fill with the white frosting then
snip off the tip of the bag so the frosting flows out.
First, make the base of the nose by piping a ¾-inch
spiral of white frosting above the rim on each cupcake.

2. Fill one of the pastry bags with beige-colored frosting and the other with brown-colored frosting, twist the ends tightly, and squeeze gently until the frosting starts to come through. Take the beige pastry bag, hold at a 45° angle, and pipe outward around half the rim of a cupcake, squeezing a little and tilting the bag upright to form the quills.

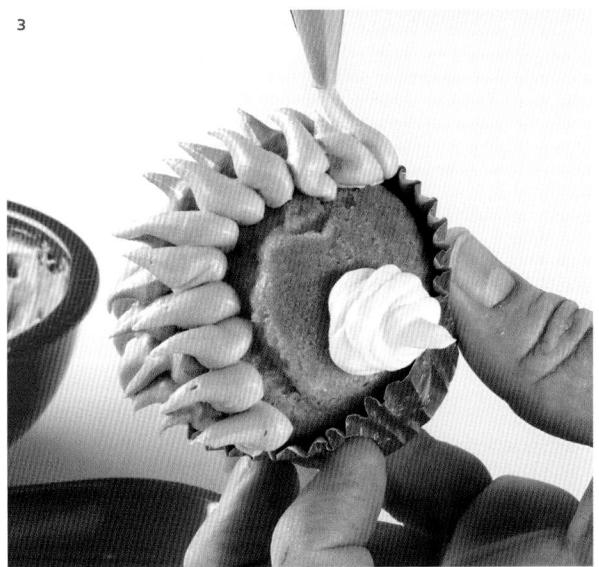

3. Now take the brown frosting and pipe more spikes overlapping the beige quills to form a second row. Repeat, alternating the colors to cover the cake until you reach the nose.

4. Place the chocolate "eyes" into position above the nose.

5. Cut the corner off of a mini marshmallow and place it on top of the white frosting to form the tip of the nose. Repeat the decoration with the remaining cupcakes.

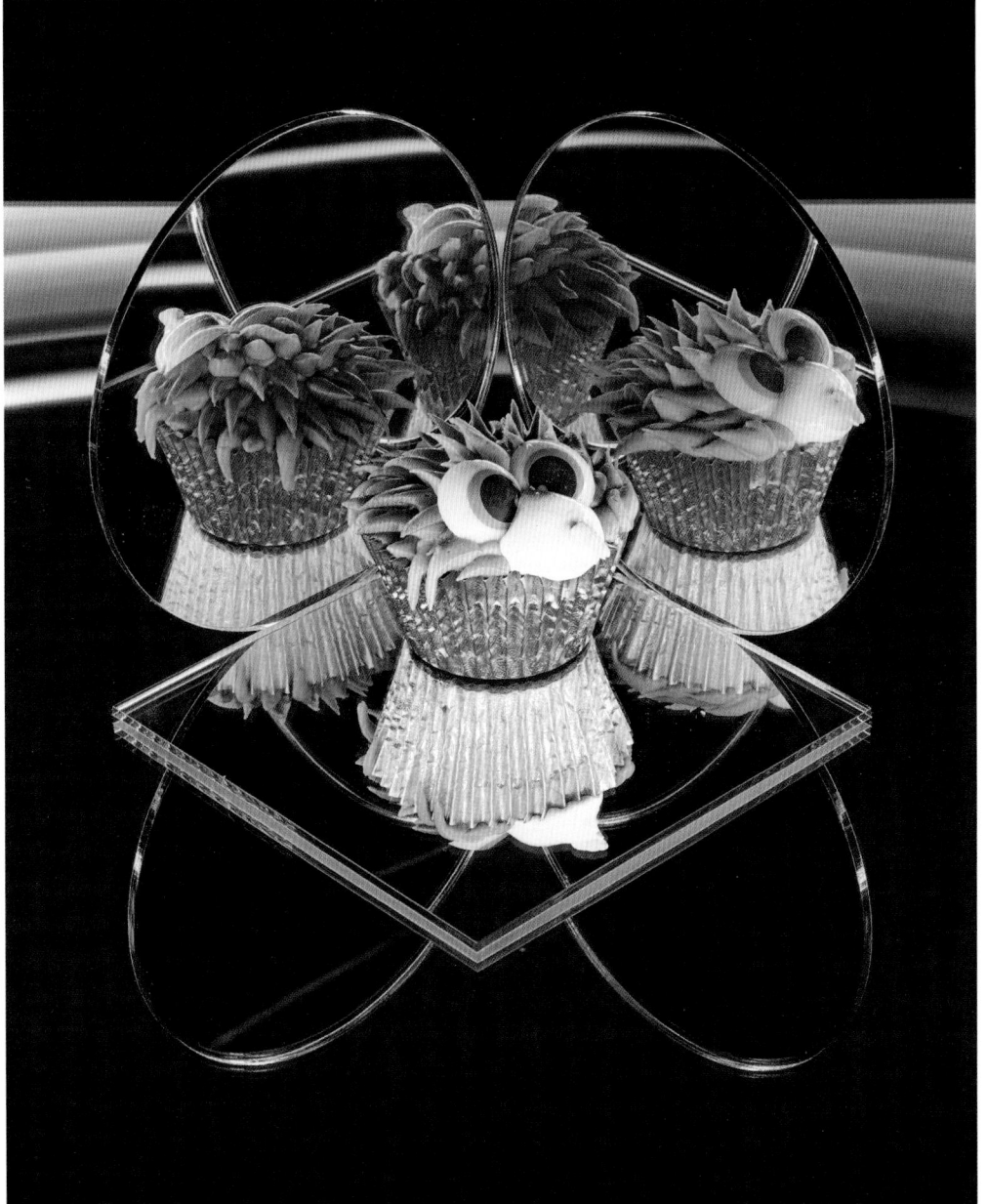

SUMMER FLOWER CUPCAKES

FOR 12 CUPCAKES

You will need:
small metal spatula
1 quantity Vanilla Buttercream
or Cream Cheese frosting
(see pages 84–5), colored
with violet edible food
coloring paste
12 chocolate or vanilla cupcake
bases (see pages 14 and 62)
pastry bag fitted with a plain
¼-inch tip
½ quantity Vanilla Buttercream
or Cream Cheese Frosting,
1 tbsp colored with black
edible food coloring paste
(for the stigma), the
remainder colored with
orange edible food coloring
paste
6-inch square piece of waxed
paper

1. Using a small metal spatula, cover the top of each cupcake with a smooth layer of the violet-colored frosting.

2

2. Fill the pastry bag with orange frosting. Twist the end tightly and squeeze gently until the frosting starts to come through. Holding the bag at a 45° angle, start at the rim and pipe a petal shape by squeezing the bag across the cupcake toward the center. Twist upward to finish. Repeat around the cake to cover.

3. Now pipe a second layer on top of the first layer.

4. Make a miniature pastry bag with the waxed paper by rolling it into a cone shape and folding the edges over. Fill with black frosting then snip the tip off of the bag so the frosting flows out. Pipe tiny dots in the center of the cupcake to form the stigma, piling them to build up some height. Repeat the decoration with the remaining cupcakes.

3

4

POKE-IN-THE-EYE CUPCAKES

FOR 12 CUPCAKES

You will need:
3½oz white chocolate
12 dome-shaped chocolates
  (such as Lindor)
small paintbrush
edible rainbow dust in red
  (see page 127 for suppliers)
boiled water, cooled
edible glitter in blue, green, and
  black (see page 127 for
  suppliers)
1 quantity Vanilla Buttercream
  or Cream Cheese Frosting
  (see pages 84–5), colored
  with edible coloring pastes
12 chocolate or vanilla cupcake
  bases (see pages 14 and 62)
6-inch square piece of waxed
  paper
piping gel, colored with red
  edible coloring paste

1. Melt the white chocolate in a heatproof bowl placed over a saucepan of barely simmering water, making sure the bowl does not touch the surface of the water. Dip the dome-shaped chocolates into the white chocolate until completely covered. Leave on a plate in the refrigerator to set.

2. After 2 hours, remove from the refrigerator. Using a small dry paintbrush, dust red edible rainbow dust onto the white chocolate eyeballs.

3. Lightly brush a circle of water on one side, then paint edible blue or green glitter over the wet circle. Paint the center with black edible glitter.

4. Using the tip of a small sharp knife, score from the center of the eyeball outward several times to create a veined effect. Spread colored frosting onto the cupcakes and place an eyeball on top of each one.

5. Make a miniature pastry bag with the waxed paper by rolling it into a cone shape and folding the edges over. Fill with red piping gel and snip off the tip of the bag so the gel flows out. Pipe the gel into the center of the eyeball and let it drizzle down over the frosting. Repeat with the remaining cupcakes.

CHOCOLATE HONEYCOMB CUPCAKES

FOR 12 CUPCAKES

You will need:
6 pieces of bubble wrap, each measuring 4 x 8 inches
7oz semisweet, milk, or white chocolate, melted
1 quantity Vanilla Buttercream or Cream Cheese Frosting (see pages 84–5)
12 chocolate cupcake bases (see page 14)
small paintbrush with soft bristles
edible rainbow dust in gold (see page 127 for suppliers)
edible glitter in gold (optional)

1. Wash and dry the bubble wrap and place it, bubbles facing up, on cookie sheets that will fit in your refrigerator. Pour the melted chocolate onto the bubble wrap, dividing the chocolate equally between each piece.

2. Use a knife to spread the chocolate evenly, then place in the refrigerator for 1 hour to set. Meanwhile, frost the cupcakes.

3. Once the chocolate has set, carefully peel off and discard the bubble wrap.

4. Use a small dry paintbrush to highlight areas of the chocolate honeycomb with gold edible rainbow dust.

5. Snap each chocolate piece into 4 so you have 24 pieces. Push 2 pieces into the frosting on each cupcake. To finish, if using, dust some edible glitter in gold down the sides of the frosting.

SNOWFLAKE CUPCAKES

FOR 12 CUPCAKES

You will need:
cornstarch, for dusting
small rolling pin
1½oz white ready-made
  gum paste
snowflake cutter (see page 127
  for suppliers)
small paintbrush with soft
  bristles
boiled water, cooled
edible glitter in silver (see
  page 127 for suppliers)
pastry bag fitted with a plain tip
1 quantity Vanilla Buttercream
  or Cream Cheese Frosting
  (see pages 84–5), colored
  with red edible food coloring
  paste
12 chocolate or vanilla cupcake
  bases (see pages 14 and 62)

1. Dust a little cornstarch onto your work surface
to stop the gum paste from sticking to it, then roll
it out to a thickness of about ⅛ inch.

2. Using a snowflake cutter, cut out 12 shapes and leave them to dry in the refrigerator for several hours, or ideally overnight, until hard.

3. Using a small paintbrush, lightly brush cooled boiled water all over the surface of a snowflake. Cover it with edible glitter and shake off the excess, then leave to dry for a few minutes. Repeat with the remaining snowflakes.

4. Fill the pastry bag with frosting, twist the end tightly, and squeeze gently until the frosting starts to come through. Hold the bag vertically and slowly pipe a ring of frosting around the edge of a cupcake, then continue in a spiral until you reach the center and the cupcake is covered. Stop the pressure, then push the bag down and up sharply to finish.

5. Frost the remaining cupcakes in the same way then position a glittery snowflake on top of each one.

CHRISTMAS TREE BAUBLE CUPCAKES

FOR 12 CUPCAKES

You will need:
bauble mold (see page 127 for
  suppliers)
cornstarch, for dusting
1½oz white ready-made
  gum paste
small paintbrush
edible rainbow dust in gold (see
  page 127 for suppliers)
boiled water, cooled
edible glitter in gold (see
  page 127 for suppliers)
pastry bag with ¼-inch plain tip
1 quantity Vanilla Buttercream
  or Cream Cheese Frosting
  (see pages 84–5), colored
  with green edible food
  coloring paste
12 chocolate or vanilla cupcake
  bases (see pages 14 and 62)

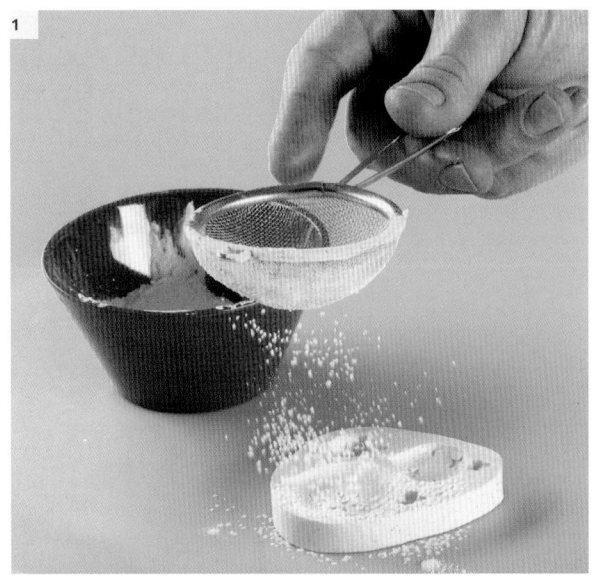

1. Dust the inside of the mold with a little cornstarch. Coat your fingertips with cornstarch, take a small ball of gum paste, and press it tightly into the bauble mold. Pop out the shape and repeat until you have 12 baubles.

2. Using a small dry paintbrush, brush the excess cornstarch off the bauble shapes. Leave them to set in the refrigerator for a few hours, or ideally overnight, until hard.

3. Once they have set, use a small paintbrush to paint the ornament "fixture" at the top with edible gold rainbow dust. Then lightly brush the rest of the bauble with the cooled boiled water, carefully avoiding the part you have painted with rainbow dust.

4. Sprinkle edible glitter over the bauble, shake off the excess, and leave to dry.

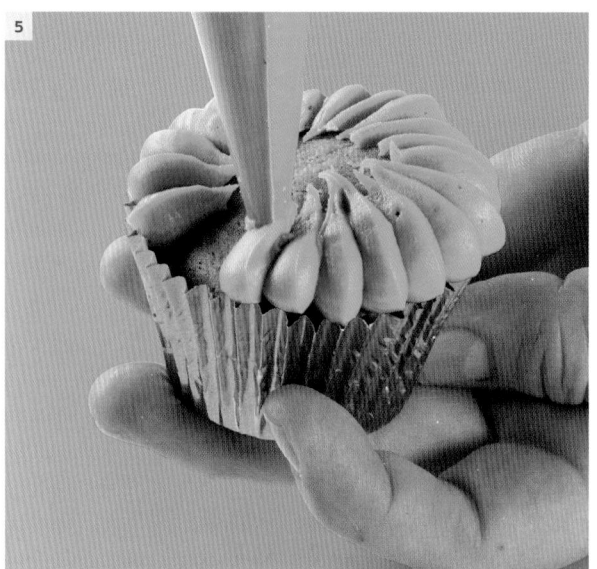

5. To create the Christmas tree effect, the frosting needs to be free-flowing and not too stiff. Fill the pastry bag with frosting, twist the end tightly, and squeeze gently until the frosting starts to come through. Pipe a dot on the rim of the cupcake, stop squeezing, tip the bag vertically, and push the tip of the nozzle toward the center of the cupcake. Repeat around the rim, then create a second row in between the gaps and repeat until you reach the middle. Pipe a swirl in the center and arrange a bauble on top.

HOLLY LEAF CUPCAKES

FOR 12 CUPCAKES

You will need:
cornstarch, for dusting
small rolling pin
2oz green ready-made
  gum paste (see page 127
  for suppliers)
small sharp knife
small paintbrush with soft
  bristles
boiled water, cooled
edible glitter in "disco green,"
  "yellow," and "super nova
  purple" (see page 127 for
  suppliers)
pastry bag fitted with a ¼-inch
  plain tip
1 quantity Vanilla Buttercream
  or Cream Cheese Frosting
  (see pages 84–5), colored
  with red, green, and/or
  yellow edible food coloring
pastes
12 chocolate or vanilla cupcake
  bases (see pages 14 and 63)

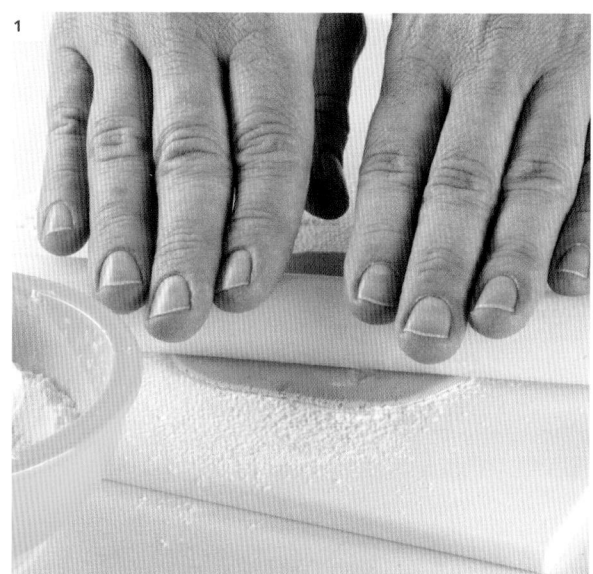

1. Dust a little cornstarch onto your work surface
to stop the gum paste from sticking to it. Then roll
out the gum paste to ⅛ inch in thickness.

2. Using the tip of a small sharp knife, carefully cut out 12 holly leaves. (You may find it easier to make a paper template first to cut around.) Leave them to dry in the refrigerator for several hours, or ideally overnight, until hard.

3. Using a small paintbrush, lightly brush the cooled boiled water over the surface of the holly leaves. Cover with edible glitter and shake off the excess, then leave them to dry for a few minutes.

4. Fill the pastry bag with frosting, twist the end tightly, and squeeze gently until the frosting starts to come through. Hold the bag vertically and slowly pipe a ring of frosting around the edge of a cupcake. Continue in a spiral until you reach the center. Stop the pressure, then push the bag down and up sharply to finish.

5. Poke the holly leaf into the top of the frosted cupcake. Frost the remaining cupcakes in the same way and arrange a holly leaf on top of each to finish.

INDEX

USEFUL CONTACTS

Cake Craft Shop
www.cakecraftshop.co.uk

Supplier of edible food coloring pastes; edible glaze spray, and sugar decorations and flowers.

Candy Direct, Inc.
www.candydirect.com

Online store for all types of candies.

FPC Sugarcraft
www.fpcsugarcraft.co.uk

International supplier of silicone rubber molds, including rose and bauble shapes.

Global Sugar Art
www.globalsugarart.com

Online store for all baking and cake decorating supplies, including edible food coloring pastes, edible glitter, gum paste, icings, and piping gel.

N.Y. Cake & Baking
www.nycake.com

Online store for all baking and cake decorating supplies, including edible food coloring pastes, edible dust and glitter, icings, piping gel, and silicone rubber push molds.

Pfeil & Holing
www.cakedeco.com

Online store for baking and cake decorating supplies.

Squires Kitchen
www.squires-shop.com

International supplier of silicone rubber push molds; snowflake, flower and holly leaf-shaped plunger cutters; ready-made icings and pastes; edible gold leaf and edible confectioners' glaze.

Sweet Factory
www.sweetfactory.com

Online store for all types of candies.

Wilton Homewares Store
www.wilton.com

Online store for baking and cake decorating supplies.

ABOUT THE AUTHORS

Eric Lanlard, master pâtissier and twice winner of the prestigious Continental Pâtissier of the Year at The British Baking Awards, has earned himself an international reputation for superlative cakes with an impressive A-list clientele.

Having trained in France, Eric moved to London where he ran the pâtisserie business for Albert and Michel Roux. He stayed there for five years before launching his own business and now creates cakes for his private clients at his cake emporium Cake Boy.

Eric is an experienced TV presenter with two series of *Glamour Puds* to his name. He has also appeared on numerous UK TV food shows including *The Taste*, *Masterchef: The Professionals*, and *Market Kitchen*. He has also presented his own TV series *Baking Mad with Eric Lanlard* for Channel 4.

He is author of *Chocolat, Tart It Up!, Home Bake* (Mitchell Beazley), and *Master Cakes* (Hamlyn) and runs regular classes at his London cookery school.

Canadian-born **Patrick Cox** relocated to London in 1983 and quickly made a mark with his footwear designs. Within a decade, his was the label on fashionable feet all over the world.

After 20 years in the shoe business he was ready for a sabbatical, and in 2010 he launched Soho baking venture, Cox Cookies & Cake, with Eric Lanlard.

STARFELL

Willow Moss & the Vanished Kingdom

⭐

DOMINIQUE VALENTE

HARPER
An Imprint of HarperCollins*Publishers*

Library of Congress Control Number: 2021944408
ISBN 978-0-06-287947-9

Typography by Jessie Gang
21 22 23 24 25   PC/LSCH   10 9 8 7 6 5 4 3 2 1

First American edition

First published in Great Britain by HarperCollins Children's Books in 2021
HarperCollins Children's Books is a division of HarperCollins Publishers Ltd,
HarperCollins Publishers, 1 London Bridge Street, London SE1 9GF

THE GRIMOIRE GAZETTE

The official Enchancil newsletter
reporting on the state of magic across
the wilds of Starfell

Letter from the Editor

Well, chins have certainly been wagging about the appointment of the new leader of the Brothers of Wol, Silas Wolbrother! His leadership has kicked off with a radical new amendment to the treaty between magical and nonmagical citizens—magical children below the age of thirteen will now be allowed to attend nonmagical schools for the first time in Starfell's history.

Head of the Enchancil (Enchanted Council) Celestine Bear believes that Silas's appointment as leader of the nonmagical community will ensure a happier era for us all. In an exclusive interview (page two), she says, "Look at what Silas has achieved in such a short time. Admittedly, it's not something we magical folk ever actually asked for, so it's a total surprise, but what a win! Who knows? One day we may even be able to convince the Brothers that a school of our own won't result in them being blown to smithereens. It's just so promising!"

However, our notorious twelve-year-old correspondent Willow Moss disagrees. Gazette readers will no doubt be familiar with the young witch's wild stories—for example, her accusation that the very same new High Master "stole a day" (which, conveniently, no one can remember).

"Silas cannot be trusted. The Enchancil has been tricked by him somehow," she claims, adding that he is "actually a wizard—who wants to steal everyone's magic." Apparently, Willow discovered Silas's "diabolical plan" while on a trip to the realm of the undead a few months ago.

"Clearly, young Willow has lost her mind," counters Bear. "Everyone knows that it is impossible to simply 'visit' Netherfell—unless you want to lose your soul! The girl is delusional."

However, some Enchancil members were concerned by Willow's claims—as she was backed by the infamous and powerful witch Moreg Vaine. At Moreg's request, Willow was allowed to address the Enchancil with her latest tale some months back, despite being underage, and she has been sending the Gazette a steady stream of letters about it ever since.

Yet fears died down quickly after Moreg went silent

on the issue. In fact, she has been completely off the radar for the past three months.

Bear adds, "Thankfully, sense seems to have prevailed and most now agree that this rumor about Silas boils down to the fact that Willow is either rather unwell or has a desperate need for attention. The fact that Moreg has slunk off—well, that should speak for itself. She's probably embarrassed that she was ever taken in, if you ask me." More on pages three, four, and seven, and find Willow's latest outrageous letter on page nine.

Another occurrence that has gotten lips flapping this week is rising tension between the elvish city of Lael and the town of Library, as a priceless scroll has been stolen from the bookish town. Many elves believe that the scroll contains the location of the vanished elvish kingdom of Llandunia, which disappeared, along with Queen Almefeira, during the Long War.

However, most Library historians believe that this is just a myth, as no one has been able to decipher the scroll in over a thousand years. "It could be something as boring as an old elvish recipe for bread," said one of the Secret Keepers, Copernica Darling, when pressed. "Still, it is an ancient, unique artifact and that makes it very valuable. We are offering a reward for its safe return." More on page ten.

Speaking of strange thefts, there has been a string of these recently. Homes around the Midnight Market, Lael, and Howling have fallen victim to burglary—including my own home, though the only thing taken was an old eyeball I was saving for a rainy day. Enchancil enforcers believe that the suspects could be linked to a group of pirate-wizards who are trying to reclaim the Ditchwater district within the city of Beady Hill, which was granted Forbidden status earlier this year. . . . More on this on page eleven.

Finally, in Troll Country (see our double-page spread on pages twelve and thirteen), new attempts to expand troll territory into dwarfish lands have been met with resistance.

Magnus Pack, a spokesdwarf, says, "We will not give so much as an extra toehold to those flat-footed monsters. To see our beloved forests trampled by their clubs and heavy feet? They must be mad."

Troll chief Megrat hurled a studded club at me when I asked for a comment. I was given to understand by her daughter, Calamity, that this meant I should run, so I did.

Rubix Grimoire
Editor in chief

The hare was a scrawny thing with long limbs, patchy gray fur, and an ear that looked like it had endured some chewing.

It was perfectly ordinary, apart from the fact that it was glowing faintly blue and was, in fact, a ghost.

The witch kept a watchful gaze pinned on it as it followed after her from a distance.

Then she reached inside the pocket of her new portal cloak and, after a bit of rummaging, took out a bedroll, a cheese sandwich, and a rolled-up newspaper. She was saving the crossword for later.

It would be some time before she knew again the full comforts of home. . . . For now, there was business to do—a witch's business, which is always her own.

Up above the purple marshes, the sky had turned to pewter and the part of herself that had taken a moment to listen to the song of a passing sparrow heard a storm begin to brew.

One that had little to do with the weather.

1

A Blundering Beginning

IN A BLISTER of a village called Mild, where the sun was hunkering down for a sulk, Willow Moss was having a bad day.

See, it was her first day at a new school—a school that was governed by the Brothers of Wol. And, while first days at a new school are always a bit tough, Willow's seemed destined to set the record for Worst Day Ever and, with the day being young, there was always the chance that things could actually get *worse*.

As far as thoughts went, this wasn't exactly a comforting one. But that's the trouble with thoughts, you know? The bad ones grow like spiky weeds, and if you aren't careful to prune them, you'll be left with a mind full of thorns. And what Willow was thinking right then was that if she could do it all over again, she would go about things a bit differently. . . .

For instance, she might have reconsidered entering the school grounds on the back of a flying broomstick named Whisper. . . .

She had realized this was a mistake rather quickly.

Thanks to the screaming . . .

. . . And the way the students scrambled to hide beneath their desks when she entered the classroom. There was also the boy in the corner making the sign of Wol at her as if to ward off evil. Then there was the fact that the teacher had flattened himself against the wall when she turned to him, arms raised above his head, as if Willow were a dangerous viper poised to strike.

Not exactly *ideal*.

The second thing she might have reconsidered was bringing along the monster from under the bed.

Oswin, the monster in question (and her best friend), chose that precise moment to pop his shaggy head out of the hairy green carpetbag she was carrying. His green, lamp-like eyes squinted in the daylight as he harrumphed, "WOT a bunch o' cumberworlds. . . . Yew'd fink they'd never seen a witch afore. 'Tis not like yer gonna ketch 'em all an' turn 'em inter stew or sumfink. . . ." A low belly rumble followed this pronouncement, and he added, a little mournfully, "Actual-lys, I could jes' *murder* a bowl of stew abouts now. . . ."

This, unfortunately, elicited more panicked wailings.

"It's a talking cat!"

"Why is that cat green?"

"Did it just say it wants to turn us into STEW?"

"Oh Wol, it's changing color!"

"Oh, the smell! Oh, save us. . . ."

And that sort of thing.

Willow fished out the StoryPass from her pocket. It was a compass-like device from the town of Library that was supposed to help with novel cataloging, but offered useful life advice as well. The five points were: "One Might Have Suspected as Such," "There Be Dragons," "If I Were You, I'd Run," "Turning Point," and "Cup of Tea?"

It was currently pointing to "One Might Have Suspected as Such."

Willow sighed, then pushed Oswin's head—which had turned from the color of pea soup to a violent blood-orange—back in the bag.

"I is not A CAT . . . I is the monster from under the bed! Honestly, wot do they teach kits in skewls nowadaisies?" he hissed.

"Just leave it," Willow whispered, pinching the bridge of her nose.

There was a harrumph from Oswin—who was in fact a kobold, a subspecies of monster. Alas, he did look like a cat, but calling any attention to this resemblance made him rather upset—and this, in turn, made him change color. Sometimes, if you upset him enough, he *blew up* . . . which would only make the situation worse.

This was not at all how Willow had hoped things would go today.

Before she'd left home that morning, Willow's father, Hawthorn, had given her a packed lunch that included two gumbo apples and a sandwich filled with eel-liver paste. It was one of those situations in which the phrase "it's the thought that counts" was sure to apply. Hawthorn's almond-shaped eyes, which looked so much like Willow's, had sparkled.

"Oh, Willow," he'd said, beaming. "I still remember my years at school rather fondly, despite all the scars. It will be such fun to compare notes."

Willow had felt momentarily uneasy as she nodded and smiled. She did not enjoy lying to her family, pretending she had come around to the idea of attending school, but she could see no other choice.

Her wrist still ached from writing urgent letters about Silas to the *Grimoire Gazette* that were dismissed or ridiculed. The editor, Rubix Grimoire—once an ally, and the guardian of Willow's good friend Essential—had seemingly turned against Willow altogether. And Moreg Vaine, the one person who might have been able to persuade the Enchancil of the truth, was nowhere to be found. All of this had caused Willow more sleepless nights than she could count.

She was tired of being ignored. Tired of having no answers. She needed to find out for herself why the Brothers of Wol had suddenly changed their minds and allowed magical children into their schools . . . and why nobody else seemed confused by this reversal.

In her hairy green carpetbag, Willow had packed enough clothes and food to last for a few days, and she'd left a note in her bedroom telling her family she wasn't coming home until she'd gotten to the bottom of what was happening.

So a better, more well-thought-out plan might have been for her to try and *blend in* a bit more with the nonmagical children—to keep her head down and her eyes and ears open. Instead, she was standing out in a rather worrisome way. But Willow couldn't help thinking that Oswin had a point. The class's reaction to her was a little . . . puzzling.

The village of Mild was only about five miles away from Grinfog, where Willow's magical family lived, so she'd assumed they would've heard about her. Yet, considering most of the children's reactions, she might as well have come from somewhere as far away as Starfell's second moon, Hezelbob (which was said to have spun off several thousand miles away from its first moon, Jezelbob, many eons ago in the luminary equivalent of a family spat). Perhaps it was more than that, though—perhaps they *had* heard of her, but were still afraid?

Thankfully, a small handful of nonmagical children from Grinfog were looking just as puzzled as Willow was by the panic. Willow recognized a boy with green eyes and dark-brown skin named Peg Spoon, who she often saw down by the river, fishing. He shot some of the others a bemused look before giving Willow a small wave, which she returned.

Willow then took a deep, steadying breath and gave the teacher an encouraging look. "I'm Willow . . . Willow Moss? There's no reason to be scared. . . ."

She looked from him to a little girl who had started crying and back again. The crying got louder. The teacher's eyes continued to bulge.

"Erm. Blink if you can hear me," she said.

The teacher dutifully blinked.

Willow tried to explain. "Um . . . my mother wrote a note?" She held it up like a white flag declaring a cease-fire.

The teacher seemed to recover slightly, finally unsticking himself from the wall to take the folded-up piece of paper from her.

"I'll just sit down over here, all right?" suggested Willow, heading to a vacant desk near the center of the classroom. She was surprised and pleased when Peg came to sit next to her.

"Y-yes," squeaked the teacher as he began to read the letter, the blood draining further from his face.

Dear Sir,

We are proud to be sending our youngest child, Willow Moss, to attend your school. What a time to be alive! We—her parents— are delighted at the amendment to the treaty. I can only imagine your own excitement—I just wish I was there to witness it!

I can't foresee a teacher of your fine caliber having any doubts about managing someone with a magical ability. (I'm sure there will have been rigorous training for this new endeavor, and I trust that only the most stalwart of educators have made the grade.) However, if you experience even a momentary twinge of concern, have no fear! I can reassure you that in sending you Willow, who is the least dangerous of my three witch daughters, there will be no risk of her blowing up any of your students or sending them hurtling through the sky with her mind! (Kids, am I right?)

Admittedly, there is the small but, alas, real danger that she might make one or all of the children disappear due to an ability she acquired in recent months. (We blame puberty—it's havoc.) Nonetheless, rest assured in the knowledge that, for the most part, she has this under control (except when she sneezes) and is able to return those she has vanished fairly unscathed. No doubt this will offer complete comfort all around.

In terms of her educational background, Willow has been homeschooled by her granny—the renowned potion maker Florence Moss—who has sadly passed on. However, as my mother-in-law had lost most of her marbles before she died, due to a potion explosion in the mountains of Nach, this means you may have your work cut out for you. Sorry.

Sincerely,
Raine Moss

Resident witch of neighboring Grinfog, renowned seer, and creator of the Traveling Fortune Fair*

*Tickets available by raven, half price for the Midnight Market (sale offer for the period of the Greening Moon only)

The teacher blinked a few times as he read, then reread, the letter—perhaps in the hope that it was all some sort of dream. Finally, he looked at Willow the way someone might contemplate a large spider.

"Do you . . . um, feel well?"

"Perfectly, thank you."

He cleared his throat, then glanced at the letter again, his skin mottling slightly. "No . . . er . . . c-colds or s-sniffles at all?"

It took a moment for Willow to grasp what he was referring to. "Oh, that? I feel fine! Besides, I recently figured out that if I hold my nose when I sneeze no one seems to disappear."

Another shock wave went through the class.

The truth was that when she had done that—held her sneeze in—she had made *herself* vanish instead. Only for a minute. But Willow filed this information under "Things Best Left Unsaid."

"And the, um . . . creature? We don't usually allow . . . pets."

"A WOT?" came Oswin's outraged voice from the carpetbag, which began, worryingly, to smoke.

Willow pulled a grim face and shot back quickly, "That's all right, as Oswin isn't a pet. And he won't cause a problem." She turned to Oswin's now pumpkin-orange eye, just visible through a hole in the hairy bag, with an expression that threatened . . . consequences. The sort of consequences that resulted in a *bath*.

There was a sulky sort of grunt from inside. "Fine. But 'tis bad enough when these cumberworlds fink I is a cat. 'Pet' jes' takes the blimmerings cake. No respect, an' me being the last kobold an' all. . . ."

"Um, right. V-very well. Erm. Welcome, Willow. I am Master Cuttlefish," said the teacher, patting himself down in his nervousness, as if to assure himself of who he was. He glanced at the hairy green bag at Willow's feet, then chose to simply ignore it, which was probably wise.

Willow felt someone tugging on her sleeve and turned to find Peg looking at her with wide green eyes. Up close, she noticed that he had a smattering of freckles across his nose. "You can make people vanish?"

The spirit hare stood in the clearing.

"You have what I asked of you?" said Silas.

The hare stared at him for a long moment, then opened its mouth. It made a hacking, coughing sound, then something round and gray rolled toward him.

It was an eye.

A clouded eye.

Silas bent down and picked it up gingerly. The thing looked dead, but as he touched the eye it grew darker, like a day shrouded in fog.

The wind began to whistle, and up ahead a storm gathered.

Silas allowed himself the smallest glimmer of a smile.

"You have done well."

2
Something Windy This Way Comes

WILLOW GAVE AN embarrassed sort of nod in response to Peg's question. "You know I find lost things, right?" She had helped Peg find a few bits and bobs in the past—he seemed to have a habit of misplacing his fishing flies, as she recalled.

He nodded.

"But making them vanish started happening last year," she continued. "Do you remember . . . Elth Night?"

Peg stared, then after a moment he clapped a hand over his mouth and snickered. "So it *was* you! *You* were the reason Birdy Pondwater found herself naked at the bunfire."

Willow blushed crimson.

Technically, the old woman still had on a pair of red-and-white-striped bloomers, so she wasn't exactly stark naked, but yes: Willow had somehow, accidentally, made the old woman's dress vanish . . . in public.

She closed her eyes, wincing at the memory. It was not one of her finest moments. When she opened them, Peg was still staring at her, looking amused.

"I believed you when you said it wasn't you. . . . You know, before the villagers threw their currant buns at you, and your sister dragged you off." He grinned, revealing a dimple in his cheek.

Willow fought back a grin herself. "Juniper didn't drag me off. She . . . er . . . marched me firmly away from the stampeding horde."

"Oh, right . . . that's totally different."

"Yep."

They shared a grin.

"Erm, but it turns out it *was* me . . . though I didn't know that at the time. My magic started to go a bit haywire—or at least that's what I thought was happening. It's a long story, but I've developed the other side of my ability. Now, as well as finding things, I can make them disappear. People too . . . though mostly by accident. I can't quite get it right on purpose."

She didn't tell Peg that when she tried, she usually made the wrong person vanish—like her mum when she was really aiming for her sister Camille. It had caused more than a few awkward moments at home, and plenty of time spent in the attic, where she was apparently supposed to think about her behavior while Camille gloated at her from the stairs . . . and so the cycle repeated itself.

It was quite a relief that her sisters were too old for the new mixed schools.

To Willow's surprise, instead of looking scared at the prospect of vanishing, Peg's face split into a mischievous smile. "It's a pity you haven't got it nailed down just yet," he said, casting the teacher a sideways glance. "That could come in handy. You have no idea how boring Cuttlefish can get when he puts his mind to it. And he *always* puts his mind to it."

Willow chuckled softly.

Peg's face turned serious for a moment, and he whispered, "It's wild that you're here, though. My mum couldn't believe it when she heard that they'd changed the rules. . . ." His smile faltered, and he looked a bit sheepish. "She's a bit, er . . . old-fashioned."

Willow nodded. She'd guessed as much. His mother, Begonia, always wore a "witch-resistant necklace." It was made out of goat hair and wigweed sprouts and was supposedly meant to protect the wearer against magic. It didn't work, but Willow would never tell Peg that.

When she was little, Willow had passed Begonia in the street, and something about the way the woman had clutched at her necklace had struck Willow as odd. She'd gone to find Granny Flossy—who had been brewing up a potion for improved digestion that would later destroy part of the greenhouse—to tell her about what had happened.

Granny had moved aside a long strand of green hair and looked up at Willow in surprise. "That necklace Begonia wears? It's jes' old bits and bobs strung together—they sell them at some of the markets. I've even made a few of them meself in me time, ter smooth things over when us magical folk started moving inter their towns. It won' do much apart from keep the fleas off her. Best not ter let on, though," she'd said, tapping the side of her nose. "Sometimes ye've got ter let people have something ter believe in, so their fears don' take 'em over."

Willow had been a bit shocked. "You've made them yourself—even though you know they don't work? Isn't that, well, a bit . . . wrong?"

Granny Flossy had considered the question while cutting up a bunch of grumbling Gertrudes for her potion—probably to disguise the bad taste. The purple juice stained her fingers. "Fear is a dark mistress, and it don' play fair, child. It'll take up all the room in yer brain if yer let it, so it's a kindness ter find ways ter help people keep it at bay. 'Tisn't exactly right or wrong, but a bit of both—like life itself, which is a mix too. You see?"

And Willow had. But she knew that not everyone would.

She looked at Peg, who seemed a bit embarrassed. "I wish she wouldn't wear that necklace," he said softly. "I mean, she knows there's nothing to fear, really. . . ."

"It's fine, Peg. I don't mind."

Part of Willow wished she had a load of those necklaces now, so that she could offer them to the rest of the class and make them feel better. But a bigger part of her wished that they wouldn't want them, that the children would see for themselves that they didn't have to be afraid just because she was a bit different.

Peg sighed. "I mean, it's silly that Mum's still a bit wary of witches. All I've seen your family do is help people, and she knows that too, I think. . . . She even said that you have a right to learn just as much as any of us. But considering how scared people are, it's a bit weird that they changed things, um, so suddenly, from one week to the next." He looked embarrassed. "Um, not that they shouldn't have."

Willow was quick to reassure him. "No, you're right. It *is* weird. . . ."

She thought once again of how little her own parents had listened to her concerns, and how much it had convinced her that something wasn't right. . . .

A few weeks ago, her parents had attended an Enchancil meeting informing them of the new legislation. When they'd come home and told Willow the "happy news," it was like waking up in a house that you thought you knew, only to find yourself tumbling down a set of stairs you never realized existed.

They'd looked blissfully happy about the idea of sending their youngest daughter to a school governed by the Brothers of Wol—an order now headed by the person Willow and her friends had discovered was actively trying to steal everyone's magic and start another war.

"You can't be serious?" Willow had cried. "Why on Starfell would you choose to trust Silas, after everything that's happened?"

Willow's mother had tutted. "The Enchancil has cleared all that up. It was just a silly misunderstanding. . . ."

"A . . . *misunderstanding*?" Willow had stared at them both in shock. Just two weeks before, when Silas had been appointed, her mother had said they needed to find Moreg and that it was time to take a stand against the Brothers . . . and now this? Suddenly she thought it was all right to send her youngest child to a school run by these people?

"Oh yes, my dear, it's nothing for us to worry about it," her father had said.

Willow had blinked, looking from one parent to the other. From underneath the table, there had been a faint "Wot?" from Oswin, who seemed as confused as she was.

Willow stared. "But . . . we *know* what Silas wants, and

he's getting even stronger—he's overthrown the Brothers of Wol. Can't you see how suspicious it is that he's now inviting magical children into his schools?"

Raine had huffed. "Overthrown? Don't be silly. He's been voted in as leader. That's how it works. And as for 'suspicious,' you just sound paranoid. Things change. This is what real progress looks like! You simply got the wrong information, that's all. . . ."

Willow had stared at her parents in disbelief. "The wrong information? When my friend *saw* Silas's own memories, proving that he's trying to become the most powerful magician in our history? That he's planning to rip all the magic out of Starfell?"

"Yes, that's just nonsense. It's why we need to send you all to school, you see, so you can sharpen your minds, accept the truth."

Willow had spluttered, "Accept the truth? The only truth that needs accepting is that Silas *must be stopped*!"

Why were her parents acting like this?

Willow's father had shaken his head benignly. "Oh, Fetch," he'd said, using an unfortunate nickname that Camille had started when she was little and Willow still couldn't quite shake off. "It's all going to be just wonderful, you'll see."

In the weeks that followed, Willow had tried her best to get through to her parents, but they'd only looked at her with slightly vacant expressions whenever she brought up Silas or his plans. Willow had been forced to conclude that something odd had happened at that Enchancil meeting. . . .

She turned to Peg. "I was starting to worry that I was the only one who thought it was weird that the Brothers suddenly wanted us in their schools!"

It was good to have someone agree with her. It hadn't occurred to Willow that it must have seemed very odd from the nonmagical community's perspective too.

"Nope," he said, then jerked his head in the direction of a few of the other children who were still cowering beneath their desks. "I bet they think it's odd too . . . if I were to take a wild guess."

Willow gave a hollow laugh.

"But maybe it's nice that it's happening," he said.

Willow looked from Peg to the other children, who had now picked up their chairs and desks to get as far away from her as possible. Somehow, she thought, despite Peg's kindness, "nice" was a stretch. In fact, she was a bit worried that the Brothers were trying too hard to make things seem "nice."

Master Cuttlefish called for their attention as he picked up a box from the floor.

"Instructions and workbooks from the Brothers of Wol, for our n-new undertaking," he said. "We were instructed to only open this box if one of you actually showed up." He broke off, cleared his throat, and took out the instructions. As he read, he picked up several pieces of chalk from within the box and muttered, "Ah! That is a relief. I wondered if the Brothers had completely lost their minds. . . . Though of course I shouldn't have doubted their wisdom. . . . Oh yes, indeed. I see now."

From near Willow's feet there came a faint "Wot's 'e on about?"

"I don't know," whispered Willow, feeling the hairs begin to prickle on the back of her neck. She shared a confused look with the kobold, whose green eye was just visible through a small hole in the carpetbag.

The teacher straightened, and it was as if all his earlier fear had left him. The color returned to his cheeks, and he called out, "Nigel?"

The ginger-haired boy at the back who had made the sign of Wol at Willow squeaked in reply, "Yes, master?"

"Please come over here and help distribute these."

Nigel hesitated for a moment, as it meant passing Willow, but then went to help Cuttlefish hand out the thin blue volumes to the class.

When one of them landed on Willow's desk, she stared at it. In the middle was a large *W* embossed on the cover in red.

But before she could open the book, the sky outside suddenly turned the color of an old bruise. The air crackled with electricity and the classroom door was flung open, slamming against the wall with an enormous crash.

"Oh nooooo," cried Oswin. "Oh no, oh, me greedy aunt! Wot new eel is this?"

Willow blanched. What new "eel" indeed?

The air had turned cold, and the wind began to howl as something wild, something blue, something utterly *terrifying* came hurtling toward them.

It was a tornado.

Everyone began to scream bloody murder. Wind whipped through the classroom, overturning desks, blowing papers everywhere, and frosting everything with ice.

The hairy green bag began to shake as Oswin zipped himself more securely inside. "I really should 'ave stayed under the bed today," he whimpered.

There was an eerie wailing sound, loud enough to break glass, and, as the swirling mass came closer, everyone gasped in shock.

Right in the center of the whirlwind was a girl.

3

Twist Howling

FROST SPREAD ACROSS the floor as the girl spun into the classroom.

Willow shivered violently in her thin green cloak, her eyelashes crusting with icicles.

And then, quite as suddenly as it had appeared, the wind and the cold and the swirling blue tornado died down, revealing a tall girl around Willow's age. Her hair was white and appeared to crackle as it quivered around her head in a kind of electrified cloud. She inspected the class with piercing blue eyes—the kind that seemed not only to see you but to take an X-ray too. Then she calmly told the icy wind, which was now swirling more gently by her side, "*Selia*—scatter now."

And it did, departing in an intricate swirl of mist and ice.

When the girl saw the many pairs of fearful eyes, like peeled grapefruits, pinned on her, she frowned.

Everything she wore—from the long white dress that brushed the tips of her black pointed lace-up boots to a thick cream cardigan—was twisted. Yet despite the fact that she looked a bit like she'd been dragged backward through a hedge, met the resident wildlife, gotten into a fight and *won* . . . she was somehow still elegant. Willow was reminded of the way an old house can sometimes seem both stately and slightly dilapidated at the same time.

The girl's pale eyes took in the fallen desks, and she sighed. "Skiron can be a real menace indoors. North winds, you know?" she said.

None of them did know. They all blinked at her in horror.

Unfortunately, the fierce, swirling, frosty wind that was lurking just outside the classroom door seemed to take sudden offense at the girl's words. A screeching, earsplitting noise erupted, making all the children clap their hands over their ears, as the wind gusted itself into a furious frenzy and hurtled inside once more.

The girl tapped her foot impatiently, lips pursed. "Skiron, it's not like you to be so sensitive. Honestly, you're embarrassing yourself."

This, unfortunately, made things worse.

The door began to slam violently on its hinges, and the wind swelled to three times its size as it spun like a top into the center of the room. Everyone screamed as desks and chairs and children started to rise into the air.

Clouds of condensation left their mouths and ice crystals hardened on the floor. Inside the hairy green bag, Willow could hear Oswin's teeth chattering, along with a muffled "Oh nooo, oh, me 'orrid aunt . . . Oh, fings is turning blue which should not be blue. . . ."

Some of the children managed to hold on tight to their desks or chairs, their legs floating behind them, but others were thrown roughly against the walls, their screams reaching a deafening pitch.

Willow winced as Nigel, the ginger-haired boy, was gusted upward, and there was a nasty cracking sound when his head met the ceiling.

This made Willow's entrance seem like a breeze in comparison. She gingerly got out of her chair, fighting hard against the fierce wind, and edged toward the girl. Willow's lips were turning blue from the freezing cold, and she wasn't sure what she was going to *do* exactly, but she hoped to help.

However, it soon became clear that help was not needed.

The girl used that strange word again: "*Selia*." But nothing happened. She raised an eyebrow, then said in a low voice that was only mildly terrifying, "I am going to count to three, but it would be better for us both if you decide to be reasonable and obey the command before that happens."

The wind was being—there was no other word for it— stubborn. At that moment, in sulky response, it knocked over a big wall display that featured the children's artwork.

The girl's eyes glittered. Thunder rumbled as if from nowhere, and it took a moment for Willow to note that it had come from the girl's open mouth as she boomed, "ONE!"

Everyone flinched.

"Oh noooo! Don' make her count ter free!" cried Oswin, the top of his head peeking out of the bag. "Oh, me heart!"

The wind, it seemed, agreed. It beat a hasty retreat through the classroom door.

With that, the temperature returned to normal. The frost melted away as suddenly as it had appeared. The classroom furniture and a handful of children came tumbling to the floor with a crash.

The windswept girl, however, made no comment. Perhaps she was used to this. Instead, she turned back to the class as if it were completely normal to have thunder coming out of your mouth. "Sometimes you have to bring the thunder to avoid the lightning," she explained. Then she smiled, which was also a bit terrifying.

"To tell you the truth," she added, rubbing her throat, "it does rather burn when it comes out. My aunt Dot says gargling with salt water helps strengthen the vocal cords, but so far nothing. . . . Then again," she said, snorting, "she's got the west wind—the gentlest one, which brings along spring, you know? It's not like she ever needs to call on the thunder when her wind, Zephyrus, ignores the command to scatter. She can summon a slight drizzle and hers just flies away, absolutely terrified. Skiron, on the other hand, is one of the toughest and the fiercest—that's why he's mine." She smiled again.

Willow's mouth had been hanging open, and that's when the girl finally noticed her. She seemed a little amused or surprised—it was hard to tell. "Were you coming to help?"

"Um, y-yes."

The girl stared. "Can you tame winds too?"

"Er, no . . . ," admitted Willow. "Not at all. That was, well, brilliant, what you did. I just thought maybe you could use a hand?" Then she blushed. "Um, but obviously you had it under control."

The girl's pale eyes regarded her for some time. "Yes, I certainly did," she said, then she frowned. "But you didn't know that. You came to help, despite having no ability to do so . . . which tells me something. You're either a bit odd, or you're a witch." Then she smiled, as if making up her mind. "Probably a bit of both."

Willow didn't know whether to feel insulted or not, but she could tell that, if anything, the girl seemed to warm to her. Besides, if Willow were honest with herself, she'd lost the battle with being "a bit odd" a long time ago.

She decided it was best to change the subject. "I can't believe another witch has lived near me this whole time!"

The girl looked askance. "A witch? I should think not."

Willow blinked in surprise. "B-but—"

"I'm an elf."

Willow's eyes shone in amazement as she noticed the girl's pointed ears. "Oh!"

Elves kept themselves to themselves, so she'd never actually met one before. She knew they were excellent craftspeople and traders of magic, though, and some of the best magical objects and devices—like Moreg's portal cloak—came from the elvish city of Lael. The girl's storm magic also made a little more sense now, as it was only elves who seemed to have some control over the weather. (Well, elves and Moreg Vaine, who could make lightning and thunder strike too—though, to be fair, not *out of her mouth*.) And, unlike humans, who didn't always get any magical ability, all elves did, though no one really knew why.

Elves were also rumored to have some kind of collective magical power called elfsense. Willow wasn't sure how it worked, but then, not many humans did.

"I'm Twist Howling," said the girl, holding up her index finger. Seeing that Willow clearly didn't know what she was meant to do, Twist broke into a small smile, and she picked up Willow's hand to touch her finger to Willow's own. A small bluish-green spark emitted from them both, which took Willow by surprise.

"Knew you were a witch," the elf girl said.

"I'm Willow Moss," said Willow, still a bit puzzled by the sparks.

The girl's eyes widened in surprise. "YOU'RE Willow

Moss?" She grabbed Willow's hand, pulling her closer to get a better look.

The way Twist was staring made Willow feel a little awkward. There were some people in the magical community who had heard of her now, mostly due to the reporting in the *Grimoire Gazette*—which, unfortunately, made her sound like she needed to be carted off somewhere.

"Er, yes. I've, um, been mentioned in the Enchancil newsletter . . . a few times."

Twist let out an odd barking laugh that made a few of the children jump in their seats. "A few times? It's been every week without fail for the past three months." Then she frowned. "They don't seem to like you much."

Willow didn't know what to say. It wasn't untrue.

"Well," Twist carried on, "you're the reason I came to this school. I wanted to track you down. I need to talk to you."

Willow's eyes bulged, and she took an involuntary step backward.

From the hairy carpetbag there came a whispered "*Oh no.*"

Which was probably what Willow's knees would say too, if they could speak.

The fiercest person she'd met since *Moreg Vaine* had come to track her down?

4

An Elvish Legend

"REALLY?" SAID WILLOW, finally managing to pull her fingers from Twist's grasp. "Um, w-why did you want to talk to me?"

But Willow wouldn't learn why just yet, as right then there was the sound of a throat being cleared rather loudly.

It was Master Cuttlefish. He had managed not to stick himself to the wall at Twist's arrival, and it appeared that his impatience at her continued interruption of his lesson had, at last, outweighed his fear.

"If you two have quite finished getting acquainted? Not to mention destroying my classroom before we've even started our first lesson?" he added sarcastically.

Willow blushed. "Sorry," she said.

Twist, however, did not apologize. She merely stared at Cuttlefish until he cleared his throat again and said, a bit more politely, "I—I presume you're also starting with us today?" His tone implied that he wasn't exactly thrilled about this.

And, to be fair, given the state of his classroom—which now looked rather worse for the wear, the children windswept and disheveled with tracks of tears down their faces, skin mottled from screaming—he might have had good reason to feel put out.

Twist nodded. "Yes. I had a note, but there's a strong possibility it got blown away. . . ."

"You don't say," he muttered. "Well, never mind. I think I get the gist: new student, magic, lucky me."

Willow shared a look of surprise with Oswin, who muttered, "Someone 'as 'ad a change o' heart."

Willow agreed. Cuttlefish had indeed made a remarkable recovery in his approach to magical children in a relatively short space of time, considering his earlier fear of her.

"Class started twenty minutes ago, Miss Twist. Do not be late again," he said.

Twist didn't reply. She simply cocked her head to one side and stared at him with those odd piercing eyes of hers.

After a rather awkward moment, as Cuttlefish grew ever paler, he suggested weakly, "Er, p-please. T-take a seat."

The rest of the class gave them both a wide berth, setting their now-righted desks and chairs down as far away as possible. Only Peg stayed near, giving them both a shaky smile. He touched his throat for a moment and Willow wondered if he was thinking about borrowing his mother's necklace after all. . . .

Cuttlefish handed Twist one of the blue books. Then he turned, walked over to the classroom door, and drew a small X on it with chalk. Once done, he addressed the rest of the class as if this were perfectly normal behavior.

"Welcome back, everyone. Before we get started on the new curriculum, I think a brief recap of what we learned last year might be helpful for our old and, er, new students," he said, and his voice took on a monotonous drone as he began going over what they had covered the year before, most of which seemed to involve methods of farming.

Within minutes, Willow was finding it hard to pay attention . . . and she wondered if the Brothers of Wol's plan was simply to bore magical children into submission.

"Told you," whispered Peg. "He takes being boring seriously."

Willow grinned, then introduced Peg to Twist.

Twist nodded at him in greeting, then cocked her head at the chalk on the door, whispering, "What's with that? Is it something to do with the lesson?"

Peg shook his head. "No idea! First time he's ever done that."

There was a harrumph from the hairy carpetbag, and Twist turned to it in confusion. "That's Oswin," Willow said quietly. "He's a kobold. I'll explain later."

From within the bag, Oswin muttered, "Can yew smells that? That chalk smells a bit weirds."

"What?" asked Willow, but she was distracted when Cuttlefish asked the old students to take out their notebooks and summarize some of last year's lessons. A boy at the back of the classroom was asked to outline the history of farming in Grinfog, and he started on a long monologue about the types of apples they grew in their county. A girl with pigtails was next, describing the different harvesting methods and how they had changed over the years.

Willow found herself stifling several yawns.

"Oh no," whispered Oswin. "I'm actually gonna be bored ter death. The Flossy Mistress always made learnin' much better than this—excitings . . . 'cos yew never knew if she wos gonna blow the roofs off again or not."

Willow felt tears smart in her eyes.

"I miss that," Oswin said mournfully.

Willow had to bite her lip to stop it from wobbling. "Me too," she whispered.

Granny Flossy's lessons had been about life and, despite what her mother thought, Willow knew her grandmother's wisdom was probably a lot more valuable than knowing the various types of apple rot, which Peg was now reluctantly reciting.

Before Willow could get swept away in her memories, though, she was interrupted by Twist.

"Willow, like I said—I need to talk to you. This week's *Gazette*—did you read it?"

Willow nodded. "Look, I know everyone thinks I'm sick or mad or making things up to get attention, but that's not true. It's Silas—he can't be trusted."

Twist stared at her as if she were an idiot. "Course he can't. We all know that."

Willow blinked in confusion.

Twist went on, "By 'we,' I mean elves. I don't know why all the other magical folk have suddenly decided to accept everything Silas and the Brothers are saying. . . . I mean, it doesn't make sense, does it?"

"Exactly!" cried Willow in an agitated whisper. "That's what I've been thinking. It's like something happened at the last Enchancil meeting—since then, it's as if all the grown-ups have just decided to blindly trust Silas and the Brothers, ignoring everything else. I mean, until then my parents had been quite suspicious of them."

"Interesting. . . . We elves haven't had a seat on the Enchancil for years. We were thrown off after a bit of an incident. My aunt Tuppence lost her temper when she caught someone lying. . . . She *may* have overreacted a little, blasting him with a bolt of lightning—you know, the usual stuff— but maybe that explains why the elves feel differently . . . because they weren't there?"

"That would make sense!" said Willow, though a small, dismayed part of her was picturing Twist's aunt blasting someone with a lightning bolt. . . . But she managed to push that thought aside for the moment. "My parents have been impossible to reason with ever since that meeting. That's why I came here today—to see for myself what the Brothers are really planning with this new idea to mix magical and nonmagical children together. Something about it just feels . . . weird. I don't know what they're up to, but I want to find out."

Twist smiled. "Well, I figured you'd be trying to do just that. I was sure I'd find you here."

Willow stared at her in surprise. "So . . . what *did* you want to talk to me about?"

"It's about Silas. I think he stole the scroll."

"What scroll?"

Twist looked impatient. "The ancient elvish scroll that was stolen from Library!"

Willow frowned. She vaguely remembered there had been a string of burglaries throughout Starfell lately, including the theft of an old scroll, but she hadn't paid much attention, to be honest. She had other worries to focus on—like the fact that all the grown-ups seemed to have lost the power of rational thought, for one.

"Why do you think Silas has taken it?" Willow asked carefully. Then she frowned, recalling what the *Gazette* article had said. "No one has ever been able to decipher that scroll, right? They said it could be something as simple as an old elvish recipe for bread or whatever." Willow remembered that part because it had been a quote from Copernica Darling, a librarian and Secret Keeper she'd met once when she visited the town of Library.

To her surprise, Twist let out a short laugh. "They're lying! That's their job as Secret Keepers. *Of course* they know what the scroll says!"

Willow blinked.

"Okay, well, not in detail," Twist continued. "I don't think they've lied about not being able to translate it properly. But all elves know that it contains the last words of Queen Almefeira and the truth about what happened to the vanished elvish kingdom. . . ."

Willow had heard the stories over the years about the kingdom of Llandunia that had mysteriously disappeared during the Long War, and the infamous scroll that had appeared afterward with the queen's seal. She'd always thought it was just a story, really—a fairy tale about a beautiful queen and a land that had gone missing a thousand years ago.

"But isn't that just a myth?"

Twist gave her a hard stare. "No," she said firmly. "Though humans love to dismiss my people's history as mere fairy tale."

Willow stared at the elf as she took that in. "So you think Silas knows this, and wants to try to find the kingdom? Why?"

Twist darted a look over her shoulder. A boy at the back of the class was still going over crop-rotation methods. Twist's white-blond hair seemed to crackle as she leaned nearer to Willow and whispered, "Because there's a part of the story that no one knows, and it's linked to Queen Almefeira's staff."

"Her staff?" echoed Willow.

Twist nodded. "It was said to have enormous power—even the ability to bestow the gift of magic. Now, when the kingdom vanished, so did the queen, and so did her staff. Most people know this." She leaned closer still. "But the part they don't know is something I just found out. It's the reason I came to find you, Willow. There was another side to her staff, a darker one: *it could take magic away*."

Willow gasped, the color draining from her face. "How do you know?"

"I found something, back in Lael. It will be easier to show you. But I think you're right. Silas *is* going to try to steal everyone's magic—he just needs to find the staff first."

Willow paled. "This is how he plans on doing it."

Twist nodded. "And what's worse is I think he's probably quite close to finding it. Think about it: That's why he was so keen to suddenly allow us into his schools. He's about to get his hands on a staff that can strip away magic—so he's started to round up the first people he can use it on."

Willow blinked in horror as it all became horribly clear.

Twist meant them.

Magical children *like them*.

"High Master?" said the young acolyte, approaching the raised stone dais hesitantly.

Flames suddenly ignited from the torches on either side of the marble seat on which Silas sat, his fingers steepled.

"You may have an audience," replied Silas.

It was the official welcome, and the young acolyte should have felt relieved, but instead he glanced at the flames and swallowed.

There had been rumors circling the Brotherhood, before Silas became the new High Master. Whispers behind locked doors. Whispers about his strange . . . abilities. They had been told that he was blessed, that he had been touched by Wol himself. Anointed. It seemed . . . unlikely. Why him, why now . . . after all these years?

The acolyte dared not even think it, afraid it would show on his face . . . but he couldn't help himself. So much had changed in the Brotherhood. So many new "blessings" and "gifts" had suddenly been discovered—like the glowing manacles that could ensnare a witch. The way these tools worked seemed odd—akin almost to the devices used by an unnatural—and they all led back to Silas. There was a simpler explanation, the acolyte knew. One he wished he could stop thinking of now that it had occurred to him. . . . What if Silas had simply been cursed with magic?

Over the years, there had been talk. Strange incidents that

happened behind closed doors. Accidents. The old High Master had brushed them aside, refused to do anything about them.

They used to say that Silas was a foundling. Some said his mother was a witch.

But no one spoke of that anymore. Not now that he was High Master. Not now that he had changed so much in such a short time. He was only a few years older than the acolyte, but one would never be able to tell that now: his face had hardened and lost all traces of the softening effects of youth. His hair, once straw-colored and thatch-like, had been shaved, as was the custom of all High Masters. Yet he had gone a step further, not keeping the ring of hair. It was unusual, a practice that only the High Masters of old had done.

At his throat he wore a strange kind of amulet hanging from a piece of twisted brown leather. It was gray and clouded, and, as the acolyte watched, its surface seemed to shift like fog.

It was another of the strange "blessings" that had appeared in recent months.

As if reading the acolyte's mind, Silas looked at him and said, "You have been wondering, Elsen, about my blessing."

Elsen stepped forward quickly, desperate to deny his misgivings, and almost tripped over his long brown robe. His mind raced. Who had he told? Just one or two Brothers, he supposed. How much would they have told Silas?

"High Master, I was only curious . . . that is all."

"Curious about Wol's blessings? Curious enough to question a . . . god?"

Elsen's eyes widened in fear. "No, master. Oh no—never that." He was effusive in his denials.

To Elsen's surprise, Silas waved his hands in dismissal. "It is natural to wonder, of course."

Elsen breathed a sigh of relief.

"Step closer, and I will show you Wol's blessing."

The boy hesitated. But then he walked the few steps toward the High Master, trying and failing to avoid Silas's penetrating eyes. He noticed that he had stepped over a faint chalk line, which seemed odd; the High Master was so particular about cleanliness and presentation. . . .

Before he reached the top step, there was a screeching sound, and he was knocked into the air, crashing down a few feet away.

He lay on the stone floor, winded, dazed, and confused.

Silas stood up, and Elsen could see that his robes were very different from the old High Master's. These were long and black, and instead of the single arrow in the center there was another more ancient symbol, of a spiral stick topped with a pair of half moons surrounding a circle.

He walked nonchalantly toward the boy and looked down at him.

The young acolyte was blinking up at him in surprise. But there was no fear in his eyes. Not any longer.

"I have been chosen, you see. Chosen by Wol to be his successor," said Silas.

The boy's eyes appeared almost blank, but he readily agreed. "Yes, High Master. I see now."

"Good," said Silas. "You may spread the word."

"I would be honored to."

5

The Vision for the Future

"WE'VE GOT TO stop him!" cried Willow. "We can't let Silas find that staff!"

There was the smallest flash of lightning, and Twist nodded, fast.

"Oi!" called Peg, snapping his fingers. Willow and Twist looked at him in surprise.

"EXCUSE the interruption!" called Master Cuttlefish sarcastically, gaining their attention at last. "Now that we've finished going over what we learned last year, and I trust our new students took notes"—he gave them a meaningful look—"we will make a start on our new curriculum. If you could all turn to the contents page."

Willow opened the slim blue volume, then blanched. There on the page was everything that they'd feared and *more*.

"This can't be right," breathed Peg.

Willow read on in shock.

Why magic is unnatural

What constitutes a Forbidden area and why we need more of them

What lessons can be learned from the Long War—and where we went wrong

Why we need to start with magical children first

Magical draining—barbaric or a necessary kindness?

How real unity will begin when we are all exactly the same

The vision for the future: a magic-free world

Willow's eyes were drawn to the words "Why we need to start with magical children first," and then widened at the perhaps even more ominous ones: "Magical draining— barbaric or a necessary kindness?"

"This is mad," said Peg, looking at Willow and Twist.

"Wot? Wot is it?" asked Oswin, his now pumpkin-bright ears inching out of the carpetbag, making a few children gasp in horror.

Ignoring them, Willow showed him the book. As the kobold read, his fur turned oddly pale and green, as if he were about to be sick. "Oh noooo! Oh, me greedy aunt! These cumberworlds is planning on doings us all in! We needs ter skedaddle!"

"Yes!" said Willow.

"So a kobold is . . . a talking cat?" breathed Twist, momentarily distracted.

Oswin whipped around to glare at her, his eyes turning into angry slits. "No they is NOT! I is the monster from under the bed. Or the monster in the bag, or the stove. . . . I moves arounds a bit," he admitted. "I is the monster in the room yew is in, when I is in it," he decided at last.

Willow shook her head impatiently. "We don't have time for this, Oswin! We have to get out of here." Her heart was pounding in her ears.

He nodded. "Sorry."

Peg had started to shout, holding up the book in distaste. "There's nothing wrong with magical people! This is barbaric!"

There was a low murmur from the other students. Some, it seemed, like Peg, were also a bit concerned.

"How can we go from lessons on farming to . . . witch-hunting?" asked one.

"What do they mean, 'magical draining'? That sounds a bit dangerous. My third cousins have magic. We're not exactly close, but I wouldn't want to actually take their magic away. . . ."

Alas, others seemed to think Cuttlefish had every right.

"About time!"

"I always thought they were strange. It makes sense that magic is unnatural."

Willow had heard enough. "We're leaving," she told the teacher, standing up. "There's no way you'll get away with this."

To her surprise, Cuttlefish smiled. "By all means, leave. I'm sure you'll soon have a change of heart, though," he said, toying with the piece of chalk he'd used earlier to draw an X on the classroom door.

Oswin gasped. "Oh noo! Oh, me greedy aunt! I suspectred somefing fishies. He's used Gerful chalk," he spat, glaring at the teacher with his large, lamp-like eyes. The kobold had turned a blood-orange color in his outrage. "I knew that pale carbuncle was acting shifties—'twasn't natural that 'e suddenly found 'is courage. 'E din't! Not till he opened that box!"

Oswin was speaking about the box from the Brothers of Wol, which had contained the books, as well as the instructions and the mysterious chalk. . . .

At Willow, Twist, and Peg's confused looks, the kobold explained, "It controls the mind . . . makes yew believes anyfing someone wants yeh to."

The three of them gasped.

Cuttlefish nodded. "It's nothing to worry about. It's all going to be perfectly fine. . . . The Brothers have thought of everything. You see, when you exit through the door marked with the chalk, you won't remember any of your concerns. The chalk puts the mind in a more agreeable, receptive state. . . . You'll remember only the lessons we teach you, and you'll be happy about them too. It's genius really."

Willow gasped. "That's brainwashing!"

The teacher shrugged. "Some brains could do with a bit of a wash."

They stared at him in mute horror.

"You can't drain their magic and think we'll just be okay with that!" cried Peg.

Willow's heart started to thud painfully in her chest. There was a buzzing in her ears and she felt faint. Were they too late? Had Silas already gotten his hands on the staff?

"That's not happening today, dear boy. The Brothers are working on their cure, which will take some time," said Cuttlefish. "It won't be me who performs the miracle. It will be High Master Silas, the new leader of the Brothers of Wol himself. I believe he's very close to uncovering the method that will help rid Starfell of this unnatural affliction."

It took a long while for Willow's breathing to return to normal.

"He doesn't have it yet," she whispered to Twist, some color returning to her cheeks.

"Thank Starfell," breathed Twist.

"It's only a matter of time," Cuttlefish said, tapping the book. "But our first goal, really, is to help you to see how important it is that we rid the world of this infection, and that's where *you* all come in. . . ." He turned to the rest of the class.

Peg screwed up one green eye as he considered something the others hadn't. "That's not just for them, is it?" he said, pointing at the chalk X on the back of the door. "It's for all of us, so no one else remembers how wrong this is—otherwise there'd be chaos when the news got out to our parents!"

There was a burst of excitable chatter at this.

"It's for the magical people, Peg, not us," said the boy called Nigel.

"Not strictly true," said Cuttlefish, shaking his head. "Peg is correct. I always knew you were smart, boy. When you all leave class today, things will be a bit hazy, but you'll feel content, as if everything is as it should be."

"You can't do that!" cried Peg. "You can't make us all go along with this . . . It's madness. Magical people are just different!"

Cuttlefish looked calm as he explained, "Yes, we can. And we must. You see, the last time we tried to rid the world of magic, the nonmagical community showed compassion, tolerance—like you're doing right now, Peg. But the unnaturals preyed on this weakness, and that is why we were never able to stamp out magic. We were weak when we needed to be strong and united. We won't be doing magical folk any favors if we're too soft and let them carry on being diseased when they don't have to be."

"Diseased!" cried Willow. "We're not diseased!"

"Yes, yes . . . I know *you* believe that, but that is why

you're here. We want to help! With this chalk, we will all be on the same side, and over time you'll all come to believe, as you should, that these words are true," Cuttlefish said, tapping the front of the book again. "High Master Silas has had a vision about all of this—it's how he was led to the chalk. It is a gift from Wol, bestowed on us so that we can come together at last. Don't you see?"

A few of the children slowly nodded, but Willow was glad to see that a lot of them still looked suspicious and upset.

"Wot a cumberworld. 'E finks it's some kind of miracles. Don' even occur to him 'e's bein' hoodwrinkled—fed some ol' dangerous magic that 'as been med to look like a blesserings," whispered Oswin.

Willow nodded. She knew Oswin was right. Once again, Silas was using magic and dressing it up as a holy gift.

Then she gasped as she realized something else. She turned to Twist and hissed, "The grown-ups!" But Twist looked blank. "The Enchancil meeting—the one about the school plan. That's what must have happened!"

Twist's eyes widened. "Someone must have used that chalk!" she breathed.

Willow nodded. "I'm sure of it. Someone has infiltrated the Enchancil. It's why the adults are all suddenly on Silas's side!"

"That makes sense! My aunt said that Celestine Bear was never the type of person who would have just taken the

Brothers at their word. . . . She thought it was odd."

Willow nodded. "And Rubix—it didn't seem like her to buy into all of that either."

"They've been brainwashed!"

"We have to get out of here!" cried Twist.

Willow didn't need to consult the StoryPass to know that it was most likely suggesting "If I Were You, I'd Run."

But the chalk on the door presented a major problem. How were they going to get out?

6
Travel by Tornado

"I THOUGHT YOU might say that," said Cuttlefish, going to his desk and opening up the box on the floor again. "But I'm afraid I cannot tolerate any more of this disruption. Caraway, Hessan, Gertie, and Clementine," he called.

Willow wondered briefly if these were some kind of weird expletives. But they turned out to be students—the biggest ones—who stood up, looking uncertain.

"I need your help securing our unruly students with these, so we can continue our lesson without their magical interference." Cuttlefish stepped forward with two pairs of iron manacles that were glowing faintly blue.

Willow gasped. She recognized those. They were another of Silas's magical devices, made specifically to lock up witches and wizards—the Brothers of Wol had used them to try to seize Moreg Vaine.

"These manacles are blessed by Wol, and they prevent a person with magic from using their abilities," Cuttlefish explained to the students he had called forward. "You have nothing to fear—just restrain them so we can keep them under control."

Caraway, Hessan, Gertie, and Clementine looked relieved. Two of them took the manacles and began to advance with determination toward Willow and Twist.

"Those aren't blessed!" cried Willow. "It's magic!"

"Trust me—it's Wol's blessing," said Cuttlefish. "Seize them!"

Willow grabbed her carpetbag, shoved the blue workbook inside, and jumped up from her desk. She and Twist leaped away from Cuttlefish and the students—but they were closing in.

Peg dashed toward the door and tried in vain to rub out the chalk.

"Can we try water or something?" asked Twist, ducking away from one of the approaching students.

The kobold popped his head out of Willow's bag. "No— won't make no difference. The on'y way is for 'im to break the charm 'imself."

The part of Willow's mind that wasn't occupied with the terror of those manacles took a moment to appreciate just how valuable Oswin was at times like these. He had a wealth of knowledge about magic since he'd spent most of his adult life roaming Starfell, looking for a new home after kobolds were banished from their homeland.

"Can you summon the chalk with your abilities, Willow? Maybe if we have it, we'll be able to break out?" asked Peg, his eyes wild.

Willow shook her head. "I can only summon it if it's lost! We'll have to get out through the window!"

The trouble was the window was on the other side of the classroom, and she and Twist were cornered! But they could make it if she could just get hold of Whisper. . . . She dived toward her broomstick and grabbed it in triumph. She leaped on, Twist scrambling on behind her.

"Stop that this instant!" shouted Cuttlefish, rushing forward and leaping at Twist, knocking her off just as Willow flew toward the ceiling, out of reach.

"Oh no!" cried Willow as Twist stormed toward the teacher, her hair beginning to crackle.

"Don't worry about me!" called Twist. "I'll be with you in a second."

Cuttlefish took a step backward in fear at the look in the elf girl's eyes, before racing after Willow again—perhaps in an effort to get as far away from Twist as possible. . . .

Willow swooped down beside Peg, shouting, "Get on!"

The boy quickly clambered on behind her, his eyes huge.

"Don't you dare take Peg with you! Get back to your desks immediately!" Cuttlefish screeched, again taking a flying leap toward Willow and Peg and managing to claw at the carpetbag.

"Oh noooo! A curse upon yeh," wailed Oswin, a paw shooting out of the hairy bag to swipe at him.

Cuttlefish roared and held on tighter, despite the sharp pricks from Oswin's claws.

"I'm not sure we'll be able to hold them off!" cried Willow, darting a kick at one of the boys who was trying to pull at her leg, the glowing manacles in his other hand.

The other student with manacles had paused for a moment at the look of fierce revenge in Twist's eyes, but somebody else had bravely stepped forward in an attempt to seize her by the wrist. It was the biggest one, who had a dopey look on his face.

Twist nodded and, as if she were batting off a fly, she managed to fling the boy across the room with a bolt of electrical energy. The others hesitated before coming after her—Twist was obviously very strong—but there were five of them.

In her thunder-voice that made them all shudder, Twist boomed, "SKIRON!"

Suddenly the door burst open with a crash and the great icy-blue wind swept into the classroom.

Twist smiled at it the way one would at a beloved but somewhat naughty child. "Stop them!" she said, pointing to Cuttlefish and the others.

And the wind, which seemed to swell with pride and purpose, lifted the teacher and students into the air and began to spin them like tops. Wasting no time, Willow aimed Whisper at the row of windows at the back of the classroom. Alas, Skiron's force was so strong that Willow and Peg went flying off course and crashed into the wall. Willow winced as she scraped her arm.

Peg inched his way off the broom, fighting against the strong current, and managed to open the window with some difficulty. There were icicles in his dark hair and his lips had turned blue. Willow held on tightly to her broomstick, steering it firmly toward Peg and battling the gale that threatened to suck Whisper into the same spinning vortex as the teacher and the four students. Peg eventually managed to climb back on.

Twist raced toward them at high speed.

"C'mon, Twist!" cried Willow encouragingly. At last, Twist managed to get a grip on the broom. "Skiron—let's get out of here!" she shouted, calling the wind that was having a blast spinning Cuttlefish and the students in the air.

Skiron dropped them in a heap on the ground, then gusted toward Willow, Peg, and Twist. In a second, it had enveloped them all, and they began to whirl inside the deep-blue tornado as it spun out of the window, Peg dangling off the end of the broom by one hand.

Oswin's familiar cries were drowned out somewhat by the

howling wind. "Oh no, oh, me greedy aunt Osbertrude . . . THAT'S ALL THIS FLYIN' STICKS NEEDED . . . A BLIMMIN' TURBO-CHARGE . . . I DON' WANNA DIE AFORE I HAVE THAT STEW!"

If you listened carefully, though, beyond the eerie wail of the wind you could hear the sound of someone else shrieking. Peg clutched on to the broom for dear life, eyes closed tight, while he yelled, "OH WOL! MY MOTHER IS GOING TO KILL ME. . . . SHE SAID TO STAY AWAY FROM WITCHES, NOT RUN AWAY WITH THEM!"

7
The City of Elves

It was early afternoon, and the sun had abandoned its sulk, the sky turning a bright cornflower blue—not that any of them noticed as they flew over the village of Mild at high speed, Peg and Oswin competing in their hollering.

Twist had let Skiron die down now that they were away from the school, but she called out, "We need to get to Lael as quickly as possible. There's something I have to show you, Willow, and we must tell my aunts what happened at the school so they can get the word out."

Willow barely had time to ask her what she meant by "as quickly as possible" before all the air suddenly vanished from her lungs. Skiron had picked up speed, whirling even faster than when they'd left the classroom. Before they knew it, they were shooting through the air so fast everything turned into a blur.

The wind was icy and cold, and from within the hairy green bag Oswin whimpered, "Oh nooooooooooooooooo. I don' feels wells."

Neither did Willow. Ice was forming on the ends of her hair and around her nostrils, and she shivered violently, but she wasn't sure if that was from the cold or from trying desperately not to give in to the nausea.

"I HATE THIS SO MUCH! AAAAAGHHHHH!" yelled Peg. "THIS WILL TEACH ME FOR TRYING TO BE NICE TO NEW PEOPLE!"

They passed streaks of green and blue—forests and lakes that were just blurs to them all—and then, after just moments of being hurtled through the countryside, they arrived outside the tall iron gates of a vast, sprawling city.

And if the world hadn't been spinning so much, they might have stopped to appreciate how beautiful it was. But it was as if they had just climbed off the longest, fastest roller coaster in existence and were now too busy bringing up their breakfasts on a small patch of grass just outside the city walls. Oswin didn't get that far and was sick inside the hairy green bag. Willow and Peg staggered about as they tried and failed to regain their balance. Peg fell over, only to be sick again. There were spots before Willow's eyes.

Twist looked a little uncomfortable and tried to make a joke. "I'm sorry. I forget that not everyone is built to travel by tornado."

No one laughed, and the elf looked uncharacteristically awkward.

Willow fought for air as her world continued to spin. Bending over, clutching onto her knees, she whispered, "It's fine. We'll be all right."

"Speak fer yerself," groaned the kobold as he climbed out of the carpetbag. He had turned a very pale green, his furry ears drooping forward. He zipped up the bag with some distaste, then picked it up, giving a small shudder when it sloshed around somewhat. "This is jes' not my day," he said mournfully.

"You can say that again," said Peg. He dry-heaved once more, his head in his hands.

"Water," said Twist. "That's what you need."

Willow nodded. Water would be good. And for the world to just stop spinning. . . .

Twist nodded. "Follow me."

Willow reluctantly straightened up. And then she blinked, gasping aloud. She had finally clapped eyes on the vast city before them. Despite the fact that she was still shaken from everything that had happened that morning, she couldn't help marveling at the sight. "It's beautiful," she breathed.

The city wound around a large hill, and everything was made out of white marble, from the tall, polished walls that encircled the perimeter to the intricate houses sculpted from it. They appeared to change color, from palest pink to blue and gold, wherever the sun touched them.

"Wow," said Peg, stopping to take it in, like Willow. "I've never seen anything like it."

"I suppose it is pretty," said Twist, cocking her head to one side and looking at the city critically. Her electrified white-blond hair listed ever so slightly to the right as she did so. "I just think of it as home. Funny how you can take things for granted."

Willow nodded, though a part of her wondered how you could ever get used to something like *this*.

They followed Twist toward the city's entrance, and the enormous pair of blue iron gates sprang suddenly apart as they approached, despite the fact that no one was there to operate them.

Willow and Peg gasped.

"It's part of the elfsense," explained Twist as they passed through.

"Elfsense?" asked Willow. She'd heard of it, but never understood it.

Twist nodded. "It's weird—I've never had to explain it to anyone before. Elves are just born with it, you know? We can sense when another elf is nearby, and we sense other things about each other too—like deceit, or when someone is sad."

"You can read each other's minds?" breathed Peg in shock.

Twist laughed, as if that were absurd. "No—it's not like that. It's just the surface stuff really."

"Like thoughts or memories?" asked Willow, thinking of her friend Nolin Sometimes, who, as a forgotten teller, could read other people's memories when he was near them.

"No, it's more about the emotions we feel. We can't tell what another elf is *thinking* exactly, or what might have happened to them, but we'd be able to know how they *felt* about what they were thinking or saying—or sometimes *not* saying . . . Do you know what I mean?"

"Mebbe," said Oswin. "I can always tell when someone is lyings. Fings turn differents colors."

"They do?" said Willow. She knew that Oswin could always spot a lie, just like he could tell when something magical was approaching, but she hadn't known exactly how.

He nodded.

The elf gave him a small smile. "It's a bit like that for us too. We see emotions as colors, though most of the time we sense a mixture of shades, because people tend to feel a mix of things, I suppose."

Willow frowned as she tried to follow. She realized that it made sense: people often experienced a range of emotions at once. Now she could feel a sense of fear that Silas was close to enacting his plan, anxiety for the magical children across Starfell, plus a bit of guilt for running away from her family again. She still felt slightly ill too, and yet also full of wonder at their beautiful surroundings. Emotions were strange, complicated things.

Twist nodded. "But it's why we can't hide things from each other as elves, you see? It's what makes elves so direct at times, and it can make us a bit skeptical of humans, as you're so good at hiding what you feel, even from yourselves."

Willow stared at Twist. She hadn't quite figured out what it was about the elf girl that had unsettled her at first, but now she understood: Twist *was* direct—incredibly so. Initially, Willow had thought that she was just rude. . . . She seemed to say things that perhaps you wouldn't normally voice— like, for example, that the person in front of you seemed "a bit odd." (*Well, to be fair, pots and kettles*, Willow thought.)

Then there was the fact that Twist had flat-out told Willow that she'd come to find her after reading about her in the paper. Most people would have tried to find a way of making that sound a bit less like they were stalking you. . . .

Twist also seemed so capable, so sure of herself—so in charge, despite the fact that she looked like she'd never come into contact with a hairbrush in her life, or an iron. She carried herself as if it was desirable to have hair that electrified around you in a cloud, or clothes that looked like they were put on backward . . . and somehow it worked.

But Willow didn't think this was arrogance. It wasn't like her sister Camille's inflated opinion of herself, or the way Juniper acted as if everyone around her owed her something. Twist didn't appear to think she was better than anyone else or need to make anyone feel less than her—she'd listened to

Peg with just as much respect as she had Willow, and she'd done the same with Oswin. She was simply self-assured, with no pretenses or disguises. She recognized her abilities and didn't bother trying to hide that she was strong and powerful and capable. She saw no reason to make herself smaller just so that others might feel more comfortable or less frightened. Willow wondered how that must feel—to fully accept yourself, even the wild, odd parts.

Good, she suspected.

"Can't believe I've gotten to meet an actual elf," said Peg. "Or visit Lael. So the whole city is made of marble?" His dark skin had lost its ashen appearance at last, and with his restored health had come his restored curiosity.

Twist grinned at him. "I haven't met that many humans before—or a kobold! So this is new for me too."

They all smiled, apart from Oswin, who looked at the carpetbag with a bit of a frown. He wasn't used to walking around in the daylight, but a bag full of sick meant that for once Willow wouldn't have to carry him.

They followed Twist up a long winding lane. Even the streets were marble, though different in hue than the houses and walls—a pale-blue color, threaded very lightly with gold. Here and there were trees and plants in polished marbled pots. While Willow's heart was always moved by the wildness of nature, from the colorful forests of Wisperia to the awe-inspiring beauty of the Cloud Mountains, she found she was just as moved by this city of stone. She soon realized why.

"Marble is sentient, you see, as are crystals and other minerals. They're more alive than other materials such as, say, tin or iron, which we find hard to commune with. Some elves can, but marble and crystal are felt best. You see, marble forms part of the elfsense too—it feels what we feel, and it responds. It's been shaped by thousands of elvish hands and minds over the years, and it knows who we are. It will remember us long after we've gone."

"That's incredible," breathed Willow.

"Completely," said Peg, who looked utterly entranced. "Wow, look at that!" he cried, pointing at a pretty street ahead.

Each of the houses was like a work of art, rounded in shape and topped with a green spire that featured moons or stars. Some of the homes were vast and sprawling while others were smaller, almost cottage-sized, but each one was finely sculpted out of the pale marble. What was really unique was that each home had some kind of intricate, colorful figure mosaicked into the walls as an adornment, and amazingly, they appeared to move as Willow, Twist, and Peg neared. Seamlessly skittering across the walls were elves, woodland animals like fawns and rabbits, and intimidating figures like fire dragons or water nymphs.

"I've never seen houses with moving designs like this before!" said Willow, admiring a life-size winged horse that seemed to gallop across the walls in shades of blue and green and gold, glowing brightly in the afternoon sun.

"Each home has one—it's a family emblem," explained Twist. "It represents the spirit of the people inside. Like this one." She pointed to a large house that had a stag leaping from one wall to the next. He was blue with dark inky eyes, and, like the others, he was able to move effortlessly across the pale marble walls like a shadow. "That's the Swift family. They're known for being strong-willed and loyal to a fault."

Twist then led them up a marble street lined with tall, slim purple trees.

"And up here is where we live—the Howling family," she said, pointing to a three-story marble house with tall blue windows and an unusual spire. The spiral piece of steel was topped with a crystal orb, framed on each side by a half-moon shape.

But it was the home's emblem that made them all gasp. It was the most wondrous they'd seen yet! It was the profile of a beautiful elvish woman with wild hair floating above her head in shades of white, black, red, and brown. Her eyes were closed, and her cheeks were puffed out as she blew several differently hued winds: one that was blue flecked with icy white; an orange one with cascading russet leaves; a green one with swirls of tiny white blossoms; and a golden-yellow one . . . All the colors of the winds wound around the house, billowing over the walls as Willow and Peg stared in wonder.

"It's incredible," breathed Willow, whose heart almost

stopped when the figure turned around to look at them and smiled.

"Oh, me greedy aunt," whispered Oswin.

"She's called Föhn. She represents my aunts and me, and the four winds we tame—the north, south, east, and west—and their accompanying seasons."

Föhn blinked a pair of startling green eyes, and then suddenly her mouth opened wide as if she'd been spooked, and she swept away, taking the four colorful winds with her toward the back of the house.

Twist closed her eyes and winced. Then, shoulders drooping, she turned around very, very slowly.

In the distance, there was the sound of thunder and the crackle of lightning. The sky turned dark and gray. The wind began to howl. A heavy storm was brewing. . . .

"Trolldash," said Twist. "I'd hoped to give you a bit of a breather before *they* came. Sorry."

"OH NOOOOOOO! Oh, me 'orrid aunt, oh, 'tis the worst day EVER!" cried Oswin.

"What is it?" asked Peg and Willow.

But before Twist could answer, they saw exactly what it was.

Three tornadoes whirled toward them, and inside each was an older female elf, eyes wild. From their wide-open mouths, they were spewing thunder and rain, and they looked ready to swallow them whole.

8

The Howling Aunts

Twist sighed as the elves tore toward them. "I would like to apologize in advance for my aunts," she said with a grimace.

The force of the aunts' combined wind magic caused Willow, Peg, and Oswin to stumble backward. Rain was falling on their heads and Oswin was trying and failing to cover his fur with his paws.

"Oh nooo, oh, these 'orrid aunts are worser than the worst!"

Wind whipped around their faces, cold, then warm, like it was confused, and the sound of the three elvish women speaking at once was deafening. Willow could see why Twist looked momentarily cowed.

"Feeling satisfied, are we?" said one of the aunts. She was shorter than the others, and plump, with a bob of yellow hair.

"I CANNOT BELIEVE you sneaked off EVEN after

we specifically forbade it!" said the one with black hair. She was tall and imposing and wore a long black gown and very sensible shoes.

"Not even a hint of REMORSE!" said the aunt with long, curly red hair and a pair of blue spectacles that pointed up at the corners. She wore a satin and chiffon gown studded with tiny diamantés and shoes that were the very opposite of sensible, with high, slim heels.

They must be using elfsense, thought Willow. Despite what Twist said, it seemed a lot like mind reading . . . and it didn't seem at all pleasant.

"I sense A LIE TOO," said the black-haired aunt.

"I sense it too!" the others cried.

Willow and Oswin shared worried looks. . . . What lie?

"It was just a tiny white lie to the teacher. I pretended I had a note," explained Twist. "It's the school's stupid rule that you have to bring a note. . . ."

"So you crept away, even though you knew that it could be wildly dangerous—that you might even risk losing your magic!" said the black-haired elf.

"YES! It was worth the risk. I had to find out if I was right, and I was, SO THERE!"

There were several booms of thunder and flashes of lightning. The winds howled and Skiron dashed into the fray, twisting with the others—a green one fluttering with blossoms, and another that was sun-colored and hazy, like a lake on a hot summer's day.

Willow, Peg, and Oswin clapped their hands over their ears at the high-pitched whirring of the winds.

"What did you say?" hissed the aunt with black hair.

"I said, 'SO THERE'!"

More shouting, thunder, and flashes of lightning ensued.

Skiron gusted into a frenzy, eclipsing all the other winds. Willow, Peg, and Oswin held on to each other for dear life as the force of the swirling tornado blasted them.

"We don't have time for this." Twist's pale eyes narrowed, and she looked even fiercer than usual. "I am going to count to THREE," she declared.

"HOW DARE YOU?" cried the aunt with black hair. "I'll FIZZLE you here and now, child!" A bolt of lightning burst out of her mouth and singed the hem of Twist's dress, making Willow, Oswin, and Peg jump back in fright.

"Oh noooooo," whimpered Oswin as he clutched Willow's leg.

Twist was the only one who hadn't moved an inch. Then she smiled, as if her aunt hadn't just tried to burn her to a crisp. "Well, it was worth a try."

To Willow's absolute shock, the aunt who had made lightning shoot out of her mouth started to laugh—a great, booming, thundering laugh that was almost as scary as the lightning—and the others soon followed suit. The air stilled as the winds, at last, died down.

"Cheeky miss!"

"Chip off the old gale!"

"Count to THREE. HO HO HO!"

"Just like her mother!"

They all suddenly fell silent at this, their faces sad. "Couldn't control her either," said the one with yellow hair, dabbing at her eyes. "Followed her instincts too!"

Everyone's eyes were suddenly misty, including Twist's. "I'm sorry for making you worry, Aunts!" she cried, rushing forward to embrace them.

"Nutters, the lot of 'em. Look wot they did ter me tail," Oswin sniffed.

Willow saw that the tip was singed. She had to swallow a smile. The kobold was indeed having a bad day. "Sorry, Os," she said, giving his head a pat. Showing just how upset he was, he let her.

The aunt that had released a lightning bolt rushed forward to Willow and Peg to introduce herself. "I'm sorry about all this. I'm Tuppence Howling, one of Twist's aunts. I hope I didn't frighten you too much." She held out her index finger and touched it to each of theirs, smiling when a small blue spark came from Willow's.

"You mean when you tried to FRY YOUR NIECE? Not at all," said Peg.

"Don't be silly, boy. If I wanted to fry her, she would just be a puddle of ash. I have perfect control over my bolt-ability." She frowned, her eyes boring into Peg's. "I resent the accusation."

Peg recoiled and Willow felt a stab of sympathy for him.

"Really?" muttered Oswin sarcastically. He turned around to show the elf his backside, where, like a griddled steak, the tip of his tail was smoking. "Burned to a crispid." He glared.

Tuppence's eyes widened. "Oh, um . . . I'm really sorry."

Willow and Peg fought hard not to laugh. Peg didn't win. The kobold glared at the boy, who bit his fist to hide his chuckles.

The aunt then peered more closely at Oswin and gasped. "Why, you're a kobold!"

"Mebbe," said Oswin, glaring at her from between Willow's legs. "Who's askin'?"

"My goodness, you really are. I thought you'd all but died out, I mean apart from—" At Oswin's glower Tuppence broke off and frowned. "Never mind."

Twist introduced the rest of them. "So you've met Tuppence. This is Griselda"—she gestured to the aunt with red hair and glasses—"and Dot." She pointed out the aunt with yellow hair. "Aunts, this is Willow Moss."

"Oh!" they all gasped. "So you found her."

"I did," said Twist.

As Griselda opened her mouth to say something else,

Twist held up a hand. "I know there's a lot to discuss—but right now it can wait. They all need some water and a sit-down. I, er, gave them a lift over. . . ."

"Ah, poor mites. Lost their breakfasts?" asked Dot.

"Every bit," said Twist, who didn't seem all that sorry about it. She turned to Willow, Peg, and Oswin. "Follow me. I'll get you that water, and then we'll tell my aunts about what we found out. Because we're going to need their help."

"More than just ours, if you've been proven right, Twist," said Tuppence.

9
The House That Seemed Alive

WILLOW AND THE others followed after the elvish women as they marched toward the marble house. The wide blue doors flung themselves open.

"*Selia*," said the elves together, and each of the winds stayed outside.

The elvish home was every bit as beautiful inside as out. The hallway was marble too, in shades of palest blue and green.

Willow's own home was cluttered with tables, chairs, and shelves crammed with books, teacups, old potions, and things from her mother's Traveling Fortune Fair. (These included crystal balls, gauzy shawls, and black candles, which people believed helped Raine to commune with the dead. . . . None of them made a difference, but they were all part of the "ambience," as her mum said—or, as Willow privately thought, helped to "drive the price up.")

Unlike Moss Cottage, Howling House was wide, open, and airy, with the occasional gilded table in the corner or plant in a pot, a few of which seemed to be opening their eyes to get a better look at them. There was a large green sofa piled with cushions and, just as Twist was directing them to it, a small marble side table with gold chicken legs came scurrying toward them. It was topped with several glasses of water.

Willow's mouth fell open.

"Thanks, Scratch," said Twist, handing the glasses around.

"That table has feet!" cried Peg.

"Yours don't?" asked Griselda, flicking back her long red curls as she arranged herself on one of the velvet couches, high heels dangling over the side.

"Er, no," said Peg.

"Mmm, humans are strange," said Dot. "I'm not sure I could live in a dead house."

"A dead house?" asked Willow.

Dot paused. "One without thought or feeling. Scratch is part of this place, like the bathrooms or doors, and they all respond to our needs."

"Is it like . . . a charmed house?" Willow asked, thinking of Rubix's star-shaped home, Pimpernell's tower, or even the wizard Holloway's copper boat, *Sudsfarer*.

"Well, yes, in a very crude way," said Tuppence.

At the same moment, Griselda snorted, "Not at all! Charms are a bit vulgar, if you ask me."

"Sisters, don't be rude," said Dot with a motherly sort of smile that revealed the dimples in her round face. She rolled her eyes at Peg and Willow. "It's rather a touchy subject," she confessed. "A charm is a kind of awakening. The witch who performs it searches for the small fragments of soul that exist within the material, lying dormant. The difference with elfsense is that our homes and objects are never forced to awaken—they simply begin to respond out of choice. Do you follow?"

Willow and Peg frowned, and Tuppence tried to explain as Dot hurried off to the kitchen.

"When something is charmed," said Tuppence, "it's cajoled and flattered into doing something it wouldn't usually do."

"So it doesn't want to be charmed?" asked Willow.

"I wouldn't say that," said Griselda, pushing up her rhinestone glasses. "It's a charm because it has found the witch who uses it charming." She grinned and they all grinned back.

"The charmed object doesn't mind, but it isn't exactly behaving naturally," said Tuppence, pushing her sister Griselda's high-heeled feet off the couch and giving her a hard stare.

Griselda gave a dramatic sigh, then sat up straight. "My feet are sore," she complained.

Tuppence raised a dark eyebrow and gave Griselda's heels a pointed look.

Griselda muttered, "It's not always sensible to be sensible, especially when it comes to pretty shoes. . . . Something you'll never understand."

Tuppence turned back to Willow, ignoring her sister. "Elvish marble or crystal, on the other hand, comes alive of its own free will. And, when an elf wants to build a house, they have to wait for the right stone. You can't just go to a quarry or a mine and choose what *you* like."

"You can't?" said Peg, surprised.

"Well, you could, but then the house would never respond to you," said Dot, reappearing with a plate of strange-looking fruit. She was followed closely by Scratch, who was piled high with all manner of vegetable snacks and dips.

"How do you know which is the right marble?" asked Peg.

Dot offered around the plate of weird fruit. "Whirl-hip?" It was bright purple with red seeds, and as Willow bit into hers she gasped. It was sweet and slightly spicy, with an almost cinnamon-and-honey taste.

"When a material like marble or crystal chooses you, it changes color beneath your fingers," Dot said, setting the plate on Scratch's surface. She reached down to touch the marble floor, which began to glow a faint green. "See? That's when you know it wants to be yours too—and that it enjoys its role. Only a house that likes its occupants will anticipate their needs, and help their guests too." Dot gave Scratch a pat, and it wriggled a bit from side to side like a dog wagging its tail.

"Why is Lael made mostly of marble then?" asked Peg. "If other materials can respond the same way?"

"Well, marble is easier to obtain. The vanished kingdom was mostly made of crystal, so I've heard, but nearly all the crystal mines are exhausted now. . . ."

"And iron isn't exactly pretty," added Griselda. Tuppence rolled her eyes, but Griselda shrugged. "What? It's true."

Elf houses seemed incredible. Willow couldn't imagine what it must be like to simply voice a need and have her house try to cater to it. She had a sudden wild vision of a toilet running after her and had to stop herself from laughing out loud. . . . She wasn't sure about *that*.

"Fascinating as all this no doubt is to our guests," interrupted Twist with her customary directness, "they aren't here on a social call. Like I said earlier, Aunts, it's as I feared. The Brothers of Wol have only let magical children into their schools because they plan to strip them of their magic."

10

The Consequences of Magic

Twist's words caused an air of seriousness to descend on the room.

"Oh Wol, no!" cried Tuppence.

"Does he have the elf staff already?" wailed Griselda.

"Has he found the vanished kingdom?" exclaimed Dot.

"No," said Twist, "not yet . . . but that's his plan, I'm sure of it."

"That's what the queen's staff was called? The elf staff?" asked Willow, and Twist nodded.

"What's a staff got to do with anything?" asked Peg, thoroughly confused. "I don't remember Cuttlefish saying anything about that."

"Remember he said that Silas was working on a 'cure'? A way to strip magic from people?" said Twist. "Well, we think we know how he's going to do it—and it involves an ancient staff that once belonged to us elves."

Twist filled Peg in about the long-lost elvish kingdom, the stolen scroll containing the queen's last words, and how, shortly after the theft, Silas amended the treaty to allow mixed schooling.

"And, as we've found out, they're planning to take away children's magic. It all adds up—Silas stole that scroll, and now he's after the staff."

Tuppence looked disturbed. "So this teacher just *told* you that they're planning on removing children's magic?"

They nodded.

Willow produced the small workbook that she'd taken from the school, anticipating moments like this when proof might be needed, and handed it over. The aunts passed it around, each one clutching their chest and gasping as they read what the Brothers of Wol planned to teach children.

"B-but that's ludicrous!" cried Dot.

"And utterly foolish too, on his part—considering that everyone will now know their plan. I mean," Tuppence said, holding up the small book, "why advertise the fact that they want to rip away children's magic? Why tell everyone?"

"Because they is using Gerful chalk," said Oswin.

The aunts gasped.

"We had to break out of the classroom window. The teacher marked the door with the chalk, and if we'd gone that way . . . well," said Willow, clenching her jaw, "we would have been fooled into believing that this was all a good idea."

Dot glared at Twist. "You see now why we didn't want you to go? Look what might have happened! You could have been brainwashed—and taken somewhere to have your magic stolen!"

Twist glared back. "It *is* happening. . . . This is his plan. That's why I needed to go—to team up with Willow, who's been right all along. I'm glad I did, because now there's a chance we can stop him. But we can only do that by helping—not by staying home, not by burying our heads in the sand or pretending everything's all right!"

Dot stared at Twist, then she took a seat, her face downcast. "You're right." She looked at her niece with new respect laced with sadness. "I wish I could keep you safe at home, though."

Twist's eyes softened. "I know that, Aunt Dot."

Willow looked at them. "It wasn't just Gerful chalk our teacher had. He also had manacles that had been magicked. The nonmagical folk have been told that all these things are 'blessings from Wol'—and they seem to believe it. I wonder how many Brothers of Wol even know the truth about Silas, and just how dangerous he really is."

"Hang on," said Peg, standing up. "Were those things really *magic*? And what do you mean, 'the truth about Silas'?"

Willow blew out her cheeks. "Silas is a wizard."

Peg sat back down with a thud. "Now I've heard it all."

"Yew tellings me," said Oswin.

"A wizard?" repeated Peg. Then he looked at them all skeptically. "Are you sure about that? I mean . . . it just doesn't make any sense. AT ALL. The Brothers of Wol are *against* magic. Aren't they trying to 'cure' it?"

"I know it seems that way, but that confusion is what Silas is relying on, so no one suspects him," said Willow. "But it's the truth—Silas was born with magic." She filled them in on everything that she'd discovered. "He was brought up in Wolkana with the Brothers of Wol and didn't know who his parents were. So, when he developed a fizz of magic, he was raised to be ashamed of who he was. They told him to pray for it to be taken away."

Peg wasn't the only one who winced at the idea.

"It wasn't until many years later that he found out that he was the High Master's son, and that his mother was a witch. In fact, he's the nephew of one of the greatest witches alive, Moreg Vaine."

"No!" cried the aunts in shock.

"You can't be serious!" gasped Twist.

Even Peg looked surprised. "Oh, Wol! I've heard of her. . . . Doesn't she pickle children in ginger and have tea parties with the dead?"

"'Tis jes' rubbish mostly," admitted Oswin. "'Cept the tea parties. Thems is real. Though they is not much of a party—more like a visits to a nightmare where yew coulds lose yer soul. We all went, actually," he added brightly.

Peg and the aunts blinked at him.

"Um, anyway," said Willow, who didn't think that now was the time to explain Netherfell to poor Peg, "Silas's mother died when he was a baby, so Moreg left him with his father, the High Master, to be raised by the Brothers of Wol."

"Why on Great Starfell would she have left a baby—who, with a bloodline like the Vaine family, stood a good chance of having magic—with the Brothers of Wol?" cried Dot, who had gone pale.

"Surely she must have known how he'd be raised!" cried Tuppence. "I've always thought of her as shrewd, a few steps ahead, but never . . . cruel."

Willow shook her head, her face flushing slightly as she felt herself prickle with defensiveness. Moreg was many things—practical, quirky, slightly off her rocker, yes . . . but not cruel. Besides, she did nothing, nothing at all, without a reason. However, Willow could understand the aunts' confusion. She had asked Moreg about this herself the last time she'd seen her—before Moreg disappeared.

Willow had opened the cottage door in surprise to find the witch staring back at her—impossibly tall, with the ability, somehow, to make someone's knees decide to take an impromptu holiday.

"Cup of tea?" she'd suggested. It was the same thing the

witch had said to her the first day she'd shown up on Willow's doorstep and decided to change her life forever.

Willow had smiled, then fished out her StoryPass. The dial was currently suggesting a cup of tea too.

Moreg had taken a seat at Willow's scrubbed wooden table, a cup of hethal tea in her hands, and looked at her with eyes like razors. "I know what you're thinking," she'd said.

Willow was startled. There was, after all, a rumor that the witch could read minds—a rumor Willow had tried to ignore.

But Moreg had continued, "Because I've been thinking it too. Ever since we got back from Netherfell, I've been asking myself, why? Why does Silas want to steal everyone's magic? Why does he feel the need to be all-powerful?"

Willow had nodded. "It's like he hates magical people—which doesn't make sense to me, because he's magic himself. After he realized he was lied to by his father, why wouldn't he have just come over to our side?"

Moreg looked at the floor. "I think because it happened too late. They'd already convinced him that magic was unnatural, that it was a curse. . . . And that's my fault. I never would have placed him there if I'd known what was going to happen."

"So, erm, why *did* you leave Silas with the Brothers?"

"When I discovered that my sister had died, I should have raised her baby myself. . . . And I would have. But I had a vision—I saw things changing. I saw Silas with the Brothers, as a new leader. I saw him wielding *magic*. I thought that I was seeing a happy vision of the future, Willow . . . not this. Never this. I hope you'll believe me."

"Of course I do," Willow had cried.

"You see, I made the mistake of projecting my own hopes into the visions I was having. I believed, naively, that if the High Master realized that his own son had magic, it might put an end to this animosity between the communities. That if he could see that there was nothing to be afraid of, it would pave the way for peace. I thought perhaps we were halfway there, considering he'd already fallen for my sister—but, of course, it didn't work that way.

"The High Master liked Molsa *in spite* of the fact that she was a witch. He wished that she didn't have that 'affliction,' and Silas was raised to be ashamed of that part of himself— as if it were something he could simply wish away. When Silas found out that he was my nephew, and that I didn't take him in—didn't spare him that pain and suffering—well, I think he felt rejected not just by me, but by the entire magical community.

"He has become so twisted. He knows he's been lied to, yet he still believes what he's been taught—that magic is unnatural. But then, of course, he found out the hidden truth about Wol—that the "god" they'd worshipped all along was in fact a wizard too, like him. So Silas decided to do what Wol tried and failed to achieve—to rid every last living creature within Starfell of magic, and in the process take all that magic for himself. To become something else, something more—like a god.

"If I've learned one thing about human nature, Willow, it's that we all see the world though our own imperfect lens—myself included—and so a seer's vision of the future is clouded by that, becoming imperfect and subjective too. I regret my decision to give up Silas, but I did what I thought best at the time. In life, we must move forward, looking back only to help navigate the way. What we must do now is stop him."

Before Moreg had left, the witch's eyes had turned white for a moment as she experienced a vision, then back to black. She'd said, "You might want to fish that whistle out from under your bed. Who knows when you'll need to summon a troll army?"

Willow had blinked. She'd forgotten all about the troll whistle. She'd been given it some time ago by the troll chief while trying to find the missing Tuesday.

It had now been months since Willow had seen Moreg, but she had carried the troll whistle in her bag ever since.

Willow explained everything that Moreg had told her. Even now, after all this time, after Moreg hadn't come forward to clear Willow's name, Willow still believed in her.

"This can't be right!" said Peg, standing up again, his hands in his hair. "Someone would have known. Someone would have stopped him!"

"We've tried—but look at the trouble he's gone to," Willow said. "Remember the chalk! It's like no one can think for themselves, so he's just getting away with it. . . . But he won't. Not if we stop him, and we will somehow."

Peg shook his head. "I feel like my head's spinning. This is a . . . lot to take in."

Dot came forward and touched his arm. "We could take you home. Would you like that?"

Peg looked from Willow to Twist and the aunts, then shook his head slowly. "No. I don't know. . . . This is scary, I won't lie. But, if I went home, I couldn't pretend that this was okay . . . Like Twist said, I feel like I should do what I can. I may not have magic, but maybe I can help somehow."

"If you're sure?" asked Twist.

Peg nodded. "I'm good at one thing—puzzles, logic. It might help."

Willow nodded, remembering that it was Peg who'd figured out that the Gerful chalk wasn't just for the magical children—that it would be used on everyone. "Practical makes perfect," she said, using one of Moreg's favorite phrases.

Peg cocked his head to the side, confused. But the elves all nodded.

"Oh yes," said Tuppence. "Solving something without

magic—well, that's sometimes the hardest and most valuable form of power there is." She stood up, taking the booklet that Willow had shown them. "I'll take this, if you don't mind. I think we'll be doing the rounds with it, trying to get the word out to the magical community."

"I'll go to Dwarf Territory. If the Brothers are using Gerful chalk, we'll need dwarfish dust. It protects against mind control," explained Griselda.

"Good thinking," said Dot. "I'll go with Tuppence, and you lot can come with us."

"No," said Twist. "I have to show Willow the mural. Then I need her to try and find the vanished kingdom!"

Pandemonium ensued.

At the aunts' cries, their winds whipped inside the house to investigate, stirring up a trail of leaves, blossoms, and ice. It began to rain, then snow, then autumn leaves fell from nowhere, followed by a warm summer breeze—all in seconds.

"It's all right, Skiron!" cried Twist.

The aunts called out to their own winds too, each giving the command for them to scatter outside again: "*Selia!*"

Peg wrung out his wet shirt, muttering, "I don't know how I'll ever explain any of this."

"You can't ask Willow to summon a whole kingdom! It would be madness—you don't know what mayhem you could cause!" cried Griselda.

"An earthquake!" gasped Dot.

"Or an avalanche, or a tsunami . . . People could die!" breathed Tuppence.

"I didn't think of that," said Twist, who looked stricken.

Willow had to admit that very, very distantly a tiny pebble-like idea had been rolling around in the back of her mind. She'd been wondering about whether it would be possible to simply *find* the kingdom using her magic . . . considering that it *was* lost.

But, thankfully, she had learned one lesson from trying to find a missing day: magic wasn't something you could simply play with. There were consequences to forcing something to reappear.

"I agree," said Willow. "I think if I were to bring the kingdom back—and I'm not saying for sure I *can*—we'd need to first know where it's been this whole time, if that makes sense. You can't just summon something back and not expect there to be consequences. Things don't vanish to nowhere—they're always *somewhere*, and you've got to negotiate how you bring them back or things could go . . . wrong. Catastrophically wrong. For example, if a lost book is under someone's bed, buried under a pile of socks, it won't matter too much if I summon it. Maybe the sock pile will just rearrange itself a bit. But who *knows* what could happen if I summon a whole kingdom?"

Twist's and Peg's eyes were huge.

"I hadn't thought of that," admitted Twist.

"Well, at least Willow has," said Tuppence. "That's reassuring."

Willow nodded, but she didn't explain that she'd learned that lesson the hard way. . . . When she'd been on the verge of summoning back the missing day with her magic, Moreg had stopped her just in time. Apparently, if she'd done it, she could have unraveled the fabric of Starfell itself—and *ended the world*.

Sometimes it was best to quit while you were ahead, especially when people were starting to think you were smart.

Then Willow had a new thought. . . . She closed her eyes for a moment and raised her hands to the sky.

"What are you doing?" cried Peg. "You just said—"

Willow opened one eye. "That I couldn't summon a whole *kingdom* without consequences, yes. But a staff? Well, that might not be so bad."

"Oh! Good thinking!" cried Dot.

"Go on then," said Tuppence.

Willow closed her eyes and tried to focus. With her particular skill, she was used to having an audience, as her customers lined up outside the cottage door every morning looking for her help to locate their missing possessions. But there wasn't usually so much *pressure*.

She took a deep breath, put Twist and her aunts out of her mind, and began to search.

There was something there, but the more she pulled, the

more she met resistance. She tried once more—and was suddenly pushed back with such force it was as if she'd touched an electric current. She landed spread-eagled on the marble floor, and a deluge of briny water and several lengths of seaweed fell from nowhere and landed in her still-outstretched hands.

Willow opened her eyes and sighed, looking like a drowned rat. "Well, it was worth a try. It's under some kind of heavy protection."

Tuppence and the aunts nodded. "That makes sense," sighed Griselda.

There was a skittering sound as Scratch came hurrying toward Willow with a towel, a dustpan and brush, and a mophead on its tabletop.

"Thanks," Willow said, taking the towel. Scratch began sweeping up the scattered leaves from the aunts' magic, and then quickly mopped the floor. She was bemused when afterward it began picking seaweed from her hair with its chicken-like feet. When it had finished, it edged toward Oswin, who scurried out of its way, the carpetbag in his arms. The table drummed a foot as if it were impatient, and then backed away.

"Well, we learned one thing from that at least," said Willow.

"Wot?" asked Oswin. "Tables can use their feet to combs 'air?"

She grinned. "Not that. Wherever the staff is, it's underwater, and protected, which means I don't think Silas has it yet."

They all breathed a sigh of relief. That *was* good news.

"But there's a lot riding on that 'yet,'" said Tuppence, standing up. "We don't have time to lose. There must be hundreds of scared children out there and we need to act quickly." She put her hands on Twist's shoulders. "You were right—and we should have trusted your instincts. But please, please be careful."

Twist nodded. "We will."

Griselda stood too, wincing in her high heels. "Send a raven if you need us."

Tuppence looked at her. "Oh, for Wol's sake! Change your shoes, you vain elf."

Griselda straightened her long, beautiful gown and pushed up her rhinestone spectacles. "I'd rather make an impression," she said, then winked at the girls.

Willow couldn't help grinning back.

They watched the aunts as they departed through the open door in their whirling tornadoes of gold, orange, and green, and then Twist turned to Willow.

"Come on—I need to show you the wall. It's trying to tell me something . . . I just don't know what."

11

The Mural

"A WALL IS trying to tell you something?" Peg frowned, then shook his head. "Actually, after everything I've seen today—including moving pictures on houses and elves who can practically read minds, command winds, and make lightning come out of their mouths—well, sure. Why not? Why wouldn't a wall be talking to you?"

They all started to laugh as they headed out of Howling House.

"It is a bit mad," admitted Willow. "I've never seen anything like it either."

Peg laughed even harder. "And you're magic!" Which set them all off again.

When they had at last recovered, Twist shook her head and gave a wry grin. "I meant the mural. It's on a wall in the city center."

"Oh," said Willow, remembering that Twist had said something about a mural earlier. "What is this mural?"

"It's how I worked out the secret about Queen Almefeira's staff—the fact that it could take away magic. You see, it's not just *any* old mural. It was created in marble a thousand years ago by the descendants of the queen, soon after the old kingdom vanished. You know how elvish marble will only respond to the one family it chooses?"

They nodded.

"Well, this mural responded to *me*."

Willow was frowning, not quite putting the two facts together, but Peg got there first.

His mouth fell open as he gasped, "You're royalty! It responds to you because you're the queen's family too?"

Oswin's and Willow's mouths also flew open in shock.

"Wot?" cried Oswin.

Twist nodded but waggled her hand in a "sort of" motion. "Yes. But very, very distantly. I mean, it's not recognized today. No one's going to bow when any of us go past—elves are governed by an elected body nowadays. But, yes, my aunts and I are elvish royalty *technically*."

"Wow," said Willow.

"I'll say," agreed Peg.

There was a sound of scrabbling feet behind them, and they turned to find that Scratch the table had followed them outside. It started circling Oswin in a very determined way, as the kobold yelped, "Oi, stop that! Get away from me."

But the table ignored him and made a dash for the hairy green bag at Oswin's side. It managed to slide the bag onto its tabletop and scurry quickly away on its long chicken legs, back inside Howling House.

"Oi! Yew cumberworld, that's mine! Come back!" hissed Oswin.

"Don't worry. He's just going to clean it," said Twist. "He'll bring it back. Scratch has a heightened sense of smell." Then she gave a wry smile. "For something without a nose."

"I'm not sure you need a heightened sense of smell for . . . you know," said Peg, cocking a head in Oswin's direction.

The kobold turned to give him a highly affronted look, which lasted for much longer than was strictly necessary. Willow made no comment.

"We should go," pressed Twist.

Oswin grumbled, "Takin' fings from a kobold. No respect . . . I is a fearsome monster. . . ."

Twist stared at Oswin pointedly with those piercing eyes of hers. "Are you quite finished?"

Oswin blinked and stopped his grumbling at once, going to hide behind Willow's legs.

Willow thought she could stand to learn that trick, especially at night when she was trying to sleep.

"Your bag should be ready when we come back," Twist told the kobold. "Come on."

They followed her into the city as the sun began to set and the sky above turned pink and apricot. Outside, lamps fixed into the marble walls began to glow amber as they walked by, sensing them before they even approached.

They followed a winding marble street, where they could see elves sitting outside cafés, drinking wine, while others leaned against their balconies, talking and laughing. Many of them waved at Twist as she went by.

They passed bookshops where elves were reading in big comfy chairs, cups of tea balanced on their knees.

There was a large outdoor theater where some elves were putting on a play, dressed up as strange woodland creatures. Beautiful music was being played by a Mementon—a creature with skin made of wood, whose kind were known to be the best broom makers in Starfell. This one was tall with russet-colored hair and long nails, and he was playing what looked like a broom-guitar beneath the shade of a vast purple tree that had been strung with fairy lights.

It all seemed so alive to Willow, who'd grown up in a village where, unless it was a festival like Elth Night or harvest time, all outdoor activities faded as soon as the day did.

Twist took them to the heart of the city, where they entered a walled garden that smelled of roses and jasmine. The marble walls lit up as they entered, casting a rosy hue that bathed them in pink candlelight.

In the center of the garden was a large fountain, featuring

an elvish woman made of copper that had turned green over the years. Soft music played in the fountain, and the spray filtered down into a large pond covered in pink and white lily pads.

It was beautiful.

"The mural is here," said Twist, leading them to the back of the garden.

The mural was massive, covering every inch of the enormous wall at the back, and it was extraordinary. Willow could only imagine the time and incredible skill something like this must have taken to create. It was a huge mosaic made up of small tiles in shades of rich turquoise, green, silver, pink, and gold, though Willow noticed that many of the tiles were missing.

The mural depicted the elvish queen standing in a forest clearing. She was tall, with long midnight-black hair that had been arranged in a strange, intricate style. It was gathered back from the crown of her head and sectioned in three big loops tied with brass rings, while the remaining hair fell over her shoulder, all the way to her waist.

Her clothing was very different from what elves seemed to wear nowadays. The dress was beautiful, long and gathered, with loose, wide sleeves, and was tied with a sash at the waist. On her feet were simple leather shoes that were laced up her calves with ribbons. There were chips and cracks along the queen's arms, where tiles had fallen off.

All around her were hundreds of elves of all ages, staring up at her as she pointed in the distance with a spiral staff. At the end of the staff was a half-circle shape, but they couldn't make out the rest because a cluster of marble tiles were missing.

"It's Queen Almefeira, pointing the way to the elves' new home," whispered Twist. "With the elf staff."

"She sent them away?" asked Peg.

"Yes. Before Llandunia disappeared, the queen urged her people to leave and build a new city. And one of their first tasks when they were founding Lael was to create this mural. . . . The work was carried out only by her family."

"No servants or anything? That's kind of weird for royalty, isn't it?" asked Peg.

"It's because of the marble. Like I said before, the marble will choose you. While the city's walls and streets will remember us all, only the marble that chooses you will respond to you."

"So . . . how has the mural responded to you?" asked Willow.

"Come, I'll show you," said Twist.

She moved closer to the wall, held out her hands, and touched the mosaic.

Like it had back in the elves' home, the marble started to glow beneath her fingers, and then the image began to shift, coming alive, like the emblems on the houses. But this was so much more than even that. This was a hidden story.

In the center of the mural was a beautiful crystal city, surrounded by a shimmering lake. A red dragon flew over it, and the marble tiles changed from blue to pink to show the sun beginning to set. In the sky were Starfell's two moons and, here and there, between missing marble tiles, was a smattering of stars.

Then suddenly the queen was alone in the forest clearing. She turned, and it was as if she were looking right at them, as if she were trying to show them something.

As she moved the spiral staff, it was no longer obscured by the patch of missing tiles and they could see it clearly for the first time: at the end a white orb was suspended by magic, framed on each side by a half-moon shape. One was depicted in gold, the other in iron gray. It was just like the spire on top of Howling House, Willow realized.

The queen twisted the gold half-moon toward her, and the crystal orb started to glow with a bright golden light. She then took the staff and pointed the golden light at a small fluffy hare that was hurrying past. The hare paused, and then golden wings suddenly appeared at its shoulders, and it started to fly.

"That's amazing!" cried Willow and Peg as the hare flitted here and there between missing marble tiles.

The queen adjusted the staff again, this time twisting the dark half-moon. With that, the crystal changed color, becoming a deep black onyx. She pointed the staff once more at the flying hare. With a bolt of darkness, its golden wings disappeared and the hare fell to the ground. It suddenly appeared wasted and thin, like it was sick . . . like it had aged in an instant.

Then the mural changed back, becoming inanimate once more.

"That's the elf staff," breathed Willow.

"Yes," said Twist. "Most elves know the legend—that once there was a great elvish queen with a powerful staff that could give the gift of magic. But I don't think any elves knew that it could take magic away too. I think that was kept a secret—because if that knowledge fell into the wrong hands . . . it could be the end of magical folk.

"Queen Almefeira hid the truth so that only her descendants would find out. But I think, as time passed by, it was sort of forgotten—perhaps a keeper of the secret died before she could pass it on to the next generation. We knew our family made the mural, but I don't think any of us really thought about whether it would respond to our touch. It was only when I watched a play recently about the history of Lael, and it showed the royal family creating the mural, that I began to wonder about the marble.

"It felt like a way to connect to the past—which seemed important, because so many strange things have been happening that have odd links to history. The Brothers of Wol are growing more powerful and doing things they did years ago, like binding witches with manacles, or creating more

Forbidden areas to separate magical folk from the rest of the population. . . . So I came here to explore, and I discovered this!"

Willow nodded. "Yet somehow Silas has found out too," she said. "When I was in Netherfell, I learned that he'd uncovered the secret method used by Wol in the Long War to strip people of their magic. I bet it was the elf staff."

"It must've been," agreed Twist.

Peg nodded. "And he's stolen the scroll so he can use its message to find the lost kingdom. But if that does happen— and he gets the staff—will people . . . die?"

"Yes," said Willow. "This is bound to cause another war, and Silas will stop at nothing to win it. If he succeeds, magic will be ripped out of every corner of Starfell, and every person and creature. . . ."

Peg's eyes grew wide with fear. "And it looks as if it can be more dangerous than just losing an ability. Like that hare. It was fine when it was given magic, but when the magic was taken away . . . it was as if it aged, as if the queen took something else too."

Willow paled. "It was like part of its soul was taken."

They stared at each other in horror.

"We can't let Silas get the staff," said Peg.

They nodded, eyes wide.

It was now more important than ever to stop him.

12

Written in the Stars

"Wait, Twist, didn't you say you thought the mural was trying to tell you something else, and you didn't know what?" said Peg.

"Yes," said Twist. "I can feel it through elfsense. I think it could be connected to the missing tiles. Maybe, if it was fully restored, it would tell us something more."

Willow nodded. She'd been wondering the same thing. "I'll try to find them," she said. She closed her eyes and concentrated, then held her hand to the sky. A moment later, a dozen pieces of colored tile rained down at their feet.

They stared at them for a moment. Peg scratched his head and said, "I suppose we try and match the different colored tiles to the picture in the mural—like a puzzle?"

Willow nodded. "That makes sense."

"This should go here," said Twist, holding up a green tile

and placing it in a missing section in the forest scene. There was a faint glow, like a guttering candle, and then the tile fell back off into her hands. "Oh!" she cried. "How can we make it stick?"

Oswin padded closer. "Give it 'ere," he suggested.

The elf handed him the tile, a puzzled look on her face. He gave the back of the tile a lick, then passed it over with an air of nonchalance.

Twist reluctantly took it from him, pulling a face. "Ugh. It's so sticky."

"That wos the ideas," said Oswin, rolling his eyes. "Kobold spittles is a bit like glues."

Twist placed the tile in the empty space, and they watched in amazement as it fitted like a glove, held firmly in place by Oswin's saliva. It began to glow, changing from green to faintly pink—the elfsense was working.

"Brilliant!" cried Twist.

"I didn't know your . . . erm, saliva could do that," said Willow, staring at the kobold in astonishment.

He looked at her in surprise. "Why do you fink the Flossy Mistress always used ter tell me, "Get out of here, kobold, lickety-spit!"?"

It was true. Granny Flossy had said that to him. A lot.

Willow, Twist, and Peg shared a look that fortunately the kobold missed.

"'Cos she wanted me ter seals up the cracks and fings in the walls, yew see?"

"O-*kay*," said Willow, deciding not to let Oswin in on the fact that Granny Flossy had meant for him to leave the room pronto so she could brew her potions in peace—without him complaining that the room smelled funny or hiding behind furniture and warning Willow that things were likely to explode (which they were).

They got to work, color-matching tiles. Oswin licked each one before it was put in place, and then they were left with just three for the very top of the mural.

"We'll have to climb on each other's shoulders, I think," said Peg.

Twist nodded. "I'll go at the bottom. I'm stronger than the pair of you." They stared at her in surprise, and she said, "Oh, sorry—the direct thing, yes. Well, it's true. To withstand storms and the like, elf bones are a bit like marble. . . ." And then she stomped a foot down hard. For just a second it looked like she was having a temper tantrum, but it turned out to be a display of strength, as she'd left behind a sizable dent in the ground. "See?"

"Wow!" said Peg. "I mean, you don't look that strong." Then he blushed. "I mean . . . you just look like a normal, erm, girl."

Twist shrugged. "I know. Anyway, climb on," she said,

kneeling down so that Peg could clamber onto her shoulders. Then she held out a hand so that Willow could use it as a ledge to climb on top of Peg.

Swaying slightly on Peg's shoulders, her heart in her throat, Willow managed to place two tiles, but was still just a few inches too short to reach the top of the mural for the very last one. So Oswin scrambled up their pyramid to stick it in place, giving it an extra lick for good measure.

Twist placed her hands on the completed mural, which began to glow—just as Peg started to lose his balance and they all began to topple off. . . .

"Skiron!" cried Twist. "Catch them!"

And the wintry wind gusted itself up around them and broke their fall, before releasing them gently onto the ground.

"Th-thanks," said Willow, teeth chattering from the sudden cold. Then she looked up and gazed openmouthed at the mural.

The colors had intensified and the scene looked sharper now, more focused. They all stared in astonishment.

Willow scanned it for any clues. "Do you see anything new?"

Despite how much clearer the image had become, and the fact that the queen's hand and the staff were now filled in, it didn't seem to give them any information they didn't already have. They could see the dragon more clearly as it flew, along with the crystal city shimmering in the distance.

Above it the sky was fading from dusk to night.

"Not really—just more stars in the sky," said Twist with a frown. "And the dragon's long feathery body."

Peg was the one to exclaim in shock. "There is something else!"

"What?" asked Twist and Willow, turning to him in surprise.

"There! Can't you see it? That string of stars there." He pointed and they looked, frowning. "Have either of you seen that constellation before? It looks almost like a flying turtle."

Twist, Willow, and Oswin shook their heads and shared puzzled looks, not getting Peg's excitement.

"Well," said Peg, "many people still navigate by the stars—their position in the sky can let you know where you are, and where to go. You can see different constellations from different parts of Starfell—for example, from Grinfog you can see the old hag and the man who lost his shoe, as well as the big dinner party. . . ." At their bemused looks, he explained, "I'm really into astronomy, and I know all of the constellations of Starfell today—but I don't recognize that one!"

He seemed thrilled about it, and Oswin muttered, "Imagines getting exciterites 'cos yew don' know somefings."

"It *is* exciting, though," said Peg, staring up at the mural, eyes alight. "The positions of stars can change over time, so this must be a constellation that existed a thousand years ago.

If we can find out what that constellation is, and where it could be seen from, we'd have a good chance of finding out where *the lost kingdom* was!"

Willow's mouth fell open. "Peg, you're a genius! If we knew where it used to be, I *might* be able to go there and summon it back—if it was safe. . . ." She had visions of a city being split apart as the lost kingdom burst in somewhere it wouldn't fit. . . .

Twist looked just as amazed. "How on Starfell did you know that?"

"School can sometimes be useful," Peg admitted. "You know, when your teachers aren't trying to brainwash you or steal your magic."

They all laughed.

"One thing I noticed is that the moons are close together in this mural, unlike today," said Twist. "Do you think that, when the kingdom vanished, it made them split apart?"

"Maybe," said Peg. "It's like what you were saying, Willow—about how magic can't just make things disappear and reappear without consequences. Maybe the position of the moons was one of them."

"Maybe," she agreed.

"Anyway, what we'll need are some really ancient star charts," said Peg, but then he faltered. "But those might be hard to find."

To their surprise, Twist grinned. "Here? Not on your elf!

History keeps this city running. I know just where we need to go." At their looks of confusion, she said, "The Luminary. If anyone knows about stars and charts, it's the lumieres."

"Oh nooo! Oh, me 'orrid aunt, do all roads lead to eel?" cried Oswin. "Not 'em light-bending cumberworlds!"

Something had changed.

A goose flew past, a second too late. The wind changed direction. The trees shifted their roots.

The witch looked behind her and saw, once again . . . the ghost hare.

It always seemed to appear whenever she thought of going back.

A raven cried overhead, and she raised her hand to the sky. The bird began to fly toward her, one of its wings dark blue and made of what looked like smoke and shadow.

Then, before her eyes, the raven changed into the shape of a young boy.

"Moreg," he greeted her.

The witch nodded at him. "Greetings, Sprig."

They stared at each other for some time. The renewed trust between them was fragile.

"I came looking for you."

"Yes," she said simply.

"Something is wrong. People are acting strangely . . . Willow is—" he began.

"Is stepping into something dangerous—I know."

He looked surprised. "I was going to say that Willow is the only one daring to go against the Enchancil. If she's in danger, aren't you going to go and help? No one's seen you for months."

Moreg's face looked full of regret. "Every time I take a step toward her, it changes. . . ." She tried to explain. "The course . . . falters."

"So you're going to do nothing at all?"

"Sometimes that's what is required," she replied, before walking away.

Sprig looked on as she walked, his dark eyes full of confusion.

There was a cry, and he was gone, flying once more against the darkening sky.

13
Gandolfo's Circus of Wonders

"We'll take a portal walk to the Luminary—it'll be quicker," said Twist.

"A portal walk?" asked Peg. "What's that?"

"I'll show you," Twist said, and they followed her out of the walled garden to a busy square. Here neat lines of elves were lining up. Ahead they could see signposts that read:

The Luminary—gold walk

The Green River—green walk

Gandolfo's Circus of Wonders—blue walk

Each sign pointed toward a specific colored lane.

"You want to keep to the white marble till we're able to take our chosen lane and pop out at our destination," Twist said, leading them up the marble street, which was crowded with elves and a few Mementons. "There used to just be portal station points, but they got too crowded so they made whole streets into portals. It helps with the flow of traffic," she explained. Up ahead, they could see a thick ribbon of yellow alongside another of blue.

"Excuse me, we're in a hurry! The show is starting," said a tall elvish couple in dazzling robes who were bustling past.

Peg jumped out of their way and onto a blue lane, just as Twist cried, "Peg, no!"

He turned around to look at her in surprise, and then vanished into thin air.

"Oh no!" cried Willow.

"He's taken the portal walk to Gandolfo's Circus! Come on," said Twist, dashing toward the blue lane. Willow followed. Before she could even ask any questions, there was a whooshing sensation and she felt herself being pulled away from the square. Seconds later, she was standing somewhere else entirely.

Ahead of her stood a giant red-and-white striped tent, and above it thousands of tiny multicolored stars that formed the words "Gandolfo's Circus of Wonders" lit up the sky. The atmosphere was electric and the crowds were enormous. She couldn't see Twist or Peg.

Oswin skittered up her leg and into her arms. "Oh, me

'orrid aunt!" he cried as people jostled past them, tickets in hand, ready to join a very long line that snaked around the portal walk.

Willow's heart started to thud, and she let out a small scream when someone grabbed her elbow.

"It's only me," said Twist. "Sorry, someone thought it was a good idea to try pushing me out of the way."

To Twist's left, Willow saw a tall elvish man who looked as if he'd put his clothes on backward and his fingers into an electrical socket. He walked quickly past, not meeting Twist's eyes.

She, however, stared at him. "Ashamed, eh? Yep—you should be for shoving over a little girl." Then she looked at Willow and grinned. "Not that anyone would call me that."

Willow smiled. "They wouldn't dare."

Twist looked around. "Have you seen Peg?" she asked.

"No," said Willow, just as a large animal trumpeted behind them.

They turned to see an elephant topped by an acrobat. She was doing an impressive act on the animal's back as it slowly moved toward the enormous tent.

"Oh Wol," breathed Twist. "I should have explained better to Peg that the colorful lanes were portals to other places. I keep forgetting that he doesn't know much about magic! Come on." She grabbed Willow's hand and elbowed her way out of the line.

They moved through the crowds, calling Peg's name as they passed other circus performers, who were doing tricks to entertain the waiting crowds. There were card tricks, and jugglers, and a man who shifted into the shape of the person he was standing next to, making the customers laugh nervously as he did silly things while looking like them. There were winged monkeys who did a kind of aerial dance while screeching at each other, and a tall, beautiful midnight-skinned woman, who had horns on either side of her head like a ram, was dancing with what looked like a ribbon of light.

It was incredible.

There were stalls selling food, from mouth-watering sausages to sticky lemon cakes. There were bubbles of all shapes and sizes floating around a colorful stall, and someone called out, "Sip a bubble, taste the wonder. . . ."

"He could be anywhere! I've got a better idea. This way," Willow said, pulling Twist to the back of a stall where someone was selling animals made from clouds.

"Lookin' cost you nuttin', but if you touchies, you paysies," said an old woman, who was knitting bits of cloud into the shape of a winged monkey.

They nodded.

She looked at Oswin, then gave him a gummy smile. "Eh, that's a funny-lookin' cat. . . ."

The kobold glared at her. "I is not a—"

"Not now, Oswin. I need to focus," said Willow, closing her eyes as the kobold continued to glare at the old woman. She just grinned back and, needles clicking, started to fashion a piece of cloud into a furry cat.

"What are you doing?" Twist asked Willow.

"Finding him the old-fashioned way," said Willow, holding out her hand to the sky.

A moment later, Peg appeared in a heap on the ground. He was covered in glitter and there was a sausage in his mouth—which landed in the dirt, to his dismay.

"Wha—?" he cried. "I was just about to see the Crystal Peligraine!"

"Sorry," said Willow, who assumed that was some kind of circus act. "We were worried about you."

Peg stood up, dusting himself off, and admitted, "Well, it *was* a bit scary. One minute I was with you, the next I was here—at a circus!" His eyes were bright. "Absolutely wild! Never seen so many strange things. . . ."

"Never been ter the circus before?" asked the old woman. "Need some tickets?" Magically, four red tickets appeared in the air above their heads.

"Sorry, we don't have time," said Willow.

Peg looked a little disappointed, and the old woman said, "Fer half a spurgle, you can have a memento of yer cat."

"Go on then," said Peg, handing over the money and

taking a cloud balloon that looked just like Oswin, fur standing on end and everything.

The kobold turned a blood-orange color in his rage, and the old woman looked at him and said, "Word ter the wise, kobold: there's no shame in being who you is."

Smoke curled off Oswin's ears as he began to hiss, "But I is not . . ."

"A cat, no, but are yeh gon' let that rule yer life forever? You looks like one. 'Tisn't a bad thing, is it? Mebbe you could use that to yer advantage someday. Think about it."

Which was when Oswin exploded.

Luckily, no damage was done.

"Sorry," said Willow, but the old woman just shrugged and carried on knitting.

"Advice is fer free. 'Sides, he probably needed to get it out of his system."

Willow looked at Oswin after he'd calmed down. He did look better for his explosion.

"Let's get out of here," said Twist.

Willow, Peg, and Oswin followed her away from the crowds to the right portal walk, the yellow one, and they jumped onto it together.

After the excitement of the circus, it was a relief to be away from all the crowds, noise, sights, and smells. This new part of the city was quiet. A treelined canal path led toward a large marble structure at the edge of the city that was shaped like a giant crescent moon and topped with a smattering of stars. The whole building glowed a faint greenish blue.

"It was built to reflect Jezelboob, the first moon," explained Twist. At first, Willow and Peg didn't quite understand, until she pointed and said, "Watch."

A cloud passed over the real moon above, and the building changed color too, becoming shadowed and gray.

"That's amazing," said Peg. "Is that what they do here? Study the stars and moons?"

"Yes, and all sources of light. The lumieres work with light energy, harnessing it and shaping it."

Peg's mouth flew open. "You can do that?"

"Me? No." She held up her hands. "You need lumiere blood to be able to handle light. They're elvish, but also something more."

Willow thought of the Mementons, the broom makers, who were part elf, art spirrot, and distantly human. "Are they like the Mementons?" she asked.

"A little. You'll see."

"Mementons is even worser," whispered Oswin. "'Cept they don' eat humans."

"Eat humans?" echoed Peg, letting go of his kobold-cloud in shock. It drifted away from his fingers toward the sky.

"Not for centuries," reassured Willow.

"You've met lumieres before?" Twist asked Oswin.

"Yeh," he groaned. "Still got the scars."

That doesn't exactly sound encouraging, thought Willow.

"The entrance is here," explained Twist, leading them up a set of stairs at the side of the crescent-shaped building.

Unfortunately, a sign on the door said:

CLOUDED MOON BREAK, BACK AFTER THE FOG

Helpfully, there was a bright display written in moon-glow with the various moon phases and activities.

First Crescent: Now   *Last Crescent: 40 days*
New Moon: 30 days   *Greening (full) Moon—23 days*
Eclipse: 276 days   *Fog: to clear at midnight*

"Ah," said Twist. "Well, we could grab something to eat while we wait?"

At Twist's words, as if on cue, Oswin's and Peg's stomachs began to growl.

She grinned. "Come on," she said, and led them back down the steps.

Twist took them up a street that ran alongside a winding canal full of curved glass boats. Lights began to glow in lanterns set along the canal path as they walked by.

"The lumieres live in boats made of glass because they don't want to miss any changes to the stars or moons," Twist explained as they passed one that was strung with strange wind-chime ornaments made of glass that tinkled in the breeze.

They could just see the outline of someone sitting on the roof of the boat, gazing up at the clouded sky above. The figure was playing a lively tune on a strange-looking brass instrument with strings that made a sound like a banjo.

Twist led the others to a small café with tables and chairs that overlooked the canal. The place was full of life, with elves chatting, laughing, and eating together.

Willow, Twist, Peg, and Oswin sat at a table outside, next to a large ash tree. Skiron started gusting through the air, and several of the customers began to complain of the cold, with one or two of them shooting Twist a pointed look—which she shot straight back.

"You know, Dot never gets dirty looks when her wind gets a bit overexcited," she grumbled. "Must be nice to tame a warm westerly wind."

A waiter came to take their orders, and they enjoyed several courses—nut and leek soup, nettle pie, and chocolate cake with fern nuts and blue cherries.

"I feels like a kobold again," said Oswin, patting his tummy. "All I 'ad to eats today was a sandwish wiff eel-liver paste and two gumbo apples, plus a loaf of bread, some cheese, and twelve crackers."

"Which was both our lunches," Willow pointed out.

"And all the food I'd taken to last us a few days."

"Oh," said Oswin. "Sorry."

Willow sighed. "That's okay," she said. Missing food wasn't exactly new when your best friend was a kobold.

Though eel liver would never be top of her list, she felt a small pang, thinking of how her father had made the sandwiches himself. And how excited her parents had been at the thought of her going to school. . . . She imagined them discovering the note in her room telling them she wasn't going to be coming home until she figured out what was happening. She swallowed. They were not going to be impressed.

14

The Luminary

CLOUDS HAD PASSED over the moon, Jezelbob, by the time they made their way back to the crescent-shaped building. They could see a few people standing on the roof, adjusting strange bronze instruments.

Twist knocked at the door. There was the sound of light footsteps, and then it was opened by someone who looked a little like an elvish woman, but as the light from above hit her, she began to glow a faint pearly green color, like the moon.

She must be a lumiere, thought Willow. She had long white hair and pointed elvish ears, and she seemed to be wearing a dress made of light that rippled as she walked. Her eyes were white, with tiny pinpricks for pupils.

"Can I help you?" she asked.

"We've come to find out if you have star charts from a thousand years ago," said Peg.

The lumiere's eyes widened. "And why is that?"

"Well, we've come across a constellation that we've never seen before."

"We were just wondering if there was anyone we could talk to about that," added Twist.

"You'll want archiving. Basement level." The lumiere pointed to a staircase behind her, then grimaced. "She's helpful. Just . . . try not to upset her. If you can."

They followed a set of stairs down to the basement.

"What did she mean, 'try not to upset her'?" Peg asked.

Oswin, however, was starting to whine. "Oh noooo! Oh, me greedy aunt Osbertrude! Oh squifflesticks!"

"What is it?" asked Willow, a little concerned.

But all Oswin said was, "Oh, I wish I 'ad me bag! Oh nooo . . ."

They found a small open door with a plaque that read "Archives."

In the corner of the little room there was a desk cluttered with pens, scrolls, and odd metal devices. Some reminded Willow a bit of her StoryPass.

Had she looked at the device, currently in her pocket, she would find it was now suggesting "Cup of Tea?"

A roaring fire was crackling in the fireplace, and everywhere there were piles and piles of scrolls, some on shelves that reached the ceiling, but others stacked on the floor in tottering piles.

"Oh, me greedy aunt!" cried Oswin, skittering out of Willow's arms and ducking behind her legs.

"Looks like there's no one here?" said Twist, glancing around.

"Looks can be deceiving," said a low voice coming, seemingly, from nowhere.

They whipped around. Willow's heart began to hammer in her chest. There was no one there—just a small desk.

"Oh NOOOO! Oh, me greedy aunt Osbertrude. Oh, a kobold's curse upon yeh. I jes' din't need this today."

Willow frowned. Oswin usually only got this panicked when they were in the presence of powerful magic.

There was a screeching sound as a small sliding door in the desk began to open.

"What on Wol?" said Peg as a pair of large green eyes narrowed against the sudden brightness.

"Oh squifflesticks," cried Oswin softly.

They couldn't see at first . . . and then the light hit the thing that stepped out from the desk. It was a small creature covered in green fur with several large white spots. In fact, if you didn't know better, you might even think it was a *cat*. Its ears had started to go a little orange as it peered at the space just behind Willow's legs and sniffed the air, a puzzled frown between its eyes.

Willow gasped. "ANOTHER KOBOLD?"

"Keep yer 'air on," whispered Oswin.

The creature blinked. Then its eyes widened in shock as it breathed, "Oswinifred?" Its posh, clipped voice took Willow completely by surprise.

Oswin's pumpkin-orange ears peeked out from behind her, followed by two large, rather glum-looking eyes.

"'Lo," said Oswin.

"Os-*winifred*?" whispered Willow.

"Not if yew values yer life," hissed the kobold, and Willow bit back a laugh.

The other kobold looked delighted, her eyes filling with happy tears. "It means so much to see family after all this time . . . I mean, even if it's, well . . . you."

"You're family?" cried Willow.

"Tecknikly," grumped Oswin. "This is Osmeralda, me cousin."

Osmeralda dashed forward and squeezed him tightly. Then she wrinkled her nose and said, "You know, Oswinifred, it wouldn't kill you to have a bath."

Oswin turn a brighter shade of pumpkin as he muttered, "I bave, every second Elth Nights. . . ."

Osmeralda rolled her eyes. "Oh, Oswinifred, must we always go through this?"

"Lewk, this is whys I don' visits yew, as yew is always trying ter get me ter forgets that I is a kobold . . . So, for the last time, yew cumberworld, 'tis *Oswin*, no WINIFREDS necessary."

Osmeralda rolled her eyes. "So touchy. Don't tell me you're still cross about that thing with Aunt Osbertrude."

Oswin glared at her. "I don' want ter talk about it."

"But—"

"I said I don' want ter talk about it!"

Osmeralda sniffed. "Fine." Then she looked at Willow and Twist and sighed. "I apologize for the state of me. I'm usually better presented for company."

Willow was surprised at this, as Osmeralda seemed perfectly groomed—and even smelled a little of vanilla, something she didn't think was possible when it came to kobolds. . . .

"So, to what do I owe the honor of your barging in?"

Willow and the others shared awkward looks.

"Well," said Peg, "it's about a constellation we saw."

"Okay?" said Osmeralda.

"It's unlike any I've ever seen before—perhaps it's changed over the years."

"That can happen." Osmeralda nodded.

"We know *when* it was, if that helps," added Twist.

"What do you mean?"

"The constellation we saw was in place around a thousand years ago," she explained.

"How did you see it then?" asked Osmeralda, looking suspicious.

"Nones of yer business," said Oswin.

"Now, look here, cousin. I am trying to be professional," said Osmeralda with dignity.

"We saw it on a mural," replied Twist.

The others looked at her, and she stared back. *What?* she mouthed.

"A mural? You mean the one in the walled garden?" Osmeralda asked.

"Yes," said Twist as the others groaned.

Willow felt it was perhaps not the best idea in the world to let on exactly why they needed these star charts. It would seem obvious that they were looking for the vanished kingdom—and this would surely lead to difficult questions. They didn't want to be stopped before they could get any further. Too much was at stake.

The trouble was, Willow suspected, that Twist had very little experience of lying. It must be really hard to do with elfsense.

"But you can't see any constellations there—too many tiles are missing," Osmeralda pointed out.

"Willow found them," said Twist, then she looked surprised as each of her new friends, including Oswin, put their heads in their hands.

Osmeralda looked curious. "Willow . . . Moss?"

Willow looked up reluctantly. "Er—yes."

The other kobold frowned. "The one from the paper?"

Willow winced. "Yes—but look, I'm not actually delusional or anything. . . ."

Osmeralda held up a green paw. "Of course not."

At their shocked expressions, she shrugged. "My cousin and I might not see eye to eye, but if you were going around *telling lies*—well, he'd never be able to stand being near you. He'd explode every chance he got."

"More than he already does?" asked Peg.

Osmeralda gave him what almost looked like a grin. "Well, yes, just a bit."

"Watch yerself," muttered Oswin.

Osmeralda looked at them, and she suddenly seemed impressed. "So that's what you're after—the vanished kingdom?"

They all blinked.

"You figured that out fast," said Twist, and the others groaned.

"Twist, if you struggle to lie, can you just try not speaking in the future?" said Peg.

Twist looked momentarily thrown off guard. "Er—yes. I can try that."

Peg sighed. "Well, Twist has told you almost everything, so I may as well fill you in on the rest. We don't know where the kingdom has gone, of course . . . but, when I saw the old constellation, I thought maybe we could figure out from that where it *was*."

Osmeralda nodded. "That makes sense." Then she grinned. "I daresay there's a few upstairs who would be willing to help with this. It's been eating them alive that some outsider might find Llandunia before they do—especially after the news that Queen Almefeira's scroll was stolen from Library."

"Upstairs?" asked Willow.

"The lumieres," she said, making her way to her desk. She popped a satchel over her shoulder, put on a pair of gloves, and balanced some wire-rimmed glasses on the end of her nose. Then she crossed the room to one of the very tall shelves that went all the way to the ceiling and started to climb a steel ladder.

"The kingdom went missing during the Long War, so that's where we'll look. It makes sense that the stars would have changed since then—I mean, that's when the moons drifted apart too," she said. "If you can find your constellation in one of these, we can take it to Gibb. He'll probably have an idea."

They watched as she wheeled the ladder between the shelves and stopped it with a paw. "Mmmm. These look likely," she called out as she pawed through old scrolls.

A while later, she made her way down with a large pile of

scrolls bulging out of the satchel. "Here you are—every star and moon chart we have from the Long War period. If your constellation is anywhere, it's in one of these," she said. "Gibb might have some navigational ideas. I'll introduce you."

"And Gibb is?" asked Twist as the kobold led them back up the stairs that wound their way up the crescent-shaped building.

"He's one of the oldest lumieres and, er . . . is a bit of a fan of crackpot theories like yours."

"Oi," said Oswin.

"Just saying," said Osmeralda. "No offense meant."

She led them all the way up to the roof of the building, past a group of lumieres who were hard at work shaping light.

"What are they doing?" asked Peg.

"They're catching the moon's rays. See those big devices that look like telescopes?" she said, pointing at the large brass instruments they'd seen earlier. "They catch moonbeams, and the lumieres channel the light. It helps to power the city and gets directed into the marble."

"Wow," said Willow.

"We also bring other things to life," said an old lumiere, shuffling forward. He was tall, with a very long beard, and he had twinkling, almost mischievous eyes. Like the woman they'd met earlier, his skin seemed to glow a greenish color like the moon, and he was wearing robes made of what looked like strands of light. At his shoulder, a small bird peered at them, then took flight across the starry night.

Willow blinked. Had that bird been made out of light?

"Gibbous Beam," he said, holding out a finger. Twist pressed it with her own till a flurry of sparks danced between them, red and green, and Osmeralda introduced them all.

"Mmmm, interesting," said Gibbous. "I sense some kind of mystery. . . . A plot is afoot." He looked at Twist.

She grinned. "You can't sense that!"

"Hee-hee, nope," he said, tapping the side of his nose. "The only reason anyone comes to find ol' Gibb is when they've got a mystery and they want to theorize. . . ."

"That is a fact," said Osmeralda, though she looked at the old lumiere fondly.

"Even a broken clock is right twice a day and all that," he said. "So, what can I help you with? I do sense some urgency—this is serious?" he asked.

They nodded.

To their surprise, he said, "Has this got anything to do with that Enchancil gibberish—and the nonsense about schools?"

"How did you know?" asked Willow.

Gibbous raised a pale brow. "Eh . . . not exactly a stretch. Three kids, roughly the age range . . ."

"Oh," said Twist, and she and the others grinned before returning to the serious subject at hand.

"Well," began Willow, "you're right that this is urgent."

She and the others filled him in on what had happened at the school.

"Bless me heart!" Gibb cried, and in his anxiety he made several light creatures race toward him, including what looked like mouse, a bird, and a pony. He waved his hands and they scattered.

"So, them Brothers are at it again, trying to rid the world of magic?" he asked.

"Yes," said Willow. "That's why Silas is after the vanished kingdom—"

Gibb looked from Twist to Willow. "Because something there is going to help him do just that?"

"How did you know?" cried Peg.

"Another one of his theories," said Osmeralda.

Gibb nodded. "During the Long War, magic started disappearing, right? Things got really bad. The Brothers of Wol were just about to succeed—and then suddenly Llandunia vanished, the queen disappeared, and the war was over. . . . The Brothers were defeated, and many years later magic re-entered the world. Well, I always figured that whatever started to take away magic was somewhere there in that kingdom, and without it they failed. . . ."

The others nodded, looking a bit amazed.

"So, you want to try finding it first—to stop them from doing it again?" he guessed again.

Willow nodded. "Well, yes."

"You know, I like my theories more than just about anybody, but if no one has found that kingdom in a thousand years, I'm not sure how you will," sighed Gibb.

Peg then explained about the mural and the strange constellation he'd seen.

"That's why they've come to you. They want to see if they can find out where the kingdom was, using these star charts," said Osmeralda, patting her satchel.

Gibb looked absolutely thrilled at this news. "A missing constellation that might help us find Llandunia? Well now, that is a good puzzle to solve." He danced on his feet, then hurried them over to a brass table and chairs.

"Let's have a look," he said. He clicked his fingers and a small bright moon appeared above their heads, helping them to see better.

Osmeralda carefully unrolled the charts and they began to peer at them.

"Hmm, not that one . . . or that," Peg said as Osmeralda unrolled chart after chart. "What we saw kind of looked like a flying turtle." He reached out a finger to trace the stars.

"Don't touch!" cried Osmeralda.

"Sorry."

On the fourth one, he called out, "Wait, that might be it! It did look a little like this." Peg pointed at a constellation.

"Ah yes, well, that's one we see in the west to this day— it's just changed a bit," said Gibb.

Peg gasped. "Oh! Yes, I see the tail now—am I right?"

Gibb beamed at him. "Correct!" But, seeing the looks of confusion on the others' faces, he explained further by drawing the constellations in the air for them, using spots of light. "You see, back when Llandunia was around, the stars were a bit different . . . like this." He pointed at the flying turtle shape. "But what if it's something you already know . . . just rearranged a little?"

Then he began to move the dots of light, spreading the two moons farther apart and lengthening the constellation's "body" so that it looked less like a flying turtle and more like a dragon.

"It's the old winged dragon!" confirmed Peg. "You can only see it from the west of Starfell!"

"Oh!" cried Willow, who had at least heard of that before. "Could we chart where the kingdom was based on this?"

Gibb stroked his beard in thought. "You'd need to cross-reference with quite a precise image of the stars over Llandunia in order to be accurate," he said.

Peg shook his head, looking disappointed. "The mural was just a loose representation."

"How can you be sure?" Twist asked, surprised.

"Well," explained Peg, "look at how Gibb has drawn the moons. It's perfectly to scale. But in the mural they were almost the size of the dragon. If that was off, so much more could be too."

"Oh," said Willow.

Gibb nodded. "Very wise. One small mistake and you could find yourself in the wrong city, or even country."

Willow swallowed. This meant that they still didn't know where the vanished kingdom was. There were so many different western regions of Starfell—the Mists of Mitlaire, the mountains of Nach, Troll Country, Dwarf Territory . . .

"Funny you should mention a dragon," said Gibb, interrupting her thoughts. "Of course, there'd be no human or elf alive today who'd remember where Llandunia was, but . . ." He cocked his head toward the winged dragon constellation in the air before him. "I've always thought that they'd probably have an idea. I mean, very few people have ever spoken to a dragon, but, if anyone would know, it'd be them."

Willow gasped. Of course! She had never thought of that before! "Oh! Thank you, Gibb!"

"You're welcome," he said, then laughed. "I suppose! But good luck finding one . . . I've been alive over a thousand cycles and I've never even come close."

"Hang on. What do you mean?" asked Peg.

"He means we need to talk to a dragon," said Twist. "And they're pretty impossible to find."

Willow grinned, the dragon constellation shining in her eyes. "It's hard, but not impossible. You just need to know where to look."

15
Broom and Breakfast

"YOU MEAN TO tell me you know how to find a dragon?" cried Peg.

"Yes," said Willow, and she explained about her friend Feathering the cloud dragon, and how, in their first adventure together, she had returned Feathering to his mate, Thundera, and got to meet their baby dragon, Floss.

"That's incredible," said Twist, but she was stifling a yawn. It was well past midnight and it had been a long day.

"I think we should go back to my house, get some sleep, and head out first thing in the morning," she said.

In Willow's arms, Oswin let out a snore. "I think that's a good idea," she said. Part of her wanted to just keep going, to try to find the kingdom before Silas did, but she was dead on her feet.

They took a portal walk back to the center of the city and

trudged on leaden feet back to Twist's marble house. Willow was grateful when the doors sprang open.

"This way," said Twist. "You can sleep in my aunts' rooms."

Peg gratefully stopped at an autumn-colored door, and Twist led Willow to a green one. Inside it was still warm and fragrant, like Dot's floral spring breeze.

They said good night, and Willow climbed wearily into bed, surprised to find that the sheets had already been turned down and a pair of fluffy socks was waiting for her on the pillow. She grinned. There was certainly a lot to be said for living in a sentient house.

There was a faint knock on the door, and something crept inside the room. Willow turned to find Scratch scurrying toward her on its long chicken legs. It was carrying her hairy green carpetbag on top, which it placed gently on the floor. It looked fluffy and clean.

"Thank you, Scratch," she said.

The table gave a kind of bobbing nod, then scurried back out, closing the door behind it.

In the morning, Scratch brought Willow tea and chocolate gingerbread biscuits, and Oswin harrumphed as he examined the green carpetbag.

"Smells funny," he moaned, taking things out and inspecting them—the troll whistle, a change of clothing for Willow, and Oswin's nest blanket. The latter was pretty horrid, to be honest, as it was made up of all kinds of smelly junk. Or it used to be. Oswin sniffed a tin can and pulled a face.

"That's called clean," Willow pointed out.

"Yeh, don' like that," Oswin said. Then he reluctantly repacked everything and climbed in, and despite his grumbles she heard a low sigh of satisfaction. There was a rattle from the blanket's array of cans and bottle caps as he pulled it over him.

Willow shook her head, hiding a grin, as she picked up the bag and went to find the others.

She found Twist and Peg sitting in the kitchen, eating breakfast. It was cold, the air frosty and bright.

"Scrambled eggs all right?" asked Twist, lifting a spatula in greeting.

"Perfect."

"Skiron, no! Come on, outside! Just once in my life I'd like to have some warm food," she moaned as the swirling, icy wind circled around her feet. "*Selia*," she said, and it hurried outside. The air turned considerably warmer.

As Willow took a seat at the marble table, Scratch rushed forward to help her pull out an iron chair.

"I think I might have lost my heart to Scratch a bit," Willow said, looking at the table fondly.

"Speak fer yerself," muttered Oswin from the carpetbag. "Smells in 'ere."

"Did you also get warm milk last night and an orange this morning?" asked Peg, pausing between mouthfuls of egg.

"No—I got biscuits, though, and warm socks," said Willow.

"It's the house," explained Twist. "It knows what you like."

"That's wild," said Peg. "And it explains why it brought me this." He held up a piece of paper and a pen. "It knew somehow that I was feeling guilty about not going home. I should have sent my mother a letter earlier."

Willow felt a stab of guilt. "Sorry, Peg. I didn't even think . . ."

"Me neither," Twist said.

"It's not your fault. Your aunts offered to take me home."

"We still can, if you like," said Twist.

"No, it's fine. If the house or Scratch can mail this for me, though, that would be good. . . . I still think it's important that someone nonmagic understands what's been happening."

They nodded.

"Besides." He grinned, looking at them. "It's been kind of fun . . . apart from traveling by tornado."

They all laughed.

After breakfast, they headed outside.

"If you don't mind, Twist," Willow said, thinking of Peg's

earlier comment, "Peg, Oswin, and I will travel by broom."

Twist's mouth curved into a smile. "Suit yourself."

"I never fought I'd look forwards ter travelin' by this fing," said Oswin, who looked greatly relieved.

And they set off on Whisper, flying northeast toward the Cloud Mountains. They passed over the colorful stalls of the Midnight Market, which were all closed, their proprietors waiting for the cover of darkness to sell their dodgier wares.

They flew over Radditch, the home of the Mementons who made brooms like Willow's. Willow pointed them out to Peg.

"Wow, that's incredible!" said Peg as they flew over a group of young broom makers who were sorting twigs into piles, while others were testing the new brooms. One flew pretty close, on what looked like a strange new broom with colorful leaves at the end. The broom maker had russet-colored hair to match, and waved at them before circling back to the forest below.

As they neared the city of Beady Hill, they spied some Brothers of Wol and a few soldiers on the ramparts, armed with flaming arrows.

"We can't fly over!" Willow shouted at Twist, who was hovering with Skiron close by. Willow had attempted to fly over this city once before with Moreg, but as it had Forbidden status, it was unlawful for magical people to enter or fly over. She and Moreg had faced a lot of trouble over it.

"Follow me," said Willow, and they changed direction slightly, heading toward the long, winding Knotweed River, where delicate purple flowers shaped like bells grew and played their soft, haunting music. "Don't listen to the music," Willow told Peg. "It'll lure you into the water—and there are all sorts of dangerous creatures in there."

"Yup," said Oswin, popping his head out of the carpetbag. "Merpeoples who likes ter snatch up kits likes yew. See, they has troubles having their own babies—'tis hard 'cos they is all electeric."

Peg's eyes widened.

"The only fing they is afraid of is cats 'cos there is somefing about a cat that makes 'em lose power. . . . When they founds out I *wasn't* actuallys a cat, a mer-king tried ter marry me off ter his daughter, so he could make another tribes fink they was so powerfuls not even a cat could bovver 'em. Not that I is one, as you know," he added fiercely.

Peg nodded quickly, sharing a look with Willow, who was a little surprised at the story too.

"Though ter be fair I probably should 'ave told 'em I was. . . . Might have saved me a few scars," continued Oswin, showing the boy three faint marks on his rear, which were right next to two recent ones from Twist's aunt Tuppence.

Willow and Peg fought the urge not to laugh.

Peg shook his head in amazement. "Did you know that about him?" he asked Willow.

"No, I'm always finding out something new," Willow said, grinning, her eyes alight. Oswin wasn't exactly talkative, but she did like hearing his stories.

Willow aimed Whisper up higher, away from the soft, enticing music of the Knotweed, and they followed the course of the waterway as the morning turned to afternoon. Birds kept pace with them, including a flock of pink-winged geese.

"I've never seen them that color before!" cried Peg.

"Must be because we're so close to the forest of Wisperia," said Willow, who filled Peg in on all the strange and beautiful creatures that lived in that magical place.

As they flew on, above the long green river, Willow couldn't help thinking of her friend the sailor-wizard, Holloway, who had helped her cross into Netherfell. It had been some time since she'd seen him last. She wondered if he was involved with the wizards who'd been forced out of their homes in Beady Hill's Ditchwater district and were trying to take back their land. . . .

They stopped for a quick lunch from one of the moored boats along the river. It was a long, narrow vessel that was serving fish soup with fresh crusty bread, which they ate in wooden bowls on the riverbank before continuing on their way.

They flew over the vast, colorful forest of Wisperia, and finally toward the floating Cloud Mountains, where they entered a mist so thick it was hard to see even a few feet in front of them.

"Oh nooo! Oh, me eyeballs!" cried Oswin.

Willow was struggling to steer Whisper.

"I c-can't believe we're going to meet dragons," whispered Peg.

"I heard that they, um, eat people?" said Twist, who was swirling with Skiron nearby.

"Not anymore! That's what Feathering said, anyway."

Peg looked amazed.

"I think he said something about going off the taste of them a few years ago. . . ."

There was a loud gulp.

Willow grinned. "I think he was joking."

With her free hand, she dug in her pocket for the Story-Pass. The needle spun around and around.

"That's strange," she whispered. "It's like it can't make up its mind."

"H-how will we find the dragons?" Peg asked as Twist followed behind them, whirling in the wind.

The needle in Willow's hand suddenly pointed to "There Be Dragons."

"Like this!" she said.

16

The Cloud Mountains

At that moment, a large blue shape emerged from the clouds above, followed by a red one and a smaller blue one.

"Feathering!" Willow called, waving.

"Hello, Willow! Oswin?" This was followed by laughter that sounded like a wind chime. "And who is that with you, flying by tornado?"

"That's Twist."

"Ah, elvish magic—haven't seen it in years!" called Feathering. "Follow us. We'll lead you to a clear landing path."

Willow and Twist followed the large blue shape ahead of them through the clouds. From behind them, a little voice called out excitedly, "WI-WOW?"

Willow looked behind, then grinned. It was the baby dragon, Floss, who ambled through the sky like a puppy, bouncing between the clouds.

"Look at me! Wheeee!" he said, doing a sort of somersault.

Willow laughed, delighted to see the baby dragon again.

"I can fly really high now!"

"That's wonderful, Floss!" called Willow.

She was amazed at how much he'd grown. He was about the size of a covered wagon now.

"Follow us," called his mother, Thundera, skimming through a bank of clouds toward the floating mountains. Her sleek feathers glistened in the sky like rubies.

Feathering landed first, the ground shaking with the force.

Willow and Twist circled above in the tailwind, while Thundera and Floss followed, landing with a running stop.

Willow introduced Twist and Peg to the dragons. Floss seemed very interested in the windswept girl. "Your hair is funny," he said.

"Floss!" Thundera scolded. Looking at the elvish girl, she added, "Sorry."

"But I like it," whined Floss. "How does it all stay up like that?"

Twist grinned. "The wind."

As if in answer, Skiron spun around them, freezing the air till there were icicles at the ends of Floss's eyelashes. "Brrr," he said, shaking them off.

"It's good to see you, dear friend," said Feathering, and

Willow rushed forward to stroke his feathered face.

"You too."

"We were so worried about you," said Thundera.

"Me?" said Willow.

Feathering nodded. "We flew over the Dark Woods and Grinfog yesterday to see if we could find you. On our flight paths we have seen the Brothers of Wol rounding up children."

Willow and the others gasped.

"We saw them marching long lines of children toward the fortress of Wolkana. It didn't look as if the young ones were behaving normally. . . . There was no light in their eyes—and no one reacted to seeing a dragon," said Feathering.

This was strange, as most people panicked at the sight of one dragon—so naturally pandemonium would have ensued over seeing *three*.

"They is usin' Gerful chalk," explained Oswin, peeking out from the top of the hairy carpetbag.

The irises in Feathering's eyes whirled in anger. "That is immoral! It's been illegal for centuries!"

Willow nodded. "It hasn't stopped them, though," she said, and she filled the dragons in on what had happened at the schools.

Peg shook his head. "It looks like they're moving even quicker now, though. Cuttlefish, our teacher, implied that they were focusing on brainwashing kids about magic being unnatural. It sounded as if it would be some time before the children were taken anywhere. . . .”

"I think it's because of my aunts," said Twist. "If they've assembled some people to spread the word and go after the Brothers, it might mean that they've had to move their plans forward as a result."

"Oh gosh, you're probably right," said Peg.

Willow closed her eyes. It was a horrible thought. "We *have* to find the kingdom before Silas does," she said. "Before he's able to steal all their magic."

"What do you mean?" asked Feathering. "What kingdom?"

"The vanished elvish kingdom of Llandunia," said Willow, who explained about the scroll, the staff—and the secret they'd discovered about what it could do.

"So that's what he's after—the elf staff," said Feathering.

Twist looked at him in surprise. "You know of it?"

"Oh yes, of course. I was just a hatchling, but I was around when the kingdom vanished. . . . And even back then no one really knew what happened. There one day—gone the next."

"That's what we came to ask about!" cried Willow. "To see if you remembered it."

"Oh yes, it was a beauty—a great crystal city, as tall as the sky, with streets of marble and gold winking in the twilight. The crystal would catch the light, turning pink and purple, and the queen's warrior, Vermora, could always be seen circling the sky after the hunt. Fearsome, she was, with acid breath and talons of pure diamond. She was the last of the fire dragons, even then."

Willow, Peg, and Twist gasped.

"So the queen owned that dragon?" Twist asked.

Feathering looked at her, and the elf had the grace to blush. "I mean, she had a dragon companion?"

"Yes, she did."

"But do you know where it was—the kingdom?" Willow pressed. "We only know it was somewhere in the west. I feel like if I can find out where it *was* then I could maybe try and bring it back . . . so long as I knew I wouldn't be harming anyone."

He nodded. "That makes sense. I could tell you roughly what I remember as a hatchling, but I think there are other creatures that would have a better idea. They'd be able to tell you exactly where it used to be, as they would remember it in their bones."

"Who?" asked Willow.

"The rock dragons."

Thundera sighed. "Oh, Feathering, anyone but them."

He nodded. "They're difficult beasts. I'm not sure they'll agree to help, but there's always a chance. It will require a sacrifice," said Feathering.

Peg and Oswin started wailing at the same time.

"Oh no! Oh, me greedy aunt!" cried Oswin.

"Oh why, oh why didn't I say I wanted to go home?"

Feathering made a sound like tinkly wind-chime laughter. "Not that kind of a sacrifice. A trade—rock dragons will only help if you give them something in return. They don't relish coming out in the light."

Willow wasn't the only one who sighed in relief. "What should we give them?" she asked.

"Food?" suggested Twist.

"No, nothing like that, alas. It'll be something like your memories from when you were born, or a promise to name your first child after them . . . something permanent like that."

Willow, Twist, and Peg shared looks of horror.

"I'm sure we'll manage, though. I'll help negotiate. Get on and I'll take you to them," said Feathering.

Willow hesitated for a moment. Something else, something horrible, had occurred to her just then—worse even than the idea of giving up her memories to a fearsome rock dragon.

"Feathering, when you saw children being taken . . . was it still just those under the age of thirteen?" she asked.

Feathering frowned as he thought back. "Oh . . . I don't know. Thundera?"

"Seemed a mix to me—younger and older," said Thundera.

"Oh no!" said Twist. "So they could have taken all the children, regardless of their ages?"

"I think so," said Thundera.

Willow's stomach sank to her toes. "My sisters!" she gasped.

"We can get them back. We'll help you," said Thundera.

"Th-thank you," said Willow.

"You go with Feathering. Floss and I will find your sisters and try to stop the Brothers," said Thundera. "We'll search for Essential and Sprig too."

"Oh! Thank you," breathed Willow, feeling a pang of worry for her friends.

Thundera nodded. "We'll see you soon," she said, and together she and Floss took to the sky.

"Be careful!" Feathering shouted after them.

"Always," came Thundera's response.

"Bye, Wi-wow, and fwends!" called Floss.

Willow waved, her heart torn as she thought of her sisters, but she had to carry on—she needed to find Llandunia. She needed to stop Silas before it was too late.

17
Rock Dragons

WILLOW AND PEG climbed on Feathering's back. Willow used her scarf to strap her broomstick to her back.

Peg was shaking. "Are you sure this is safe?" He gulped.

Oswin peeked his head out of his bag and muttered, "Ridin' a cloud dragon, or goin' off in search of rock dragons?"

"Uh . . . both," said Peg nervously.

"Travelin' by dragons is better than that," Oswin said, cocking his head in the direction of Twist, who had chosen to follow by tornado.

Peg swallowed. "Yes. Anything's better than that."

"Well, I am glad to see you've started to succumb to my charms, Oswin," said Feathering with his tinkly wind-chime chuckle.

"As for the rock dragons," said Willow, "I don't see that

we have a choice—we need to find Llandunia."

"They live on the last of the Cloud Mountains," Feathering explained, and with his massive wings they flew there much faster than by broom. Even super-fast Whisper was no match for the cloud dragon.

Feathering landed on a rocky outcrop. It was less misty out here, and barren. Then he made a strange shrieking sound that caused all the hairs on the back of Willow's neck to stand on end.

"It's the dragon call," he explained. "We use it when we are in need."

"And they'll respond?" asked Willow, swallowing.

Feathering shrugged a massive blue shoulder, the iris in his eye whirling as he searched the ground. "It's possible, though rock dragons follow their own rules."

Twist whirled down shortly afterward, patting her hair into place. Then she looked around with a frown. "Where do you suppose the rock dragons are?" she asked.

A deep voice, like the earth cracking open during a drought, rumbled, "We are everywhere, and nowhere all at once. From the dirt to the pebbles to the stones, we are beneath and all around you."

"Oh!" cried Willow and Peg, who held on to each other as the ground beneath their feet started to shift and shudder.

Small stones began to scatter, and rocks and boulders

rolled, gathering before their eyes to form into a giant stone dragon. There was a hissing noise as its nostrils flared, and wind gusted in and out of them. Above its huge snout, the rock dragon opened a pair of glowing lichen eyes. Its mouth opened into a yawning chasm, and Willow couldn't suppress a shudder. Should someone happen to slip and fall inside it, there might be no return.

Behind the large dragon, several other rock dragons began to form from the scattered stones.

Willow's heart began to hammer in fear.

"Oh WOL!" cried Peg, just as Oswin muttered, "Oh no," very quietly.

"What is it that you want from us?" asked the rock dragon.

Feathering began to explain why they were there. "To see your memories of what happened to the vanished kingdom of Llandunia—so that we can find it once more."

The rock dragon sniffed the air. "And why would we tell you?"

"Because," Willow pleaded, "we need to know what happened. Someone is trying to find the kingdom, someone who wants to steal magic from Starfell. I—we—want to stop them."

In the dragons' sudden outrage, there was the rumbling sound of rocks rearranging themselves. "We have sensed this!" hissed the main rock dragon. "Something is coming!"

Feathering nodded. "There will be another war—unless we act soon."

The large rock dragon fixed its gaze on Feathering. "You are not the first to know of the coming conflict. We are connected to all things in Starfell. We can sense everything that goes on in this world. We feel the change . . . like before. Something is coming . . . something that threatens us all."

"Exactly! That's why we need your help!" cried Willow.

From behind them, a low hiss of smoke came from one of the other dragons. "We should destroy the humans. They bring destruction to all creatures, big and small. They are a blight on this world."

Willow flinched.

Another stony voice echoed these sentiments. "We could stop them all—send the rocks rolling, form ourselves all across the land. End them once and for all."

"Oh, me greedy aunt!" cried Oswin.

Peg, Twist, and Willow gasped, "No!"

With her heart thundering in her ears, Willow took a hesitant step toward the main rock dragon, her hands outstretched as if to calm it. "Please don't judge us by one human. We can stop him—stop this war. If we all work together, no one needs to be wiped out."

Feathering nodded his vast blue snout. "I agree. Besides, I

don't want to see dragons at war. And, if you hurt my friends, there will be no other option."

The rock dragon turned its head to face Feathering, considering the smaller beast's threat. It was at least ten times the size of the cloud dragon. Feathering didn't stand a chance.

Willow fought for air in her anxiety. Was this all one giant mistake? It was backfiring terribly. . . . She looked at Twist, who seemed uncharacteristically cowed, her eyes full of fear. Peg was clutching the carpetbag, which was shaking, Oswin having zipped himself inside.

She took a deep breath, then swallowed. Feathering had mentioned that the rock dragons would help you if you offered a trade, something in return. She would do whatever it took to get them out of here, and to stop Silas from finding Llandunia and the elf staff.

Willow swallowed one more time. "Please help us. Please tell us where the kingdom was. I—I will give you whatever you want. Whatever you need me to trade."

"No!" cried Oswin, peering at her from the hairy green bag, which he'd unzipped slightly.

"Don't do it!" cried Peg.

Twist scowled. "Willow, we can find another way!"

But Willow shook her head. "There is no other way. I can't bring the kingdom back without knowing where it was. Who knows how many other people's lives could be in danger? I'm just one person. . . . It's fairer like this," she said, though her voice shook along with her knees. She faced the dragon again. "Tell me what you need."

The rock dragon looked at her but didn't say anything for a long time. Then, "You will pay a heavy price."

Willow felt her knees give way slightly, and her stomach plummeted.

"Nooo!" moaned Oswin.

Willow's fear only increased as the enormous rock dragon moved suddenly closer to her and sniffed. She cried out as she felt herself being sucked toward its powerful stony nostrils, but Twist reached out and grabbed her by her cloak.

Willow wondered what they'd ask for . . . a memory? A name? The thought of losing any of her memories of Granny Flossy made her throat turn dry. As much as she was putting on a brave face, she was terrified of what they'd ask.

The rock dragon took another enormous sniff and Willow held on to Twist for dear life. Willow smelled something old and dry, like dust and heat and the echo of long ago.

Suddenly the rock dragon blinked its large lichen eyes. It paused as it considered Willow in what seemed like surprise.

"You have been touched by magic," it said. It wasn't a question.

Willow blinked. The dragon was right.

When she'd saved the missing day, there had been a moment in Wolkana when all had seemed lost—Silas had the powerful lost spells, he was shielded from their magic by a protective enchantment, and Moreg's life force was trickling away. Willow had tried and tried to summon a spell scroll away from him, and suddenly magic itself heard her, and decided to take a chance. It broke its own rules, released the protection around the spell, and chose to help her. She'd managed to get the scroll and recite the counterspell to restore the missing day, because magic had seen something in Willow that day—something it hadn't seen in a long time. It had even granted her a second power—the ability to make things disappear—as a result.

"Y-you can tell?"

There was a hubbub from the other rock dragons, who inched closer to sniff at her. "I can smell it too," said one of the others.

There were nods of agreement all around. "We must help her," said one.

Willow felt a mix of hope and relief wash over her.

The big rock dragon was still considering her, still unwilling to let her know its decision just yet.

"Magic has put its trust in you. We are surprised. You are not very strong or powerful. . . . It is an odd choice."

"Yes," said Willow, who couldn't help feeling just a little insulted, though it was probably best not to argue. Besides, she knew it was true. It *was* a bit odd. She didn't know why magic had put its faith in her, but she knew that she didn't want to let it down. "Strength comes in all sizes."

The rock dragon nodded. "On that we agree. A landslide often begins with a single rock, a pebble can cause a wave, a piece of grit can create a pearl. . . . This we know. This we trust."

It seemed to think for a while. Willow stood rooted to the spot, her heart in her mouth, until it spoke again.

"We were silent the last time. We didn't wish to get involved in human matters . . . but these are not human matters anymore. Not when it threatens our world. And, if magic has placed its trust you, so shall we. I no longer require a trade. I will tell you what happened."

Long ago, when the moons lived side by side, there was a kingdom made of strange crystal in a spectrum of blues and greens edged with purple and pink. It was magnificent. It was a living organism that responded to the wants and needs of its ruler, an elvish queen who loved the palace and her crystal kingdom like a family.

She was a benevolent ruler, entrusted with a vital task—to keep the balance in the world of Starfell.

People envied her this power. Particularly a human magician who named himself Wol and, in time, managed to make himself as powerful as he could by playing on the people's fears. He convinced those who were afraid of magic to follow him. He stole spells and used whatever methods he could to grow stronger.

But there was one thing he knew would make him all-powerful. It was known as the elf staff. It could tap in to the very source of magic itself and gift it to anyone and anything of its choosing. But it had a darker side too, which not many people knew: it could also take magic away.

Wol had become adept at disguises. He transformed himself into a deer and witnessed the queen as she used the staff in this way in the forest. As an old elf lay dying, the queen recited a ritual and used the staff to gently capture his magic and send it back into the ground around the body.

Wol's desire for the staff became an obsession, until one day he managed to break into the palace. He put all those inside it into a deep sleep, using a very powerful enchantment, and he took the queen's staff as his own.

Soon he began to make himself all-powerful. He started to call himself a god, and the Brothers of Wol grew ever stronger. He built a fortress that would keep out all magicians who might challenge him, and with the help of his nonmagical Brothers, who believed they were doing what was right, he used the staff to strip the magic from all those he could. They did not see that the world was beginning to suffer, that people and animals, forests and lakes, were suffering too. . . .

But the elvish queen did. It took her a long time to manage to break into Wol's fortress, but she did so with the help of the dragon Vermora. The queen and the wizard fought, and Wol was injured.

The queen escaped, with the staff, on the back of the dragon. They flew to the forest that edged the beautiful elvish kingdom, and it was then that the queen knew she had to do something drastic to stop Wol and end the war . . . or it might mean the destruction of the world. He couldn't be allowed to use the staff for such a purpose ever again. No one could.

She called for her sisters and they spoke in quiet whispers. Afterward, she sent them and all the elves away from Llandunia to find a new home. Then she began to run as men in long brown robes—Brothers of Wol—came for her, arrows ready.

The queen banged the staff on the ground. "Vermora!" she cried, and the large, fiery red dragon canted in the sky and then landed near her once more.

"You need to take this," she said, holding out a scroll, which she placed inside a leather satchel and hung around the dragon's neck. "It will help the elves find this kingdom again, if they ever need to. Only an elf of my line will be able to decode it."

Then she pressed her forehead against the dragon's snout.

"You must be a witness only, Vermora. Promise me?"

"A witness?" the dragon asked.

"To what will happen to me when they come."

The dragon's eyes filled with pain. "No!" she cried. "I will NOT!"

"You must, Vermora. Our world depends upon it. Llandunia and the staff must be hidden, and, for the enchantment to hold, I must go with them. I must take the staff back to the

kingdom and ensure their protection. Lerisi."

The dragon closed her eyes. "Take it back," she begged.

"Lerisi," the queen whispered again.

"Don't . . . I cannot break it if you call upon a dragon vow."

"Lerisi," whispered the queen again, for the last time. Her eyes misted with tears. Then she touched Vermora's scaled face again and breathed, "Farewell, my dearest friend."

When Vermora's eyes opened, they were filled with enormous pain. The dragon watched helplessly as Queen Almefeira ran to the lake, the staff parting the water as she raced toward her kingdom on the other side.

From the forest, men in brown robes were following, arrows flying toward her.

The dragon roared helplessly in pain and rage as she watched an arrow strike the queen's chest. The sound Vermora made was as if her own heart had been pierced.

Almefeira stood in the parted lake, in front of the kingdom, breathing shallowly from her wound. Then she struck the staff on the ground, so fiercely that the crystal orb let out a blast of pure energy. Above her head, the twin moons split apart and an earthquake began to rip the ground below. The ground started to crumble and sink, taking the lake, the queen, and her kingdom ever lower, until they could be seen no more. The forest came next, the men falling into the swirling water that spun into the ground as if down a drain.

In the end, nothing was left behind except dry, barren ground that stretched for miles and miles, completely uninhabited but for rather large stony creatures who seemed utterly perplexed and a bit apprehensive about what had just happened. . . .

The creatures remain there to this day. They have changed over time, becoming even more suspicious of magic, but they live in a place that you might know today as Troll Country.

"I can't believes it," said Oswin in horror.

"The vanished kingdom was in Troll Country," breathed Willow.

18
The Vanished Kingdom

Their tale told, the rock dragons began to disintegrate before their eyes, rocks and stones falling and scattering.

"Wait!" cried Willow.

"We have told you more than was asked," called the voice of the enormous dragon.

The ground began to shake slightly once more as tiny rocks rattled across the surface. When at last they stopped, they formed into a very small, miniature rock dragon, with two small shadows for eyes.

Willow frowned.

"I think they mean for him to come with you," whispered Peg.

"Oh, um, thank you," said Willow, bending down. The creature jumped into her hands, then scuttled up her arm to rest on her shoulder. Willow looked at it. It blinked its dark eyes and then lay down, panting softly, as if it had run a very great distance.

"So lets me gets this straight," said Oswin, peering out of the bag at the dusty space where the rock dragons had been and then looking at the tiny, now fast-asleep stone dragon on Willow's shoulder. "The biggest beasts we ever met agree to helps us save the world . . . by sendin' us a rock newt?" He harrumphed.

Willow looked back at him and nodded. That did seem to be the size of it.

"Well, at least now we know where Llandunia is," she said. "And that it's probably safe for me to summon it back. I mean, there's nothing in Troll Country."

"Apart from the obvious," said Feathering.

"Yeh . . . wonder how happy they wills be ter have a big kingdom pop up in their spot?"

"Well, it's just a risk we'll have to take. I mean, we have to find it so we can get the staff before Silas does."

They nodded.

"So, next stop, Troll Country," said Feathering, and they all climbed aboard—apart from Twist, who genuinely preferred to fly by tornado.

The sun was high in the sky as they flew through the misty Cloud Mountains and past winding lakes, over forests and towns. They stopped once for food, from a tree-market just outside the forest of Wisperia that was selling lemon buns and terhu rolls. The stallholder flew up into the canopy on her stained-glass wings at the sight of Feathering, and it took a while for them to convince her that the dragon wasn't in fact going to eat her, but would quite fancy a bucket or two of currant buns. She reluctantly lowered some down to them, even though it was most of her stock for the day.

"Just a snack," said Feathering, icing on his snout.

The tiny rock dragon simply nestled further into Willow's shoulder when she offered him some food, and she wondered if rocks ate anything. Water, perhaps?

The sun was just beginning to set when they landed in Troll Country, a fiery pink beginning to paint to the sky. Twist whirled down to join them, her eyes luminous as she took in the vast size of the area.

"How will we know where to summon the kingdom, Willow?" Peg asked, staring out at the barren landscape.

"I'm not sure—it's so enormous—but it's mostly barren," she said, looking out across the desert. "I'd prefer to know exactly where it used to be before I try summoning it . . . but, well . . ."

Peg nodded. "It's just too big to know, isn't it? Is it possible there are some signs left behind?"

"I could fly around and take a look?" offered Feathering.

"But I think, considering what the rock dragons told us, Almefeira took everything along with her when she hid the kingdom. . . ."

Willow nodded. "That's what I was thinking too. Perhaps I should just try to summon it somewhere where there are no troll huts. I can negotiate some things with my abilities, but unfortunately I don't know about getting it perfectly in place. . . . It might not be in the exact spot the kingdom used to be, but it's the best we can do. . . ."

Twist had been traversing the area as Willow and Peg spoke, crossing over vast distances by tornado. She came back just in time to hear Willow's thoughts on where to summon the vanished kingdom.

"No," she said, shaking her head vehemently. They stared at her in surprise and Twist explained. "I can feel that elves have been here. It's faint, but it's elfsense, definitely."

"Oh!" cried Willow and Peg together.

"Up ahead, it was a little stronger. Come with me," she said.

They followed after her on foot for around ten minutes, and then the tall elf suddenly stopped, an odd look of amazement flashing across her face. "I feel it more here." She shook her head. "Strange, isn't it?"

"Maybe not!" Willow gasped and pointed at the ground.

Where Twist walked, very, very faintly, the dusty ground had begun to glow green, like the elvish marble back in Lael.

The tiny rock dragon on Willow's shoulder scuttled down her arm and jumped onto the ground. He walked in circles, then came to a stop and looked back at them, nodding his minute head.

Twist looked from him to her booted feet. "Great Starfell! Do you think . . . perhaps Llandunia is below here—is that what he's trying to tell us?"

Feathering nodded. "I think so."

Willow swallowed. Part of her was still terrified at the idea of bringing the kingdom back, but thankfully this open desert wasn't somewhere she would cause any real destruction. There were no homes or villages that could be affected. Besides, another part of her was grateful that they weren't too late—that Silas hadn't beaten them to it.

She looked at the others, a determined glint in her eye. "I'm going to try finding it."

They all nodded solemnly.

Willow closed her eyes, then raised her hand to the sky. The tiny rock dragon climbed back up her leg, onto her arm, then came to rest once more on her shoulder. Willow took a deep breath, and tried to silence the voice at the back of her mind that wondered if she could even do this. Who was she to try? The biggest thing she'd ever made reappear was a kitchen, and that was by accident. Even the rock dragons were surprised that magic had chosen to trust her—they could sense that she wasn't particularly strong. . . .

Then she shook that doubt away. She pictured Granny Flossy's warm eyes before she attempted a new potion, one for a day full of joy. "Child, they are quick ter tell me not to try, that since me accident I fail more times than I succeed. But here's the thing . . . right now there's a chance I win. It's only when you don' try that you lose."

The potion had gone wrong that time, but eventually she got it right—and besides, most days with Granny had been filled with moments of joy.

Willow took in another deep breath. *The only failure is not trying*, she reminded herself. Then she pictured finding the lost city, putting it back where it belonged. She painted the scene with her thoughts, until finally she saw it all in her mind's eye. She could feel it, like a secret whispering at the base of her skull.

It resisted at first—the kingdom—as if it were stuck and didn't want to move. But she pulled gently with her mind, imagining fresh air, crystal buildings, twin moons, a lake . . . and suddenly the kingdom began to respond. The feeling at the back of Willow's mind grew as Llandunia tentatively reached out for her mental picture. She was tempting it, cajoling it, with images of a different future.

For the first time, Willow could truly feel the crystal—feel how the rock was sentient, how much it wanted to see the light again, to experience the dawn, the sky, the stars . . . She gave it that extra nudge it needed by showing it Twist, the other elves she'd seen in Lael, and the incredible lumieres, weaving a whole tapestry for Llandunia of how life could be if it came back. She pulled a little harder, and this time it didn't resist.

And then suddenly a faint crack opened up in the earth.

"It's working!" cried Peg in amazement.

Willow felt a surge of hope. But she was careful to guide the kingdom, to show it that it could trust her. She gently encouraged it with her mind, and slowly but surely it began to rise. Something sharp and pointed, and topped by what looked like two crescent moons, broke through the desert surface.

"It's a spire!" exclaimed Twist. "I think it might be from the top of the palace! In the mural, it was the highest point in the kingdom."

"Yes," agreed Feathering. "It is—I see it now!"

In the next moment, more of the kingdom began to rise from below the surface as the ground parted.

Willow and her friends scrambled backward as Llandunia rose ever faster into the space around them.

"Oh no! Oh, me greedy aunt, 'tis comin' too fast!" cried Oswin.

"We need to get out of the way!" cried Twist.

Willow looked from the domed roof that was bursting through the ground to Twist and the others and nodded, eyes wide.

"Come on!" said Peg, running away from the kingdom that was bursting through the desert.

All too soon, the palace was almost halfway up, and Feathering was on the other side of it, too far away to get to them. As the ground continued to split apart and fall away, Willow and her friends .fled, Skiron lending its support, but they weren't quick enough. As a flight of marble steps appeared beneath their feet, they tripped and fell—and then looked up in horror to see a rushing torrent of lake water coming straight for them.

There was nowhere to run.

19
The Kingdom That Remembered

THE WATER ENGULFED them all.

Willow's broom, Whisper, still strapped to her back, tore loose and drifted away.

Willow fought against the currents pulling her under. She needed air, but she could see the hairy green bag with Oswin inside a few feet away. He was struggling too as he tried and failed to unzip the bag, which had begun to sink. The rock dragon clung on to her collar as she dived toward Oswin and swam with all her might. Finally she managed to reach the carpetbag and pull it toward her.

They broke the surface, Willow gasping for breath as she unzipped the bag so the kobold could do the same. He sputtered, coughing. Willow trod water as she held on to him and the bag, the water flowing fast and attempting to pull them under once more. She looked up and saw Feathering flying over. He was trying to get to them but was whipping up more huge waves with his massive wings.

"We'll meet you on the shore, Feathering!" Willow said, seeing the edge of the lake not far away, lapping at the steps of the palace.

The dragon nodded, realizing he was making things worse.

Willow looked around for Peg and Twist.

"Up there," said Oswin, pointing ahead. Willow felt a surge of relief to see her friends climbing out of the water and onto the palace steps.

The world had stopped moving at last, and the lake began to stabilize, the water growing still and calm.

It took a while, as Willow wasn't the strongest swimmer, but at last she dragged herself and Oswin to the lake edge and coughed up a torrent of water. It was some time before she was able to move the wet hair from her eyes and stare in awe at the vast, beautiful kingdom before her.

It was all shades of blue, green, purple, and pink crystal, and the palace itself stood in the center. It was huge, and made up of various domed shapes with incredible carvings cut into the rock. The streets were marble, threaded with gold, and she could see many houses in the distance. Up above, Willow saw that Hezelbob and Jezelbob were reunited once more.

Peg and Twist helped them onto a long platform at the side of the stairs, where Feathering flew down to join them.

"You did it!" cried Twist.

Willow, still spluttering slightly, pushed herself up off her knees and smiled. "Yep. Sorry for almost killing everyone in the process."

Peg grinned. "To be fair, none of us thought that through properly." They all laughed.

Twist pulled a piece of algae from Willow's hair. "Come on, let's take a look!" She beamed, and they all followed her toward the palace.

As Twist walked up the stairs, the marble glowed green beneath her feet, and the kingdom seemed to come to life.

Willow, Peg, and Oswin watched in awe as emblems on the vast palace began to wake up after centuries. Unlike the mosaic emblems in Lael, these were like statues carved into the crystal, but even more lifelike. They raced over the walls—winged horses, dragons, water nymphs, elves, sprites, foxes, and hounds. They had come from all directions, crossing over from some of the nearby houses to gather closer together for a better look.

"Salutations!"

"Hello there!"

"Friends, where are you?"

The sound became deafening as each one cried out excitedly, looking from Willow and her friends to the space behind them, an expectant look on their crystal faces.

Twist and Willow suddenly looked desperately sad.

"I didn't know they could talk," Willow whispered, her heart beginning to ache as the emblems crowded around one another, their expressions full of hope and longing.

"Neither did I," Twist murmured as tears coursed down her face. "They're looking for them."

"Who?" asked Peg.

"The elves from before . . . The ones that left."

"Oh," he said, and his face fell. "That's so sad."

As one, the emblems and the crystal itself seemed to sense what Twist was feeling: regret, sorrow, pity. They began to realize that their old friends weren't coming back. There were keening wails. Willow felt tears flood her eyes as so many emblems crowded around the palace walls, looking for answers that wouldn't come. She watched helplessly as Twist sat down on the marble steps and began to cry.

Willow went to sit next to her, feeling awful. It was her fault all the crystal emblems were experiencing this! She had caused them this pain, because she'd convinced the kingdom to return.

Her throat turned dry, and she tried to swallow, her lip wobbling. "I'm so sorry," she said to Twist, and as she sat down she felt the marble steps beneath her fingers. To her utter shock, it began to glow green like it had for the elf.

"Oh, Willow," cried Twist, "are you perhaps part elf?"

Willow shook her head, a tear running down her cheek as she looked up at the sad faces of the emblems, and she listened to the kingdom. She closed her eyes, and she felt it then: the pain . . . the loneliness . . . the terrible longing to be reunited with old friends. She didn't know what was happening exactly—but she could guess.

"It felt me, like I felt it, when I brought it here," she said. "It wants me to know that"—she took in a shuddery breath at the thought—"it doesn't mind that I pushed for it to come back, because it's better here than below. . . . It's better to know what happened than to always wonder . . . to be trapped beneath the surface . . . *to be forgotten*."

Willow wiped away the tears that just kept flowing as she felt the heart of the kingdom.

On some deep level she knew exactly what Llandunia was feeling—because it was the same thing she'd felt after the missing day was restored, when she'd discovered that Granny Flossy had died. It had been excruciating, realizing that she was gone, but somehow the not knowing—the idea of simply forgetting—was so much worse.

Twist wiped her eyes. Even Peg was welling up.

"That's very true," said Feathering, "though, Llandunia, you had never been forgotten."

"And you can have a new life," said Twist, "and make new memories."

Willow took a deep breath and squared her shoulders. They would only have that—a new life filled with new memories—if they found what they were looking for and prevented Silas from destroying all their futures.

"We need to find the elf staff," she said, standing up.

Twist nodded. "You're right."

Her words, however, caused a hubbub from the emblems, as they each tried to speak at once.

A winged horse reared up on its hindquarters. "You cannot go looking for the elf staff!"

A water nymph shook her head, then dived into the crystal as if it were water. She reappeared on another wall and cried, "It's why she buried us. Leave it where it lies."

The others shouted much the same warnings. Willow stared at them in shock.

"Do you know where it is?" she asked.

A fox stared at her mutely. A dog looked at the marble steps instead of meeting her eyes and said, "No. . . ."

Twist frowned. "You're lying," she breathed.

"Don't ask it of him," said an elf emblem, approaching from one of the houses up ahead on a long marble road. She was made of blue and green crystal and moved through the street and then onto the palace wall with ease, like she was a shadow.

"But you know where it is?" asked Twist.

She nodded.

"Please, we only want it so we can protect it. Someone is coming, someone powerful—and, if he gets here, it will be too late," said Twist.

The elf and the other emblems stopped to stare at them, then finally they all nodded. Perhaps, thought Willow, they could sense that Twist was telling the truth.

The elf emblem pointed toward the lake. "It is in there."

"Thank you," said Willow, and she turned to walk back down the palace steps. The others followed.

Willow stopped at the edge of the lake to close her eyes, and then she began once more to search for the staff with her mind.

Like there had been in Howling House, there was a blast, like an electric current, and she flew over backward.

"Willow, are you all right?" cried Twist, rushing toward her.

Willow blew out her cheeks, then stood up. "Fine." She closed her eyes once more to try again.

"Oh, me greedy aunt," moaned Oswin from near her feet. He'd opened the carpetbag and stood it upside down to dry out. "I can'ts lewk."

Willow took a deep breath, planting her feet wide apart. Twist held on to her to lend her strength, and Willow shot her a grateful smile before concentrating on the staff.

Electrical blast after electrical blast rocked them. Then, suddenly, a tall, spiral stick began to break the surface and rise from the lake.

Willow and the others cried out jubilantly . . . only to then gasp in shock as something else emerged—something with scales and fierce claws, something that was clutching the elf staff with all its might and looked utterly furious to boot. It was a fearsome creature from below. Its hair and beard were made of hundreds of tiny serpents, and its eyes and fishlike tail were gold.

"'Tis a merman!" cried Oswin.

Willow nodded. The tiny rock dragon shifted position on her shoulder, staring at the lake creature with interest.

"Please," Willow called to the merman. "Someone dangerous knows where to find you. We need to take this staff, to protect it from him."

But it didn't look like the merman was in the mood to talk or to release the staff. Instead he clung on tighter and sent another powerful electric current toward her.

"Well, that answers that," said Willow with a sigh.

"Let me try something," said Twist fiercely, with a crackle of her own storm energy. She released a bolt of lightning toward the merman, and Willow tried to summon the staff with her magic, hoping to catch him when he was distracted. But Twist only seemed to have angered him. In response, the creature's next electric shock was stronger than ever, blasting Willow so far off her feet that Skiron had to break her fall.

"Oh, he's never going to let it go!" cried Willow. "Do you think the water nymph emblem can help us?"

"I am bound to the walls—I cannot enter the lake," called

the emblem behind them. "And while I trust your purpose, I am wary of your plan."

Willow groaned and turned to her friends in despair.

Then Oswin nodded, as if he had done some serious thinking. . . . He padded away from the wet carpetbag, made his way slowly to Willow's side, and faced the lake. Then he hissed at the merman, his fur standing on end. In that moment he looked even more like a cat than he ever had in his whole life.

The creature flinched. For just a moment, the electric current he was transmitting sputtered, and then grew strong once more. Twist held on to Willow as she was nearly blasted off her feet again.

"Oswin!" Willow gasped, guessing his plan. "Try it again!"

The kobold took a deep breath, closed his eyes, and muttered, "The fings I do fer yew." Then he squared his shoulders, dashed toward the water and, holding out both his front paws threateningly, made a pretty bad attempt at a *meow*. . . .

The merman recoiled. It was just for a split second, but it was all Willow needed, and she summoned the staff toward her with all her might. From the lake, there was a deep roar of vengeance, and the merman released another bolt of electricity, knocking them all off their feet. Willow and Twist crashed back on to the steps, but not before Willow felt something enormous, and wet, land in her outstretched hands.

"I've got it!" she cried.

There were cheers from Peg, Twist, and Feathering, and the merman retreated to the depths of the lake once more.

Willow stood up awkwardly, wincing, but brandishing the heavy staff in triumph. She could feel the enormous power and energy radiating from it.

"Oswin, you're amazing, thank you!" she said.

"Fanks," he said. Then he shot them all a hard look. "But, jes' ter be clear, I is NOT a cat."

They all nodded seriously—though Twist's lips did shake with suppressed laughter.

"But you were brilliant to make him think you were," said Peg, who was perhaps remembering the kobold's story about how his appearance had resulted in him almost being married off to a mer-princess.

The kobold shrugged, but they could detect what almost looked like a catlike smirk.

Suddenly there was the sound of someone clapping.

Willow looked at her friends—only they'd all turned pale, and were staring back in the direction of the lake.

"Right on time," said a cold voice from behind Willow.

20
The High Master's Plan

WILLOW'S HEART STARTED to thud.

Silas.

He was standing on a small boat in the water, surrounded by half a dozen Brothers. Though no one was steering, they were moving at great speed toward Willow and her friends. Even from her position on the palace steps she could see Silas's smile, which was cold and terrible.

All too soon, the boat stopped at the water's edge, and he took a casual step onto the platform, his wide smile firmly in place.

"Oh no," whispered Oswin.

Silas was followed by his faithful Brothers. Each one had glazed eyes—from the Gerful chalk, Willow realized. Worse still, each one of them was holding up a pair of glowing blue manacles.

She blinked in horror. They were outnumbered.

"I must say," Silas said, "you have behaved exactly according to plan. Who would have thought when we first met all those months ago that the little girl who tried to thwart me would play such a big part in my success? I really must thank you."

Willow's heart was roaring in her chest. She frowned in confusion. "Thank me for what?"

He grinned. "For this! Bringing the kingdom of Llandunia to me. I must confess that even with all the lost spells at my disposal, I wasn't sure how I was going to locate it. And then I realized I'd never need to." He took out something from his long black robe. It was a folded copy of the *Grimoire Gazette*. His eyes flashed in amusement. "I'd just let you follow the bread crumbs . . . and you'd end up doing it all for me."

Willow paled. "But the scroll from Library . . . the one you stole . . . ?"

"Yes, I hoped that the infamous scroll said to contain the whereabouts of the vanished kingdom would catch your attention. I did steal it—well, one of my followers did, anyway. Of course, I was unable to translate it—but that wasn't necessary, my dear. All I needed was for you to *think* I could. Oh, it was so wonderful to see how easily you played along. I'm much obliged."

"Skiron, blow!" cried Twist, and the wintry wind began to gust itself into a frenzy.

Silas staggered against the unexpected gale as it whipped his black robes around him.

Immediately two brainwashed Brothers advanced on Willow and, reacting quickly, she tightened her grip on the staff and started to race up the palace steps.

Remembering that she'd managed to lose her broom when Llandunia had reappeared, she held out her other hand and tried to summon it. Instead, she was met with the blast of yet another electric current and fell over. She whirled around to see the merman back at the surface of the lake, holding on to Whisper, a cruel grin on his face.

"Blast!" she cried, getting up gingerly and hurrying up the remaining steps toward the palace.

A few of the emblems came racing over the walls, shouting instructions—though many chastened her about summoning the staff in the first place.

"Fly away!" said the hound. But Willow couldn't.

"Summon your army!" cried the winged horse. But Willow didn't have one.

She looked behind her and saw that Twist had sent a bolt of lightning after the group of Brothers who were trying to corner Willow.

"Thank you!" cried Willow, just as thunder started to

boom out of the elf's mouth and rain lashed down from the sky. Maybe she *did* have a small army, she thought, just as Feathering roared, launching himself at Silas, and the two began to do battle.

Silas's magic bounced off the beast's thick hide. But then Willow watched in horror as Silas made some complicated gesture and Feathering was flung against the palace and transformed into a crystal emblem of a dragon, trapped inside the wall behind him.

"Feathering, no!" cried Willow, racing toward him.

"It won't hold him long," reassured the winged horse emblem. "It's illusory magic—a very old trick. He's just made the beast—and us—*think* he's crystal."

"Are you sure?"

The winged horse nodded. "I'll try to convince him to wake up. Go, run," he said, and Willow did.

She ran toward the palace doors, thinking that if she could just get out of sight inside, she could try to make the staff disappear. . . . She'd need to concentrate.

There was a cry from behind, and Willow turned to find that the Brothers were recovering and heading toward her again. Oswin swatted at one of them, but more seemed to be appearing from nowhere.

"Seize her!" cried Silas. "Get that staff!"

Willow ducked out of their way, and Twist tried once

again to hold off the Brothers with her weather magic. But Silas reached inside his robe and took out a small scroll that Willow recognized as one of the ancient lost spells. He read it fast.

Suddenly there was a flash of bright yellow light, and Twist began to struggle as if she were drowning . . . but drowning in air.

Willow swung the staff around at one of the Brothers, knocking him off his feet. Peg and Oswin raced up the steps after her. Peg managed to punch one of the Brothers, while Oswin launched himself at another, scratching him on the nose. He was soon shaken off, and his small furry body was flung down the steps—but Oswin landed on his feet and once again threw himself into the fray.

Willow aimed another blow at one of the brainwashed Brothers who was coming at her once again, despite a nasty lump forming on his head. Another one had managed to restrain Peg, pinning his thrashing body to the floor.

Undeterred by the blows raining down on them, three managed to grab hold of Willow as she kicked and thrashed and waved the staff around, and one finally tore it from her hands. Oswin dived at him, only to be flung backward down the steps once more. He tried to stand up, but this time he collapsed, making a soft mewling sound.

Willow's heart dived into her mouth.

"No!" she screamed as the Brother who'd torn the staff from her hands snapped a pair of glowing manacles roughly onto her wrists.

Willow fought hard, thrashing against her restraints, but they were locked in place. She struggled to her knees, her heart thundering in her chest. She watched in utter horror as, one by one, the Brothers passed the staff between them to Silas.

Twist pointed frantically at the scroll on the ground beside Oswin as she fought for air. "Say the reverse," she tried to shout, but the kobold couldn't understand her since her strangled voice sounded like it was coming from deep underwater.

"Turn it around, Oswin!" cried Willow. "Say what's on the back!"

Oswin quickly grabbed it and read out,

"Water to air
Breath and life
Meet once more
Restore the balance fair."

Twist was released at last, and she fell to her knees, gasping for breath.

"Thank you, Oswin," she cried.

The kobold nodded, then paled as he looked from Twist to Silas. They all turned in horror as Silas held the staff in his hands, grinning widely.

Willow felt her heartbeat roaring in her ears. Silas had won!

21
Troll Army

Silas raised the staff to the sky, a terrible look of triumph on his face.

Twist tried to send a bolt of lightning at him, but nothing happened. "I'm too weak," she cried.

Willow started to hyperventilate. Silas was going to steal all their magic. They had failed! There were spots before her eyes as she gasped for breath in her panic.

"Summon your army!" cried the hound again.

Willow thought, foolishly, that their army was defeated. Silas was about to bring forth utter destruction . . . until suddenly she looked up and blinked. Was the emblem hound referring to something else? Did he know what Moreg had told her, or was he just speaking nonsense? It didn't matter. She could kiss the crystal dog either way, as his words had sparked something in her. She sat up fast, and turned to look down the steps at Oswin.

"The whistle!"

"The wissel?" he said. Then suddenly his eyes widened. He nodded quickly and then, with an enormous struggle, he half padded, half crawled to the upside-down carpetbag that had been left to dry. Socks and nightdresses and several biscuits went flying, till he found something small and hard buried at the bottom of the bag. He held it to his mouth and blew. The whistle let out a sharp, shrill cry that made them all wince.

Even Silas lowered the staff to peer around in surprise.

For a moment, nothing happened, and then . . . from far away, they could hear an ENORMOUS BOOM.

The ground began to shake. The water in the lake started to churn. It sounded like thunder or an earthquake.

"What on Starfell?" cried Silas.

Beyond the lake, whirling banks of dust clouds were forming in the air.

Something was coming. Something FAST. Something LOUD and THUNDEROUS.

BOOM. BOOM. BOOM.

Despite the Gerful chalk, a few of the Brothers looked suddenly terrified. They scrambled up the steps as Silas called, "Steady! Remain steady!" Though even he appeared to have lost some of his bravado, because suddenly they could all see what was coming: enormous creatures, as tall as the buildings, wider than several trees.

"Oh Wol!" cried Twist and Peg, their eyes wide in fright.

The huge shapes ran, leaving behind great dents in the ground. Their legs made short work of the lake, which barely reached their thighs. Their bodies were made of stone, their teeth covered with moss. They wore human bones as jewelry and, despite the fact that their knuckles were the size of bricks, they also carried studded clubs that they dragged menacingly through the water, their eyes fixed on them.

The creatures reached Willow and Oswin in a cloud of dust, followed by a wave of water that made everyone cough and splutter.

A sixteen-foot troll they knew as Verushka turned to Oswin. "You have summoned us?"

Suddenly Willow spotted a smaller troll behind the great warrior. "Calamity!" she shouted.

"Willow!" cried her friend, a smaller troll of around her own age. Calamity made her way toward Willow and, seeing the manacles on her wrists, she snapped them off immediately. "You used the whistle!" she said.

Willow nodded. "We need your help! Please stop them!" She pointed at Silas and the Brothers, who were staring at the trolls, frozen in disbelief.

Calamity nodded. "My clan don't remember you, but

they'll keep their word. No one gets a whistle unless it's been handed over by a troll—it's an ancient custom." Then she turned to Verushka and the other trolls. She spoke quietly for a moment, and then they all nodded.

"Go after them," said Verushka, pointing at the Brothers, who were now attempting to flee.

The trolls nodded. It was clear they didn't remember giving Willow the whistle, but the fact that Oswin had blown it seemed like proof enough, and meant they could rely on their help.

The trolls began to scatter, seizing the stunned Brothers in their fists and going after Silas. But he dashed down a street. He darted out of the way of one troll, who crashed into the side of a house. There was the heartbreaking sound of crystal shattering, and Silas managed to get away just in time. Willow could see him, holding the staff high in the air. He was preparing to use it!

"Oswin, hiss at the water again!" she cried.

He frowned, but limped as quickly as he could toward the lake and hissed. There was an electrical blast, and Willow staggered back, but not before she held her broom, Whisper, in her hands. "Thank you," she called, jumping on and shooting after Silas. The super-fast Stealth-Racer broom caught up and she dived at him, her hands reaching for the staff.

"What the—?" he said in surprise, pushing her back, but she clung on to the staff with all her might.

He took one hand off the staff to reach inside his pocket. Willow closed her eyes for a second, and the small box that had been inside his robes was in her left hand.

"You're forgetting that these are known as the *lost* spells," she said, and threw them onto the ground.

He glared at her and pushed her back once more, trying to wrestle the staff out of her grip.

Willow struggled with Silas as he tried to fling her off, but she clamped her hands onto the staff and managed to hold on for dear life. . . . She tried to think of making the staff vanish to get it away from Silas, but the air was dusty and it was making her eyes itch. At that exact moment . . . she sneezed.

And *she* vanished—taking the staff with her.

Silas roared in anger.

But Willow reappeared a second later, still on her broom, only a few feet away. "Oh Wol!" she cried, wishing she had a better command of her new power.

Silas took a running leap toward her, knocking her off Whisper. The staff fell out of her hands, and they both scrambled after it, each one managing once again to grab hold. Willow had caught the staff's iron half-moon, and she held on with all her strength. But Silas was stronger—far stronger—and, as she watched, he smiled terribly, clamped his hands over hers, and began to twist the iron half-moon until the crystal turned black.

"Oh, I shall enjoy this," he said. "It makes sense, really, for it to come from you first."

Willow felt a sudden jolt, and a tingling all through her body, like she'd been stung. The more she clung on, the weaker she became, but she was determined not to let go. . . . She held on, fighting as black spots started to dance before her eyes. She fell onto her knees, pulling the iron half-moon back toward her with the last bit of her strength. . . . She pulled and pulled, twisting it until the crystal turned from black to white.

Then suddenly Willow felt something give way, but she wasn't sure what. She staggered back, and the tiny rock dragon from her shoulder jumped to the ground. Her eyes desperately wanted to close in a sudden, crushing fatigue, but the look of triumph that faltered for a moment on Silas's face kept her holding on.

The earth started to rumble and shake as rocks began to roll toward the tiny dragon.

Silas looked from Willow, nearly unconscious on the ground, to the stones around him in confusion. Willow crawled away as fast as she could, using her last reserves of energy.

More and more rocks and pebbles appeared, collecting together until the once small dragon had grown enormous in size, shaping into the giant beast they had met in the Cloud Mountains.

It turned to Silas and roared. A wave of dust clouded the air, and Silas took an involuntary step backward.

"I don' believes it!" cried Oswin. "The rock newt wos the giant all this times!"

Silas aimed the staff at the dragon, but the orb was still white, and nothing happened. Instead, the rock dragon opened its cavernous mouth, and Silas was engulfed. In moments the moving, scattering rock disappeared, taking Silas along with it.

Willow watched through eyes glazed with fatigue, too weak to even lift her head from the ground. She heard the cheers. She heard the triumphant calls of the trolls and the horrified cries of the Brothers. She saw Feathering, thankfully released from his enchantment and fully restored, and heard him explaining to the others that the rock dragons would take Silas away to the Cloud Mountains . . . where they would keep him imprisoned.

But she couldn't find the words to respond. She could barely move. It would be good, she thought, to just rest a little while . . .

She felt weak—so very weak.

22

The Iron Moon

IT HAD BEEN a long journey back home, even though Feathering had flown as quickly as he could. Willow had been so tired and groggy, it had felt like her head was underwater or that everything was happening in a kind of dream, and she'd fallen into a deep sleep at some point before being delivered home.

When Willow woke up a week later, she still felt unbearably tired, but she was surprised nonetheless to find that she was clutching something in her fist . . . something no one had been able to pry from her fingers. She looked at it in surprise—it was the iron half-moon from the staff. She frowned. Had she somehow managed to wrench it off? How?

She could hear Oswin's faint snores coming from the foot of her bed. She tried to sit up, but it was hard. She was impossibly weak.

To her surprise, she saw that Moreg Vaine was standing at the end of the bed.

Willow blinked, wondering if she was still dreaming.

There was a very faint "Oh no" from the kobold, who had woken when Willow stirred.

"You're awake," said the witch. "At last."

"You're here," said Willow. Though she was groggy and her mouth was dry, she felt a flicker of happiness spread through her at the thought.

"I am. I would have come sooner, but I'm afraid Silas managed to block my visions."

Willow tried again to sit up, and the witch helped her raise herself on her pillows. "What—how?" she asked in shock.

"He used a clouded eye, of all things—the very one that used to belong to your friend Holloway."

Willow gasped. "But I thought it was useless? He said it just made the world and his mood clouded. That's why he traded it."

"Their purpose is not common knowledge, but if you have a clouded eye, or carry one on your person, it warps a seer's visions of your future. I don't think Holloway or even Rubix knew this. Every time my visions turned toward you, and therefore Silas, everything began to get muddy. . . . I started to think that it meant the problem was me, and the best thing I could do was not to come near and interfere. It was only later, when I read that the eye had been stolen from Rubix, that I figured out what had happened. Alas, I discovered it too late. But it's why I'm here now."

"It's not too late," said Willow.

"Never," agreed Moreg. "Your friends have filled me in on all that has happened. Your sisters too—I believe they are most proud."

Willow frowned, then she looked around, realizing that she was, in fact, in Camille's bed, which was bigger than her own. She was also wearing one of Juniper's sweaters. They must have tended to her while she slept, she realized.

"I asked to speak to you as soon as you awoke. I hope you don't mind."

Willow shook her head.

"We are all very proud of you."

Willow felt tears smart in her eyes. She looked away. They were words she'd longed to hear—to feel that her family, that Moreg Vaine, could be proud of her. . . . But all she felt right then was a deep sense of shame. Her lip wobbled as all the events of the past few days overwhelmed her. "No . . . you shouldn't be! I don't deserve it. I—messed up. I was the biggest fool. I shouldn't have brought Llandunia back." She thought of all the people's lives she'd put at risk, and a tear slipped down her cheek. "It was all my fault."

Moreg's dark eyes snapped fire, and she clutched Willow's hand firmly. "No! Do you hear me? I won't have that. Silas was playing a powerful game—and we were all his pawns. Your friend Twist is also riddled with guilt. She feels that if she hadn't come to find you and tell you about the kingdom, you might never have been put through this."

Willow frowned. She'd never blame Twist.

"It doesn't matter how it happened. The important thing is that you all defeated Silas—for now," said Moreg.

"For now?" Willow remembered him disappearing into the rock dragon's mouth and what Feathering had said—that they would hold him captive in the Cloud Mountains.

"I think, maybe, you already suspect what's happened? What he's done to you?"

Willow clutched the piece of iron in her palm. There was something tugging at her mind . . . something hard and painful that made her want to sob in anguish.

Perhaps if she didn't say it aloud it wouldn't be true. It was even worse than the shame she felt. This was loss, and grief . . . it felt raw and agonizing, and a big part of her didn't even want to think of it, let alone admit it.

Moreg's face was grave even as she nodded kindly, encouraging Willow to speak aloud what seemed unspeakable.

Willow took a deep breath, tears filling her eyes as the horror of it washed over her. "He took it, didn't he? My magic."

That was why she felt so weak, so ill. . . . A part of her had been stripped away.

She couldn't see for the tears that were falling now, fresh and fast.

She'd wished so much to be like her sisters—to be powerful, to be respected, to be admired . . . to have an ability that didn't cause people to view her as the "least powerful sister." And now she would give anything, anything at all, to have her simple, wondrous power back.

She took a shuddery breath and closed her eyes. Moreg patted her hand. "I'm so sorry, but yes, he did. Unfortunately, in the moment Silas had the staff and turned it black, he took your magic from you. And, in doing so, he unintentionally took the one power he would need to escape the rock dragons."

Willow blinked, then sighed. "The ability to disappear. He knows I can do it because he saw me vanish when I tried to make the staff disappear."

Moreg nodded. "And he will come back with the elf staff."

Willow sat back and closed her eyes. Then somehow, despite everything, a small, triumphant smile flitted across her face. "It won't work, though. Not without this." Willow held up the iron half-moon.

Moreg looked at it and frowned. Her eyes turned white, then back to black. She gave a small, amazed laugh. "Oh, you marvel! No, it won't. Not for its dark purposes."

Willow beamed, relief flooding through her.

"Silas might have the staff—for now—but what you and Twist have achieved cannot be underestimated. At every turn you have foiled his plans. You have soldiered on, even when none of our magical folk wanted to believe that a threat was coming. Even as they questioned your sanity, you persevered—knowing that you faced certain danger, but doing the right thing regardless. You have shown true courage and integrity, and because of you and Twist, the children of Starfell have been saved so much pain—the pain that you now face yourself."

"I must have used the very last drops of my magic to make this disappear from the staff!" Willow realized, staring at the iron half-moon.

Moreg nodded. "You sacrificed your magic, to help save everyone else's." The witch discreetly wiped her eyes. "But it won't be for long, Willow. If we get the staff back, we can get your magic back too."

Willow stared up at her, a curl of hope expanding in her chest. Moreg's words washed over her like a balm. Silas might think he'd won—but it wasn't over, not yet. Despite his cruel trick, she *had* achieved something. They all had. And she had made two incredible new friends in Twist and Peg, who she couldn't wait to see again. She'd get her magic back if it was the last thing she did. And right now that seemed, somehow, possible.

There was the sound of footsteps behind Moreg, and

Willow's sisters, mother, and father crowded into the room.

"You're awake!"

"Thank you for sending Thundera to save us!" cried Camille. "She burned down part of Wolkana and the Brothers had to let most of us go."

"Did you know they used Gerful chalk on us? I can't believe we sent you to that school!" cried her father.

Oswin handed Willow a biscuit. "Jes' imagine all the time we could 'ave saved if they jes' believed us from the start."

Willow took it and let out a small laugh.

To her surprise, her mother ruffled the kobold's fur and grinned. "Your cat might actually have a point."

"Oh, fer the last time, despite 'AVING TER PRETEND fer likes a second that I is one to save our skins . . . I IS STILL *NOT* A BLOOMIN' CAT!"

Willow grinned, in spite of everything that had happened. Then she fished out the StoryPass from her pocket. She wasn't all that surprised that it was currently pointing to "One Might Have Suspected as Such."